Praise for *12 Brain/Mind Learning Principles in Action*

In this "how-to" book, the authors offer practical suggestions for merging today's requirements for teaching to standards with recent findings from brain research. The Brain/Mind Principles articulated in Making Connections: Teaching and the Human Brain *are expanded and categorized to form the foundation for a long-term professional inquiry designed to help teachers and administrators clarify their understanding about how to improve learning for all students. To ground their recommendations in current brain research and connect them to quality teaching and learning, the authors provide consistent chapter segments such as How Do We Know This, Taking It Into the Classroom, and Implementing the National Teaching Standards. If you are a practitioner or a school leader looking for a way to energize staff with a spirit of inquiry and create a genuine quest for continuous improvement, this book is required reading.*

—Judy Stevens, EdD
Former Director of Elementary Schools
Spring Branch ISD, Houston, Texas

Renate and Geoffrey Caine, Carol McClintic, and Karl Klimek have bridged the research-based principles of [the Caines'] earlier work with a practical/pragmatic yet visionary approach to the teaching and learning process.

The text is easy to read and follow as it guides us through processing exercises to deepen understanding, gives practical examples from the real world, offers hints for working and progressing through the three instructional approaches, lists suggestions for administrative support, and offers reflective prompts for learning. All of this in an effort to create environments where powerful learning and teaching occurs for every student every day.

Anyone who had followed the work of the Caines and their colleagues will find this new work not only enlightening but very useful in the day-to-day application of the Brain/Mind Principles that should undergird any learning endeavor. Read it today and tomorrow and the next and the next . . .

—Barry K. Tambara
Instructional Improvement Coach
UCLA Center X Partnership Program
Former Director of Curriculum/Instruction
San Bernardino County (CA) Superintendent of School Office

All unconnected ideas I ever had about transforming learning and teaching are brought together here in an organic order that represents a viable path for teacher and school change.

—Margaret Arnold, PhD
Ausgsburg, Germany

Since the publication of their book, Making Connections: Teaching and the Human Brain, *Renate and Geoffrey Caine have made the case for thinking differently about learning and teaching. In* 12 Brain/Mind Principles in Action, *the Caines, McClintic, and Klimek provide the research, the processes and the design for action that will help us create renewed possibilities for education. By providing us once again with a new place to run to . . . rather than devoting our energy to "running in the same place" . . . they give us the capacity to trust our own abilities to lead and teach, as well as trusting the potential of our students to be all that they can be. The Caines have been an inspiration for me and have influenced my work for the past 10 years. [This book] continues their tradition of practical ideas that are solidly grounded in research. It is a* must read *for teachers, administrators, board members, and college/university faculty, as well as anyone who is interested in what the mind and body need for optimal learning.*

—Elsie Ritzenhein
President and CEO, Creative Sources
Educational Consultant/Facilitator and
Secondary School Administrator
Michigan

I see this book as being essential for any school or person who wants a relevant, practical guide for implementing a powerful approach to improving student outcomes. Each chapter's link to one of the 12 Brain/Mind Principles helps focus on these core understandings. Each principle is made meaningful for the reader.

The book also recognizes that many of us work in collaborative learning communities and that, more often than not, we dialogue extensively with our colleagues in the area of professional development. For me, however, the most powerful parts of this book are those that focus on student questions and engagement.

—Mark Beach
Director of Distance Education, New Zealand
Former Principal, Tahati School, New Zealand

Renate and Geoffrey Caine give form and clarity to teachers' and school leaders' wisdom of practice. [This book] gives a comprehensive picture of the principles, the needed transitions of practice and ways of being for teachers and leaders alike. [This is] an essential resource for those wanting to engage children and young people in powerful learning for a future that matters.

—Margot Foster
Manager, Learning to Learn, Australia

This is a powerful piece of modern and well-thought-through educational literature. The Caines, together with close colleagues, combine a range of work of their own as well as some of the best thinking from modern neuroscience and psychology. They provide both the theoretical underpinnings and excellent practical applications for bringing their 12 Brain/Mind Learning Principles to life within a framework compatible with a constructivist approach to education and learning.

Not only do the Caines lead us through a process of how practitioners can adapt and evolve through their perspectives and instructional approaches, they also illustrate how educational leaders can support this growth by providing the conditions for this to happen, as well as develop alongside their colleagues.

Our challenge as educators is to create the conditions in which students can learn—both in the environment we work in and also inside the minds/spirits and bodies of the students themselves. By creating an environment of relaxed alertness, they explain how we strengthen and take advantage of the biological links necessary to support great learning. Establishing what the Caines call "complex experience" as the foundation for instruction, requiring teachers to use active processing in order to consolidate learning, completes this new vision for education.

It is both challenging and at the same time clear that this book is essential reading—and living—for anyone who is committed to learning and creating learning communities in the modern age.

—Rob Clarke
Teacher, Consultant, Independent Learning
Coordinator Holland Park School
London, England

To children everywhere . . .
As educators may we join in your dance of exploration and
wholeness and commit our teaching to Gibran's words:

"Keep me away from the wisdom which does not cry,
the philosophy which does not laugh and
the greatness which does not bow before children."

12 Brain/Mind LEARNING PRINCIPLES in ACTION

The Fieldbook for Making Connections, Teaching, and the Human Brain

RENATE NUMMELA CAINE
GEOFFREY CAINE
CAROL McCLINTIC
KARL KLIMEK
Foreword by Arthur L. Costa

CORWIN PRESS
A Sage Publications Company
Thousand Oaks, California

For information:

Corwin Press
A Sage Publications Company
2455 Teller Road
Thousand Oaks, California 91320
E-mail: order@corwinpress.com

Sage Publications Ltd.
1 Oliver's Yard
55 City Road
London, EC1Y 1SP
United Kingdom

Sage Publications India Pvt. Ltd.
B-42, Panchsheel Enclave
Post Box 4109
New Delhi 110 017 India

Printed in the United States of America

Library of Congress Cataloging-in-Publication Data

12 brain/mind learning principles in action : the fieldbook for making connections, teaching, and the human brain / by Renate Caine . . . [et al.].
    p. cm.
Includes bibliographical references and index.
ISBN 1-4129-0983-X (cloth) — ISBN 1-4129-0984-8 (pbk.)
  1. Learning, Psychology of. 2. Learning—Physiological aspects. 3. Brain.
4. Teaching. I. Title: Twelve brain / mind learning principles in action. II. Caine, Renate Nummela.
LB1060.A16 2005
370.15'23—dc22

                      2004014961

This book is printed on acid-free paper.

05 06 07 08 09 10 9 8 7 6 5 4 3 2 1

Acquisitions Editor:	Jean Ward
Production Editor:	Tracy Alpern
Copy Editor:	Kristin Bergstad
Proofreader:	Theresa Kay
Typesetter:	C&M Digitals (P) Ltd.
Indexer:	Gloria Tierney
Cover Designer:	Michael Dubowe

Contents

Foreword

Educators are intrigued with research in the neurosciences from which to draw implications and applications for teaching and learning. They strive to make teaching more "brain compatible" and, as additional research has yielded insights into how the brain learns, the more congruent instruction can become.

Simultaneously, teacher educators and staff developers have generated criteria and standards to serve as benchmarks of effective teaching. Connecting research from the neurosciences, sound constructivist pedagogical practices and the National Teaching Standards, the Caines and their colleagues have again produced a treasure of brain-based classroom practices intended to enhance learning.

Designed to stand alone as a practical implementation guide for their 12 research-based Brain/Mind Principles for teaching and learning or to accompany their bestselling basic text, *Making Connections: Teaching and the Human Brain,* the authors make this valuable resource handbook teacher-friendly by providing relevant examples, genuine reflections from teachers' journal entries, frank student vignettes, and sensible suggestions for aligning school and classroom conditions and strategies with our increasing knowledge of what the brain/mind demands for maximizing learning. Demonstrating the relationship of brain-based practices to the National Teaching Standards is a value-added component.

The classroom applications are not prescriptive, however. Rather, the authors illustrate how teachers who may employ stylistic variants might implement these suggestions differently. Each chapter concludes with proposals for school leaders to empower the entire staff to apply these principles in becoming an even more potent learning community.

Educators wishing to harmonize their educational practices with research on brain functioning will find this fieldbook indispensable.

—Arthur L. Costa
Emeritus Professor of Education
California State University, Sacramento

Preface

What does it mean to use more of one's brain and one's mind?

Many people confronted with that question will be tempted to say that having a photographic memory would constitute optimum use. But if neuroscience and cognitive science are to be taken seriously, then the brain governs much more than memory alone. The "brain/mind" includes our emotions, movement, creativity, immune responses, and abilities to use language, reason, plan, organize, and dream. It allows us to experience compassion, interconnectedness, peace, and uncertainty. Add to that the fact that context and experiences influence and shape the brain/mind and that human beings have the capacity to change their own brain by using reflection, expanding awareness, and altering behavior. So the answer to the question begins with the understanding that the body-brain-mind of every student constitutes an interconnected unity that must be addressed by educators.

Given that the brain encompasses so much, what are the implications for educators? Students walking into our classrooms have all this potential. We sense it, are daunted by it, blindly try to deal with it, and ultimately are pressured to reduce this enormous possibility to teaching reading, writing, and arithmetic. Many educators and the public assume that once students can do the basics the rest will take care of itself. The question that must haunt educators and parents alike is, "What of the rest of the child?"

In addition, most education is on a collision course with the future. Despite vast amounts of research on learning, information from the brain and mind sciences, availability of the World Wide Web, and online learning supports, many teachers and their students are chained to textbooks. Despite competition from DVDs, video games, television, a peer culture largely unconnected to parental and adult guidance, and an overemphasis on a capitalistic sense of values, educators and educational policies continue to reinvent an old, outmoded philosophy of learning and teaching. One textbook as primary resource, written book reports, prescribed homework, teacher directed instruction and evaluation, and standardized tests continue to dominate in this age of information and technology. Most educators and much of the public know that there is something wrong with this scenario. But sadly, instead of moving ahead, a great deal of money and energy is devoted to running in the same place. It is much like attempting to stuff the genie back into the bottle, when he has no intention of ever going back. Fortunately, there is a way to move on.

This book is our attempt to lay out a map that shows the way. It addresses the new world to which the current generation of students belongs, and it is based on new understanding of what it means to learn in these rapidly changing times.

Several years ago one of us was doing a one-day workshop in Canada. After a very disappointing day with teachers looking for some quick answers to address the immense pressure from an administration looking for higher test scores, both presenter and participants were at an impasse. Suddenly one young man stood up. With amazement in his voice he almost shouted out, "I get it! It's not that hard. You just have to think differently!" He was absolutely right, and, we would add, you have to *want* to think differently.

One part of this book is about thinking differently. Professional development is never just about adding skills and knowledge. The essential foundation for becoming more proficient is a shift in one's view of how people learn and what teacher and administrator actually do. That is why this book is framed in terms of a developmental path for educators. The other part of this book has to do with the courage to do things that come with that expansion of vision and possibility. As we thought about writing this foreword, the four authors took time out to watch what by now is a classic movie, *Indiana Jones and the Holy Grail*. We needed a metaphor for courage. Near the end of the movie, Indiana has to pass through various tests in order to get to the Holy Grail. During some very intense moments, he has to know how to decipher the instructions by going beyond the script provided with the map. The one test that intrigued us the most was where "Indy" has to trust that a bridge, which is totally invisible, is in fact there. But it doesn't appear until he steps out as if it existed. He had to think, then he had to believe.

What this book has to offer will never be adequately understood or even be visible until you step out toward the practices we suggest to you. We argue on the basis of research and experience that meaningful learning occurs when three elements are intertwined: A state of mind in learners that we call relaxed alertness, the orchestrated immersion of the learner in experiences in which the standards are embedded, and the active processing of that experience. We also provide a series of foundational skills throughout the book. The key to making sense of the ideas and enjoying success requires taking the step of developing and using the skills.

It will take time to implement the changes we suggest. We recommend at least a year if not five of practice and study done individually and with others. In the end, as you try the ideas presented, your thinking will change along with your practice. It may not be the "holy grail" for education but it will be true to what is collectively being discovered about how human beings learn and it will lead education in this millennium. What we suggest will be in harmony with students' brains and potential and can match more fully what is known and continues to be discovered about exceptional learning and teaching. And it will provide you, your colleagues, and your students with a great deal of joy, satisfaction, and fulfillment.

We especially appreciate the support of our focus group members who met with us to read the early draft and provide much needed feedback and suggestions. Thank you Janice Anderson, Sam Crowell, Caroline Davidson, Hollis Fulmor, Linda Hargen, Barbara Klimek, Elsie Ritzenhein, and Betty Snow. All are exceptional educators in their own right.

In addition we would like to thank our many readers of the manuscript. Their comments and contributions were invaluable. They included Margaret Arnold, Lou Cozolino, Dottie Gottshall, Duncan Johnson, Tennes Rosengren, Barry Tambara, Ken Thompson, and Cindy Tucker.

We owe thanks to the several neuroscientists who continue to help educators understand the implications of their research and whose work contributed to our thinking: Robert Sapolsky, Candace Pert, Bruce Perry, Daniel Siegel, Joseph LeDoux, Antonio Damasio, and Marian Diamond, among others.

We would also like to thank our editor, Jean Ward, who never lost faith in us and kept pursuing the realization of this book and the forthcoming revision of *Making Connections: Teaching and the Human Brain*.

We want to thank Dick Debbertine for his artwork and willingness to work with our ideas. And finally, we want to express our gratitude to Hubert and Frank, and all the folks at the Aroma. Whenever we got stuck or needed to get away, they provided a place and solace for us. Thank you.

About the Authors

 **Renate Nummela Caine, PhD,** is Professor Emerita of Education at California State University, San Bernardino. She consults throughout the world, and her work with schools has been featured on the Discovery Channel, "Wizards of Wisdom" shown on PBS, and elsewhere. She is the senior author of *Making Connections: Teaching and the Human Brain,* written with Geoffrey Caine. The book describes 12 principles of brain/mind learning that summarize and triangulate research across many disciplines, including the neurosciences. John Dunworth, Past President of the American Association of Colleges for Teacher Education, says, "*Making Connections* ranks among the most significant publications in the field of teaching and learning in this century. This provocative work could easily impact the life of every learner and every teacher."

She is a coauthor of five other books, some of which have been translated into Swedish, Turkish, and Chinese. She regularly conducts leading-edge teacher training programs for educational organizations, and her work is used as a foundation for educational change in programs at school, district, and state levels. An example of an international program that capitalizes on the Caines' work is the multi-year program "Learning to Learn" being conducted by the Department of Education and Children's Services in South Australia.

Geoffrey Caine, a director of Caine Learning LLC, is a learning consultant and process coach. He has published extensively and is senior author of the Caines' most recent book, *The Brain, Education and the Competitive Edge* (2001). Arthur L. Costa, president of the Association for Supervision and Curriculum Development from 1988 to 1989, says that "this book should be required reading for any educational policymakers, including school board members, parents, legislators, as well as educators."

His work carries him throughout the United States and abroad. He conducts programs in the worlds of education, business, and government, where he capitalizes on his prior experience as a tenured member of a faculty of law in Australia, education services manager of a national software company, state manager of a national publishing company, and National Director of the Mind/Brain Network of the American Society for Training and Development.

He has given keynote addresses or made presentations to such organizations as the Campaign for Learning in the United Kingdom, the World Conference on Education for All, and the Eighth International Conference on Thinking.

Carol McClintic, MA, is a master teacher and has received many awards for teaching. She has taught preschool, elementary school, middle school, and high school and has been a mentor teacher and peer coach. She has led workshops for teachers and parents in her districts, taught numerous education extension classes for teachers at local universities, cocreated a certificate program for conflict resolution, and been a coordinator for university and district grant programs. She has been a consultant with Caine Learning since 1995, and in that capacity has conducted workshops throughout the United States.

She coauthored the book *Wouldn't It Be Wonderful: A Guide to Teaching in the Twenty-First Century*. She retired from active teaching in 2002 after 35 years in the field. In addition to her professional work she is a gardener, sings with a local group that just completed a CD, and participates in local service organizations in her spare time.

She enjoys spending time with her son Chad and her daughter Lisa.

Karl Klimek, MA, brings a diverse background to each of his experiences with educators. Having lived and worked in five states as well as studying in the Czech Republic, he accents the excitement of opportunities we all have before us. As a teacher, building principal, assistant superintendent, career and technology education director, state and federal program developer, group facilitator, consultant, and parent, he offers an enthusiastic approach to identifying what's right in our efforts and taking positive actions toward becoming even better.

He has degrees in education and leadership from Central Washington University and Eastern Michigan University. He is the recipient of several teaching awards, and has served as a planning leader in both the public and private sector.

Currently he does extensive work with the Convergence Education Foundation, a Michigan-based organization integrating technology into projects emphasizing engineering, math, and science in schools.

Wife Barbara and children Jaci, Rachel, Dan, and Susanna each bring positive energy and enjoyment his way every day.

Getting Started

The human brain/mind is much like a dynamic kaleidoscope. The neurosciences are telling us that, energized by genetics, experience, and culture, students literally learn from everything. And as educators we are beginning to see that what this generation of students is learning beyond the classroom is unlike anything past generations have experienced. All too often educators find themselves stretched between the world of the past that signifies a sense of order and security, and the world of the future that continually beckons but calls for responses shrouded in ambiguity and uncertainty.

Like cautious pioneers, educators search for guidelines and signposts that tell them where they are going. Many educators are working to the point of exhaustion only to find that their efforts are undermined by forces beyond their control. And because they feel lost at times, entities of all kinds have stepped in to tell them which way they must go. But those entities are not present in schools and classrooms on a daily and yearly basis. It is easy to believe in certainty when not confronted with the immediate and immense complexity that represents students' living in today's world.

> It is as if educators have to learn to dance at the same time that they are also being told to march in step. In the process many of them have been robbed of their joy in teaching, which is fueled by laughter, creativity, and confidence.

One major struggle is between those who advocate schools that confine teaching largely to "the basics," and those advocating a more creative, student-centered approach. Advocates of the basics are committed to streamlining all teaching so that every child leaves school with the advocates' view of essential facts, information, and skills necessary for functioning as an adult. They do not trust that student-centered learning can lead to the type of mastery they see as critical to providing success in a discipline and in life.

Advocates of the student-centered approach would hasten to add that they too want to help students succeed and master facts, information, and skills essential to academic disciplines, but that learning should be exciting and meaningful for the learner as well. Most important of all, these educators tend to be convinced of the critical role that relationship and community play in learning.

Research from the neurosciences and research on learning in general is shedding light on this debate.

WE HAVE TO BEGIN WITH LEARNING

Several people have asked us to spell out what we see as the most important changes for education. For us, the answer is clear. We must understand how human beings learn and place that understanding at the very center of teaching. This is far from easy, and the entire process can be daunting.

To make sense of the vast amount of research that has been generated in fields ranging from psychology to biology and neuroscience, the Caines developed a set of 12 Brain/Mind Learning Principles that summarize what we presently know about learning. These principles were originally spelled out in their book *Making Connections: Teaching and the Human Brain* (Caine & Caine, in press). The principles look at all learners as living systems where physical and mental functioning are interconnected (learning is psychophysiological). As a result, no one principle is more important than another. They are numbered for identification only.

On the surface each principle seems to be obvious: for example, "The brain/mind is social" (Principle #2). But each principle is also a gateway to deeper understanding. This principle, for example, can help educators better understand the link between social relationships, brain development, and learning (see Chapter 4). The principles are not separate and discrete. Each principle has a specific focus but involves aspects of the others. Each chapter in this book begins with a brain principle that summarizes research and current understanding about learning (see wheel, next page).

A Preliminary Definition of "Learning"

The principles help us understand why it has been so difficult to agree on what it means to learn. The principles show that several different processes are involved. The key to effective educational renewal is to integrate those different aspects of learning.

- For some, the primary aspect of learning is *memorization,* and the brain/mind is designed (in part) for memorization.
- For some, the primary aspect of learning is *intellectual understanding,* and the brain/mind is designed (in part) for intellectual understanding.
- For some, the primary aspect of learning is *making intellectual and practical sense of experience,* and the brain/mind is designed (in large measure) for making sense of experience.

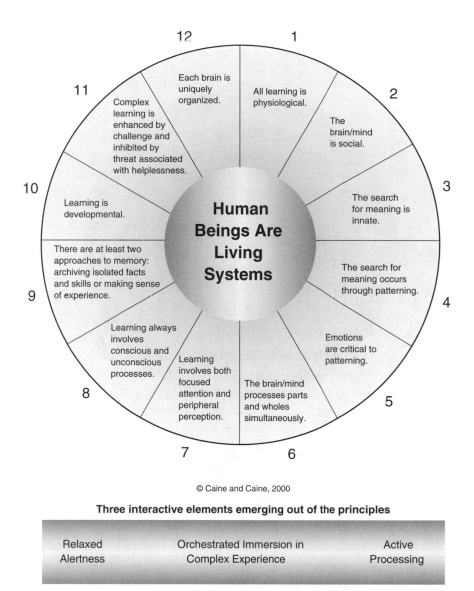

12 1 11 2 10 3 9 4 8 5 7 6

Each brain is uniquely organized.

All learning is physiological.

Complex learning is enhanced by challenge and inhibited by threat associated with helplessness.

The brain/mind is social.

Learning is developmental.

The search for meaning is innate.

There are at least two approaches to memory: archiving isolated facts and skills or making sense of experience.

Human Beings Are Living Systems

The search for meaning occurs through patterning.

Learning always involves conscious and unconscious processes.

Emotions are critical to patterning.

Learning involves both focused attention and peripheral perception.

The brain/mind processes parts and wholes simultaneously.

© Caine and Caine, 2000

Three interactive elements emerging out of the principles

Relaxed Alertness	Orchestrated Immersion in Complex Experience	Active Processing

All of these are legitimate. And as more aspects of the principles are implemented, the range of student learning increases.

LEARNING CAPACITIES

How do educators implement the principles? To begin with, the principles tell us that every learner has immense and specific capacities for learning that teachers can and must address.

The above principle, for example, "The brain/mind is social," tells us that every student has the capacity to learn through relationship with others. It supports cooperative learning, peer coaching, and having students share their work and ideas with others.

Although students will differ based on their background and genetic and physical makeup, the capacities let teachers know that every one of their students can learn more effectively if these capacities are seen as natural and are acknowledged and addressed in teaching.

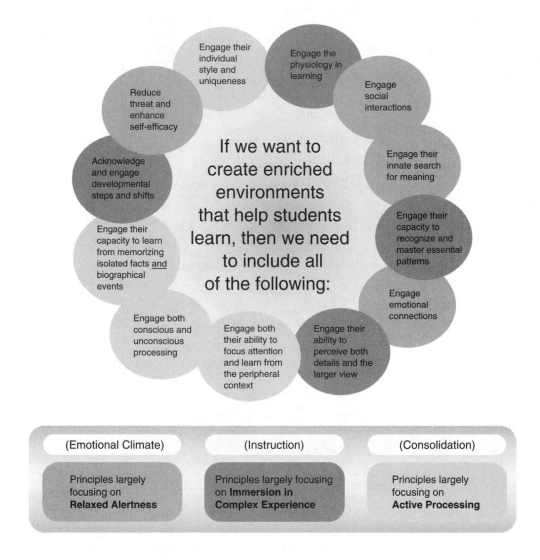

**Brain/Mind Learning Capacities
Creating an Enriched Environment for Learning**

According to Brain/Mind Learning Principles, all learning engages the following.
Our job is to orchestrate learning so that as many aspects of learning are engaged as possible.

If we want to create enriched environments that help students learn, then we need to include all of the following:

- Engage their individual style and uniqueness
- Engage the physiology in learning
- Engage social interactions
- Reduce threat and enhance self-efficacy
- Engage their innate search for meaning
- Acknowledge and engage developmental steps and shifts
- Engage their capacity to recognize and master essential patterns
- Engage their capacity to learn from memorizing isolated facts and biographical events
- Engage emotional connections
- Engage both conscious and unconscious processing
- Engage both their ability to focus attention and learn from the peripheral context
- Engage their ability to perceive both details and the larger view

(Emotional Climate)	(Instruction)	(Consolidation)
Principles largely focusing on **Relaxed Alertness**	Principles largely focusing on **Immersion in Complex Experience**	Principles largely focusing on **Active Processing**

FROM LEARNING TO TEACHING: THE JOURNEY OF THIS BOOK

All of the principles and capacities suggest that there are three fundamental components or elements of great teaching. They are the foundation for professional development and must be mastered by teachers and understood by all educators. We address each separately, but it is critical to understand that each of these elements has a profound affect on the other two and is in fact never separate.

1. Relaxed Alertness: Creating the Optimal Emotional Climate for Learning

There is an optimal emotional state for learning that is affected and moderated by the fear and pleasure centers in the brain. We call this optimal state *Relaxed Alertness.* In *Making Connections* (Caine & Caine, in press) it was defined as consisting of low threat and high challenge. The state exists in a learner who feels competent and confident and is interested or intrinsically motivated. Relaxed alertness is also a state that is present in classrooms and learning environments in which emotional and social competence is the goal. Such an environment allows all students ongoing opportunities to experience competence and confidence accompanied by motivation linked to personal goals and interests.

2. Orchestrated Immersion in Complex Experience: Creating Optimal Opportunities for Learning

The human brain learns through experience. The brain's first contact with the world is through the senses. So learning must engage our senses of sight, hearing, smell, touch, and movement (to name a few). These are naturally activated by physical experiences the learner has with the world. At one level then, *orchestration* means that teachers provide experiences that have learners interact with knowledge in ways that are concrete and physical. Teachers can help students identify physical attributes of something based on physical experience, by having students generate descriptions (what size, color, dimensions?), diagrams (draw something out to represent a physical or sensory experience), and create models (what examples are there using the same basic attributes?) of something they need to master.

The brain learns by making connections between what is experienced and what that experience means to the learner. Teaching therefore needs to require and invite learners to make connections to what is already organized and stored in their brain. That happens when students are called on to relate and understand the new in terms of what they already know and care about. This is the basis for the acquisition of technical/scholastic knowledge that is more traditionally academic. It requires students to grasp the what, how, when, and why of information based upon puzzles or dilemmas they encounter. It includes but goes beyond physical attributes of objects and fuels the search for explanations and understandings that are deeper and more complex.

Ultimately the brain needs to "own" the learning by having the learner do something with what has been learned. This means that students need to be given the opportunity and at times be required to use the information to answer personally relevant questions and to act in practical ways to solve problems and make things happen in relatively realistic contexts.

Because the brain/mind learns through experience, the teacher's job is to create learning experiences and opportunities, and to lecture only when appropriate. Experiences can be concrete or abstract in nature. All of the above—engaging the senses, making meaningful connections, and applying what has been learned—do not happen in a prescribed sequence. In any complex experience (one that includes novelty or new elements that must be linked or connected in some way) we can expect all three to be happening simultaneously. In addition, this kind of teaching and learning engages what we will discuss in a moment as actor-centered adaptive decision making. Actor-centered adaptive decision making focuses on developing skills governed largely by the brain's executive functions.

3. Active Processing of Experience: Creating Optimal Ways to Consolidate Learning

The brain is better at remembering things that are of meaning to the student. We are after performance knowledge—knowledge that the student can use. This goes far beyond standardized testing as it currently exists.

To fully capitalize on experience, there should be "in the moment," ongoing consolidation that solidifies and expands knowledge. We call this *Active Processing of Experience.*

Using teacher and peer questioning and feedback, students are continually required to think more deeply, identify specific characteristics and see relationships, analyze situations, think on their feet, develop goals and timelines, make critical decisions, and communicate their understanding.

This book is organized according to the above three elements and the 12 Brain/Mind Learning Principles. The first section begins with relaxed alertness because without the appropriate social and emotional conditions for learning, learners will not take the risks required by the kind of teaching we advocate. Part II focuses on immersion in complex experience and Part III is organized around active processing. Each chapter emerges out of one of the principles that supports the element being discussed.

WHAT ARE WE AFTER? DEVELOPING THE EXECUTIVE FUNCTIONS

What does it mean to use more of our brain? Although this is a daunting question, this book seeks to provide some answers.

All learning, from memorizing to mastering academic and technical skills, is important. Throughout this book we will, however, pay special attention to the development of what are known as the executive functions. They are the key to reaching and sustaining high standards of learning, and to raising those standards over time. We can now go back to the definition of *learning* and add to it. The primary key to learning is *developing the ability to make good decisions in the real world, based on the knowledge that people have and the sense they have made of experience.* In short, at the heart of great teaching is the development of the executive functions of learners.

A "Core" Thought

**Executive Functions: Essential but
Often Ignored Functions of the Brain**

Executive functions are largely housed in the front of the brain in what is called the prefrontal cortex. The prefrontal cortex is located approximately behind the forehead. Executive functions of the brain are currently being explored by Elkhonon Goldberg (2001) and others (LeDoux, 2002; Lyon & Krasnegor, 1999; Miller & Cummings, 1999; Molfese & Molfese, 2002). Individuals with highly developed executive functions have mastered the ability to plan and organize their thinking, use reason, engage in risk assessment, make sense of ideas and behavior, multitask, moderate emotions, work with longer time horizons, think critically, access working memory, and reflect on their own strengths and weaknesses. These processes go substantially beyond discrete, memorized skills or information. Unfortunately, developing abilities housed in the executive functions is often sabotaged by the child's social/emotional environment and bypassed by traditional teaching.

Why do we consider the executive functions to be so important?

Today's Students Are Not the Same

Although skills that make use of the executive functions have always been seen as critical, the experiences that taught students how to make decisions, apply knowledge to personally relevant questions and projects, reflect on their own thinking and accomplishments, and use critical thinking and feedback from others may well be lost in an age of instant information. The world of children growing up in the information age is profoundly different from that of most readers of this book, and of most current parents and educators. Traditional teaching and schooling is based on beliefs and values that emerge out of the past.

Perhaps most important is the belief that parents are available to act as the child's surrogate executive functions. It was always assumed that the parents were close by and it was they who could see the future and plan ahead. They were there to set goals for their children and make certain that they reached those goals. It was the parents who made certain that their children studied because "some day" they would need to know everything taught in school. The ability to think that far ahead is a cognitive function that was not expected of most children; it was assumed parents would be responsible for that. Parents were supposed to be the ones who taught their children to "not put off 'til tomorrow what you can do today" and to help children understand that learning takes time and that occasional problems are natural and can be overcome. Ideally, parents engaged their children in questions about school and the knowledge students acquired on a daily basis, and made certain that homework was completed.

The entire pace was slower and, most important, most adults were in charge of information.

Clearly, many families did not meet the ideal, but there were social structures of which most children were a part that were believed to provide a basis for maturation and development of the capacity to make important, real-world decisions.

> In recent times conditions have changed dramatically. Less than one third of families now eat together. Approximately 50% of kids grow up in a single family household (*America's Children: Key National Indicators of Well-Being, 2003.* "Population and Family Characteristics") and 60.4% of both parents work full- or part-time. So who or what is teaching critical life and decision-making skills to students?

The average student watches between three and four hours of television a night, most of which is not discussed or talked through with input from a knowledgeable and mature adult. Computers, video games, and movies add to time spent away from school (Healy, 1998). The problem with this entire scenario is that much information and almost an infinite number of "facts" reach our children. At the same time, they are rarely asked to think critically, analyze content, evaluate what is happening, or make their own intelligent decisions. Rarely are they challenged to think through a particular point of view, scenario, or action seen or experienced. Unless they are in close relationship with an adult who engages their minds by questioning their conclusions, helps them resolve personally relevant issues, or helps them see the consequences of their adopted beliefs, our students are left with facts that are not tied to real-life experience or consequences.

If parents do not engage children in thinking, teachers tell them only facts but don't tie the facts to the children's own experiences, television doesn't ask them to think and analyze, and video games provide excitement without reflection, where exactly do we expect them to develop the kinds of skills that help develop executive functions and prepare students to become responsible, thinking adults?

Educators also have to come to terms with the fact that this is the information age and information is available everywhere. Education focused on memorizing information is terribly inadequate. Any search engine (e.g., Google, www.google.com) will scan the World Wide Web instantaneously on any subject. Type in a line from a poem and the search engine will provide the name of the poem and the author. Type in the author's name and it will provide the author's other works and biographical data. Almost anything a student needs for class can be found on the Web. Learning that focuses predominately on facts and information must transition into more sophisticated learning that requires the use of that information for relevant goals and purposes.

> Educators have to understand how to create classrooms and learning that engage the whole brain, from facts, skills, and procedures to executive functions. These are not separate in the brain. Neither should they be separate in education.

Programming the Brain: The Almost Exclusive Reliance on Memorization of Facts and Skills

Let us go back to the differing views of learning from the point of view of preparing students to make decisions. The place to begin is with learning defined by mastering facts, skills, and procedures using memorization and repetition. This kind of learning has a quality to it that provides a comforting degree of certainty. It reduces things to right and wrong and serves as the bottom line for tests of all types. For example, a mile has 5,280 feet, a meter has 100 centimeters. The centers of the Moon and Earth are about 238,700 miles apart, and water is made up of two molecules of hydrogen and one of oxygen. There is no end to what we can "know" or memorize, and all of it is critical to gaining expertise in any discipline. Vocabulary, grammatical rules, and knowing how to write for different audiences are all essential skills students must master. The brain stores much of this information in the way that a "programmed" computer might (Schmahmann, 1997).

In part, the brain does learn this way. The problem, as we have shown, is that this approach to learning and teaching leaves out too much additional potential of the brain.

Developing executive functions cannot be done through memorization, and the brain/mind is not limited to being programmed by others. What the learner needs in addition is the opportunity for actor-centered adaptive decision making (Goldberg, 2001). Actor-centered decisions are the result of questions learners ask that are driven by their own purposes, needs, and interests and relate to what is currently happening. Simple examples include, "How often does my plant need water?" "How can I identify the birds in my backyard?" "What would it take to become an astronaut?" "Why did the coyote eat my cat?" and "What is gravity made of?" Most of these questions are particularly difficult to address in the classroom if the teacher is committed to direct instruction.

> Actor-centered adaptive decision making versus veridical learning and decision making.

> Goldberg distinguishes between actor-centered, adaptive decision making and veridical decision making. Adaptive decision making capitalizes on the learner's need to know and results in answers of meaning to the individual. Veridical decision making relies on what is known and/or was discovered by others. The former sparks thinking and the search for solutions; the latter relies on answers that can be reduced to right and wrong and "plugged in" or recalled irrespective of context.

How do we teach using actor-centered adaptive decision making and also teach the essential facts, information, and procedures that are a part of the formal curriculum and the highest standards? This book attempts to answer that question.

It is important to remember that development of the executive functions is a process. Anatomically these functions are present in infancy in very basic and limited ways. They reach maturity some time in late adolescence or early adulthood. Knowing what to expect of children and young adults as these functions come on board becomes critical.

SCAFFOLDING THE JOURNEY: THREE INSTRUCTIONAL APPROACHES

For education to function in this more sophisticated way, new approaches to teaching are needed, and a clear developmental path must be laid down along which educators can walk together.

This book begins with the traditional approach, which we simply call Instructional Approach 1. It then sets out to guide educators through an interim approach we call Instructional Approach 2, where new methods and practices are introduced. Ultimately, it leads to a way of teaching that utilizes aspects of the other two approaches as appropriate, but goes much further in order to accomplish what is needed. We call that Instructional Approach 3.

The latter type of teaching begins with the highest standards, but rather than teaching through direct transmission from the person who knows (teacher) to the one who doesn't (student), it embeds and consolidates essential knowledge and skills in student-centered (their questions) learning.

The differences in the three approaches are as follows:.

Instructional Approach 1

View of Learning: Memorization of facts and skills, and veridical decision making

Instruction: Largely focused on teacher presentations followed by repetition and practice

Academic Goals: Completion of assigned work, high grades based on teacher judgment and standards

Assessment: Standardized tests

Instructional Approach 2

View of Learning: Intellectual understanding supplemented by memorization, with some opportunities for adaptive decision making.

Instruction: Teacher-led experiences orchestrated around concepts and meaning; includes student choices and input on assignments, class rules and assessment (example: rubrics)

Academic Goals: Mastering curriculum and standards

Assessment: Authentic assessment supplements standardized tests

Instructional Approach 3

View of Learning: Understanding in order to make sense of experience, with strong emphasis on adaptive decision making and development of executive functions

Instruction: Real-world projects with curriculum embedded, driven by student choices and interests

Academic Goals: Going beyond academic school standards through ongoing, authentic questioning, investigation, and documentation based on experts in the field

Assessment: Authentic performance of all kinds

Throughout the book, therefore, we will provide opportunities for educators to walk the path from Instructional Approach 1 to Instructional Approach 3. We will encourage them to engage students in cooperative projects that require research, higher order thinking, problem solving, planning, and participating in defining and reaching the highest standards. We emphasize the inclusion of additional abilities such as dealing with emotional issues and becoming socially mature and adept.

To achieve this we will continually refer to the three different approaches to teaching and the beliefs that guide them. Each topic or "how to" will be accompanied by suggestions that expand upon a particular approach. They represent a developmental path, so that each approach encompasses, but goes beyond, what preceded it.

Professional Teaching Standards

In 1987 the National Board for Professional Teaching Standards was created by the Carnegie Forum on Education and the Economy's Task Force on Teaching as a Profession (the Internet address is www.nbpts.org, and the home address is 1525 Wilson Boulevard, Suite 500, Arlington, VA 22209). The National Board consists of a board of directors, the majority of whom are classroom teachers, and is a nongovernmental, nonprofit, nonpartisan, and independent organization. Support and endorsement are wide ranging, and include both major political parties. We refer to the *National Teaching Standards* in almost every chapter because they correlate so closely with what we are advocating.

In the second section of this book, *Orchestrated Immersion in Complex Experience,* we also give examples from curriculum standards. We randomly selected standards from several states in order to demonstrate how national curriculum standards relate to this approach to teaching. Most states have similar standards so only a few states are represented.

THE PROCESS THAT MAKES IT REAL: HOW TO USE THIS BOOK

To bring health to a system, connect it to more of itself. The primary change strategy becomes quite straightforward. In order to change, the system needs to learn more about itself from itself. The system needs processes to bring it together. Many different processes will work, whatever facilitates self-discovery and creates new relationships simultaneously. The whole system eventually must be involved in doing this work; it can't be done by outside experts or small teams. (Wheatley, 1999, pp. 145–146)

Professional development is an ongoing and demanding process. The principles and practices that are needed to teach children well should also apply to the development of adult educators. For that reason this is a fieldbook and a process book. There is a sequence to it, but as people work through the book they will find that every part sheds light on every other part. The result is that, in addition to acquiring specific strategies and ideas, educators will begin to make shifts in how they think about their work and how they perceive and respond to what happens in class and in the school. This means that becoming an Instructional Approach 2 or 3 teacher and leader is a transformational process.

A Resource

People are welcome to use this book as a resource to supplement or guide other processes that they have for professional development. The key is to recognize that genuine transformation and improvement always involve both formal and informal elements. On the one hand there are meetings, inservice sessions, planned activities, and so on. On the other is the need to walk the walk and talk the talk in our daily life, to live the ideas and practices in all those brief moments and unexpected interactions that are the stuff of life in the real world. We address the final section of each chapter to transformational leaders precisely because they—you—are the people for whom brain/mind learning is real and who are therefore equipped to help others along the way.

A Guided Process

We have been testing and working with change processes for many years (Caine, 2000; Caine & Caine, 1997; Caine, Caine, & McClintic, 2002).

Our experience and learning theory confirm that there are some indispensable elements for effective and sustained change.

1.   **Educators need a theory of learning that guides and justifies their actions.** They must know WHY they are doing what they are doing, both to communicate more effectively to the public and to support educators in the choices and decisions they make. *That is why every chapter of this book contains some key research and core concepts to be thought about and discussed, and most are organized around one of the Caine Brain/Mind Learning Principles.* Additional research can be found in *Making Connections: Teaching and the Human Brain* (Caine & Caine, in press).

2.   **There is a difference between knowing "about" new ways of teaching and managing and actually living and practicing them.** The successful use of more effective strategies and processes is always grounded in this new foundation. *That is why almost every chapter of the book invites educators to engage and play with the ideas and research personally—to examine their own learning and ways of communicating and making decisions.*

3.   **Educators need to see how to make suggestions practical.** *That is why almost every chapter of the book also provides illustrations and suggestions for educators to try out in the classroom and then discuss with colleagues.*

4.   **Educators need regular and safe opportunities to try things out and to learn over time.** It is absolutely essential to take time to learn, to be able to fail on the path to success, to experiment and receive feedback, to have time to grow and improve, and to be able to work together with other colleagues walking the same path. *That is why we recommend a group process that we call learning circles. That group process incorporates all of the four elements mentioned so far.*

5.   **The system needs to accommodate and support the changes that educators make.** There is, of course, much more to system change than we can address in this book. However, as a minimum, administrators and teachers need to walk hand in hand, and administrators need to support the inclusion of new ways of thinking into the everyday life of a school. *That is why we end every chapter with some suggestions for transformational administrators.*

For those who wish to follow our process, we suggest that you first browse through this book to gain a sense of what it covers. Next we suggest that you form process learning circles in order to work though this book. In general, participation should be voluntary (because no one can be forced to learn at this level). A process learning circle is an action-based, collaborative, reflective study group. Members work together to create a good learning climate, study and reflect on some material (such as the content of this book), take action in their work, and then use the group to reflect on their actions and what they learned as a result. Guidelines for creating learning circles are in Resource C at the end of the book. For more details and suggestions, refer to the book *Mindshifts* (Caine, Caine, & Crowell, 1999).

If you cannot form process learning circles, find a process partner among your colleagues or keep a personal journal. In order to give yourselves enough time, we suggest that you take a year to work through the book, and that the circles meet at least once every other week.

In addition to this structured process, there will be a multitude of other steps that you can take and informal ways to digest and to begin to implement the material in this book. Sometimes that will be a matter for your own initiative and artistry. In addition, there are times when it can be really beneficial to seek guidance from others who have walked the path before. For that purpose we can be contacted at www.Cainelearning.com and www.2perspectives.org. We are also developing some online programs and processes for those who are interested.

In tandem with the National Teaching Standards

Accomplished teachers work with colleagues to improve schools and to advance knowledge and practice in their field. They define their responsibilities as professionals to include a commitment to the continuing growth and development of their colleagues, their school, and their field. They do so because they see themselves as members of a larger learning community with responsibilities that extend beyond their classroom, including a responsibility to shape a healthy professional culture in their school. Their involvement with peers is planned and purposeful; it improves their own effectiveness as teachers, expands their knowledge of students [and] how their field connects to others, and contributes to the knowledge and skills of other teachers and education.

—Standard XII

The nature of this book requires the collaboration suggested by this National Teacher Standard. Look at the idea of learning circles. Is this a possibility for your school? How would it begin? How could you start the process of reflection as a community?

PART I

Relaxed Alertness

2

Introduction to Relaxed Alertness

Relaxed alertness is the optimal state of mind for meaningful learning.

 At the Core

People in a state of relaxed alertness experience low threat and high challenge (Caine & Caine, in press). Essentially, the learner is both relaxed and to some extent excited or emotionally engaged at the same time. This is the foundation for taking risks in thinking, questioning, and experimenting, all of which are essential to mastering new skills and engaging the executive functions. In this state the learner feels competent and confident and has a sense of meaning or purpose.

Believe in yourself! Have faith in your abilities! Without a humble but reasonable confidence in your own powers you cannot be successful or happy.

—Norman Vincent Peale (1898–1993)

Everyone knows people who have triumphed over adversity. One example is Jesse Owens, a weakling as a child who went on to win four gold medals at the 1936 Olympics. The indispensable foundation for success in every endeavor is the right state of mind. The same is true for learning. To help people learn better, the first task is to support them in acquiring the optimal state of mind; namely, relaxed alertness.

RELAXED ALERTNESS IS A PSYCHOPHYSIOLOGICAL STATE

What is a state of mind? Neuroscientist Daniel Siegel defines *state* as "the total pattern of activations in the brain at a particular moment in time" (Siegel, 1999). Any state actually combines aspects of body, mind, and emotions, so it is psychophysiological. In trying to describe a state a person might say,

- "I *believe* something to be true."
- "I *feel* something in my emotions and body."
- "I am *acting* on the basis of how I feel and what I believe."

> Of course, many people are not aware of how they feel or even what they actually believe at the moment of action, but what they do is, nevertheless, congruent with what they feel and believe.

Let's view relaxed alertness through the same lens. A person in that state might say,

- "Even though I am challenged and excited (even anxious), *I feel capable* and trust in my abilities."
- "*My mind is relatively focused and open to possibilities* despite obstacles or potential uncertainties."
- "*My actions are under my control.* I want to respond to the conditions around me."

We can get an even clearer sense of relaxed alertness by looking at the opposite state, one that has as its foundation insecurity, helplessness, threat, and/or fear. For example, an individual experiencing this might say,

- "*My body* is tense and agitated because I don't know what to do."
- "*My mind* is distracted or focused too narrowly."
- "*My actions* are not under my control. I lack a sense of purpose or meaning."

Relaxed Alertness as a Temporary State

States can be temporary, and so relaxed alertness can be a temporary state that is experienced because of a particular situation. One example could be a situation where a student comes across several items on a test that the student knows or recognizes. Under those circumstances the student would very likely experience a boost in confidence.

That sense of confidence could easily generalize to a feeling of mastery for the entire test. Teachers can do much to create a temporary state of relaxed alertness by helping students experience a momentary sense of success, but ultimately we are after something more. *The ultimate goal must be to help students be in a state of relaxed alertness as a way of life.*

Detailing the Research

We can use the term "state of mind" to refer to the cluster of brain activity . . . at a given moment in time. This moment can be brief or extended. The repeated activation of states of mind as time goes by—over weeks, months and years—into a specialized, goal directed set of cohesive functional units is what we are going to call a "specialized self" or "self state." (Siegel, 1999, p. 230)

Relaxed Alertness as a Personality Trait

It is quite possible for a state to become a trait or what Siegel calls a "self state." Over time the state becomes a part of a person's personality—it becomes a personality trait. (For a more in-depth discussion of how traits become states in the brain, see Siegel, 1999, or Perry et al., 1995.) This can happen with relaxed alertness, which gives students a substantial head start for learning. How does this happen?

We suggest that learners who are in a more or less ongoing state of relaxed alertness had their genetic makeup and their biological imperative for growth and development (one that exists in every human being and unfolds naturally) come together with certain consistent experiences over time. This combination resulted in a brain architecture and physiological response that made the state of relaxed alertness a part of their identity.

Ongoing Relaxed Alertness Is Grounded in the Physiology

One reason why developing new traits can be difficult is that personality traits, including relaxed alertness, are physiologically entrenched. In part, for instance, new patterns of synaptic connections are made in the brain and there are changes in the ways in which chemicals interact and flow throughout the body. The brain's ability to change as a result of experience is called plasticity (Diamond, 1988; Huttenlocher, 2002; see also Schwartz & Begley, 2002).

Most systems of the brain are plastic, that is, modified by experience, which means that the synapses involved are changed by experience. (LeDoux, 2002, p. 9)

In most instances traits develop through social interactions that occur over time.

Genetic studies of behavior commonly note that fifty percent of each of the personality features measured is attributable to heredity. The majority of the other half of the variability is thought to be due to "nonshared" aspects of the environment, such as school experiences and peer relationships. (Siegel, 1999, p. 19)

Once physical patterns have been set by previous experiences, only new experiences can alter them. This is where a teacher's role becomes vital. At the heart of the work of educators is creating opportunities for students to have experiences that will develop relaxed alertness.

The way to begin is to know what to look for.

FOUNDATIONS OF RELAXED ALERTNESS

Research from several different domains helps us begin to see who these individuals are who experience confidence, competence, and meaning or purpose as a way of life. We will look at research on self-efficacy, resilience, and self-regulation.

Self-Efficacy

Self-efficacy refers to an innate belief in oneself and one's ability to achieve. This belief, based on past experience, frees learners from self-doubt and criticism and allows them to believe that they will succeed at what they do. As a result, they believe that they can learn from mistakes and work harder to overcome potential obstacles. They see learning as being engaged in an ever-evolving process of becoming better and more capable (Bandura, 2000; Pajares, 1996; Schunk & Pajares, 2002).

Students with self-efficacy will

- Set higher goals and believe that they will succeed.
- Persist longer, even in situations they don't like or even find threatening.
- Visualize success.
- Possess better skills to manage emotional reactions and can use them under taxing conditions.
- Perform better regardless of ability.
- Discover more quickly what strategies work.
- Possess a more positive attitude.

One way to approach relaxed alertness, then, is for teachers and schools to create self-efficacy in all learners.

Confirm for Yourself

Consider some people you know who seem to have a strong sense of self-efficacy. Which of the listed qualities do they have? How can you tell?

How about your own sense of self-efficacy? Now look at your students and answer the same questions.

Resilience

Resilience and self-efficacy have a great deal in common. Resilience refers to the ongoing deep capacity to bounce back from failure or set-backs. People who struggle against enormous obstacles, say to return to safety after being lost in the wilderness, have resilience. The term is often used to describe students who survive poverty or other abusive environments. Resilient kids are kids who survive and thrive despite the odds (Gillham, 2000; Reivich & Shatte, 2002).

Students with resilience (see Davies, 2002)

- are likable; they have social skills and are socially competent (they evaluate their own contributions accurately and can control their impulses);
- have self-efficacy in some areas;
- have coherent moral or spiritual beliefs (can articulate and behave on the basis of moral judgment);
- have a sense of humor and a sense of optimism (can see things in the long term);
- learn from experience (make use of feedback from others);
- have more problem-solving skills;
- are independent and have a sense of autonomy (are self-directed).

Confirm for Yourself

Consider some people you know who seem to be fairly or very resilient. Which of the listed qualities do they have? How can you tell? Have there been times when you were very resilient? Now look at your students and answer the same questions.

Self-Regulated Learners: Students Who Take Charge of Their Own Learning

One area of great interest to educators is the research that focuses on the development of self-regulated learners (Boekaerts, 1996; Perry, 1998; Zimmerman & Martinez-Pons, 1990). Many of the qualities and attributes invoked in this book, and particularly our emphasis on developing the executive functions, are also dealt with in the research on self-regulated learning.

Self-regulated learners have learned how to

- sustain motivation,
- use appropriate strategies,
- be aware of analyzing their own thinking habits,

- set appropriate goals that are attainable and challenging,
- manage time and resources (see previous references).

Self-regulated learners, young and old, believe that they have the capacities and capabilities to influence and control events. Like students with self-efficacy and resilience, they are comfortable with the notion of process (the ability to see how effort can affect future outcomes) and look for the essential steps leading to success.

Having a sense of process results in being comfortable with "emergence" (waiting to see what develops) and "active uncertainty" (remaining calm because of a basic belief that the answers exist even if can't be seen right away). *This ability to see into the future and understand that effort over time pays off and ultimately affects the future is an important characteristic of powerful learners. This also allows them to take occasional failures in stride as they pursue their goal.*

Self-regulated learners, like students high in self-efficacy and students with resilience, tend to feel capable and to believe in themselves. They are also more likely to see themselves as a "work in progress." Self-regulated learning is also correlated with meaning or purpose (Stipek, Feiler, Daniels, & Milburon, 1995; Turner, 1995). *This means that these students are more likely to feel competent and confident and to engage in adaptive decision making.*

Confirm for Yourself

Consider some people you know who seem adept at regulating themselves and their learning. Which of the listed qualities do they have? How can you tell? How about your own capacity for self-regulated learning? Now look at your students and answer the same questions.

Common Threads

Let us pull the threads from these three bodies of research together. Students with self-efficacy, resilience, and self-regulation have the following sorts of qualities and capacities in common. They

- can set short-term and long-term goals and believe that they will succeed;
- persist under pressure;
- visualize a positive future (optimism);
- search out successful strategies or resources;
- have a more positive attitude;
- possess good social skills (get along with and are liked by others);
- are independent (autonomy);
- use time management, which includes being able to pursue their goals when situations change;
- know how to learn and how *they* learn;
- can evaluate themselves.

Clearly a short-hand way of describing this cluster of qualities is needed. We use the term *relaxed alertness*, and we suggest that the core features emerging out of this research can be summarized as confidence, competence, and meaning or purpose. These attributes will be further clarified in the rest of this section of the book, but we can already see how valuable these qualities and attributes are for effective learning. For instance, students would be clear about their goals, be able to persist and overcome the confusion that naturally occurs when learning new material, and be able to acquire new strategies and cope with difficulties as they learn.

In recent times, brain research has begun to confirm and explain these findings.

EXECUTIVE FUNCTIONS

As you read the list below of abilities governed by the executive functions, notice the similarities between characteristics of students with *self-efficacy and resilience* and who are *self-regulated learners*, and the capacities attributed to the prefrontal cortex (Miller & Cummings, 1999) and the executive functions of the brain.

> Students with *self-efficacy and resilience* and who have become *self-regulated learners* are using their executive functions.

Among the abilities housed in the prefrontal cortex and the executive functions are the abilities to

- engage working memory—this means that students can determine a future goal, make a plan to reach that goal (example: time management), and not be easily distracted;
- use reason, assess risk, and make sense of ideas and behavior;
- moderate emotions;
- see ahead or have a sense of an extended future;
- be resourceful and know when to seek help from others and other sources;
- demonstrate flexibility in thinking and be able to shift or add tasks;
- think critically and creatively;
- reflect and engage in self-critical consciousness and metacognition.

The executive functions are also said to house a sense of interconnectedness based on perceiving complex patterns (concepts, metaphors, and other abstractions) and complex relationships among facts or events. Some also suggest that they are involved in experiencing a sense of spiritual connectedness (Austin, 1998).

> Students with well-developed executive functions have *foresight, hindsight* (as a way of influencing present or future decisions), and *insight into self.*

> **Point of Significance**
>
> When learners take charge of their own learning and experience success over time, they are not just more successful, they are also literally growing a brain and mind that ensures future successful learning. So, developing the executive functions is the indispensable key to ongoing powerful learning and, therefore, to raising standards.

Reflection: Something to Think About

Do a preliminary assessment of your own executive functions. How easy is it for you, as an adult, to anticipate the future or use the past to understand yourself? To make it real for yourself, give an example of each.

Learned Helplessness: The Opposite

Increasing the use of the executive functions and having a sustained mental state of relaxed alertness is the ideal objective. Unfortunately, much of the time the reverse occurs. As we will see more clearly in Chapter 3, helplessness and fear lead to activating the threat response in the brain and the physiology. This response, along with the chemicals that accompany it, keeps the learner's thinking at a more automatic, survival level, which is characteristic of helplessness (LeDoux, 2002; Peterson, Maier, & Seligman, 1996; Sylwester, 2002).

Students who tend to experience a lack of power, or helplessness, have difficulty grasping the fact that learning (like life) is an ongoing process. For some people, helplessness is shown as a tendency to see the world in terms of "snapshots" that cannot be changed (Peterson et al., 1996). People are seen, for instance, as either smart or dumb. Things tend to be seen in very concrete terms, limited to what is directly observed or experienced. In Goldberg's terms (see Chapter 1), these individuals favor veridical thinking—they tend to refer to events or information as either true or false, right or wrong—including their own characteristics and the characteristics of others. Their beliefs leave little room for processing (reflecting on possibilities), ambiguity (seeing value in two or more solutions), and emergence (waiting for a solution to emerge).

Because so much of the learning of veridical thinkers focuses on what others want them to do, they fail to decide on, or to initiate, goals. They do not see that they can influence or control. When this becomes a consistent pattern for students, it is referred to as learned helplessness (McEwen, 2001; Peterson et al., 1996; Wallenstein, 2003).

We can see that students who believe that they are smart or are dumb and can't do much about it also tend to decide that success or failure is dependent on someone else's judgment. All too often when students steeped in helplessness do succeed at a task, they don't know why they succeeded because they believe they are "dumb" (as a permanent state). And those who believe that they are "smart" often don't understand when they do fail at something that they can take additional action. Many just give up. They not only give up on learning, they give up on using and developing their executive functions.

Confirm for Yourself

Consider some people that you know who often seem to be helpless. Which of the attributes described in the preceding paragraphs do they have? How can you tell? Now look at your students and answer the same questions.

Let's apply this to the relationships that are either empowered or passive. Take a moment to reflect on your own learning experiences. Think of a body of material or skill that you mastered, and a body of material or skill where you did not succeed. How did you feel in each case? What was your attitude in the two different situations?

WHAT CAN EDUCATORS DO?

One of the primary goals of this first section is to guide educators in ways that help students experience relaxed alertness—the optimal mind state for learning. That means that learners must feel competent and confident and experience meaning or purpose a great deal of the time. Relaxed alertness is one of the foundations for developing the executive functions. Of course, this state is not something that is taught independently of content or academic disciplines. It is not an "add on." Educators have often separated "life skills" from academic skills. The neurosciences are telling us that students need both if they are to use more of their brain. Opportunities to create relaxed alertness are often present and must be monitored and attended to on an ongoing basis. It refers to the physical, mental, and emotional state of the learner and the emotional climate and relationships that accompany learning.

Relaxed alertness, orchestrated immersion in complex experience (Part II), and active processing (Part III) are interactive and ongoing.

Indicators of Relaxed Alertness in the Classroom

The place to begin is to know what to look for. What can be used as evidence of confidence, competence, and meaning or purpose? Here are some preliminary indicators that you can use at every stage of your journey.

Is there evidence of confidence?

- Do students choose to work with groups based upon an area of interest rather than based only on friendship?
- Do students volunteer to share ideas?

- Do students volunteer to help someone who has been absent?
- Do students feel free to give and accept suggestions and feedback from each other?

Is there evidence of competence?

- Do students search out the teacher for feedback and advice?
- Do students feel comfortable debating issues with the teacher?
- Can students answer questions and deal with problems naturally and effectively?

Is there evidence of meaning or purpose?

- Do students take work home automatically because they want to complete something or continue their work on a project?
- Do students come to class with articles or other information (Internet, TV programs) that refer to what they are currently studying?
- Do students talk about the class, their projects, and intellectual content with others outside of class?

What about the teacher?

- Does the teacher respect students?
- Does the teacher allow students freedom to explore their own ideas?
- Does the teacher have high expectations of students?
- Does the teacher point out areas for improvement by processing student assumptions about something they have produced?
- Does the teacher listen to students, thus allowing them to pursue their own thinking?
- Does the teacher engage the rules of logic?
- Is there evidence of community (enthusiasm, laughter that is related to academic work, general atmosphere of excitement and challenge)?
- Are discussions in the spirit of dialogue?
- Can students process their experiences together?
- Is there time to get to the bottom of a frustrating situation?
- Are there procedures for bringing new members to the group?
- Is there concern for others that is expressed in action?

Relaxed Alertness and the Instructional Approaches

You will see that some of the student and teacher behaviors that reveal relaxed alertness actually depend on the instructional approach that is being used. The reason is that each approach is correlated with a particular view of the type of relationship that should exist between teacher and students. That is why understanding and proceeding along a developmental path is so important. One aspect of the increasing complexity and depth of relationship that is found at each instructional approach is summarized in the following table.

Relationship in Instructional Approach 1

The emphasis is on mastering content (skills and facts) that is readily reduced to true or false (veridical). The focus is therefore on classroom management that creates respectful and attentive students who listen to and master the facts provided by the teacher.

Relationship in Instructional Approach 2

The emphasis is on developing an authentic community that encourages actor-centered decision making and the development of the executive functions. Instructional Approach 2 teachers therefore make use of the following (some of which will be explained in later chapters of the book) with both peers and students:

- Shared decision making
- Social/emotional skills (entire community)
- Authentic questions
- Ordered sharing
- Mastering "I" messages
- Effective listening
- Class process meetings
- Processing emotional issues

Relationship in Instructional Approach 3

The emphasis is on generating a community that is capable of monitoring itself and practicing actor-centered adaptive decision making, thus naturally sustaining respect, challenge, and safety. Relationship, then, includes the following:

- Developing social and emotional intelligence using collaboration
- Reflecting and having insight into self
- Managing conflict

THE TRANSFORMATIONAL ADMINISTRATOR AND THE PROCESS FOR MAKING IT REAL

The overall task of the transformational administrator is to do for his or her colleagues and nonteaching staff what teachers need to do for their students. A crucial aspect of an effective learning environment, therefore, is the nature of the leadership. Administrators, lead teachers, mentors, and others need to prepare the way for facilitating empowered individuals who can contribute to a community that fosters a climate of relaxed alertness.

> The key to developing the optimal state of mind and climate in the classroom is to have the same state of mind and climate throughout the school.

Overall, the task is to use as many of our questions and suggestions as possible in your work with your colleagues. In part, you can support them in their classroom endeavors. And, in part, it is a matter of having the same philosophy and practices in all your out-of-class interactions.

The first step is to take stock.

1. Use the indicators in this chapter to assess what sort of climate and state of mind exist in the school as a whole. Take some time to do this, and invite others to participate.

2. Self-assessment. The hard truth is that we cannot guide beyond our own limits. Clearly there is a developmental path for administrators as well, and they need to gain a sense of where they are on that path.

We suggest that you take some time to do this. Browse through the book and talk it over with some colleagues. See if it makes sense.

The second step is to create process learning circles. These circles were introduced in the previous chapter; more details can be found in Resource C.

In tandem with the National Teaching Standards

Teachers develop students who challenge assumptions, initiate projects and activities, take risks, share insights, persist in their exploration of difficult material, and demonstrate a commitment to learn the topics under consideration.

—Standard V

Resilience, self-efficacy, and self-regulation are precisely the sorts of capacities that students need to have in order to meet Standard V. In essence, by creating relaxed alertness and working to enhance the executive functions of students, educators are developing the foundations for the "mental operations, habits of mind (Costa & Kallick, 2000) and attitudes" indispensable for high standard learning.
An additional standard, below, emphasizes the need for the implementation of the steps as outlined in the transformational administrator.

Accomplished teachers work with colleagues to improve schools and to advance knowledge and practice in their field.

—Standard XII

Engage their individual style and uniqueness

Engage the physiology in learning

Reduce threat and enhance self-efficacy

Engage social interactions

Acknowledge and engage developmental steps and shifts

Engage their innate search for meaning

If we want to create enriched environments that help students learn, then we need to include all of the following:

Engage their capacity to recognize and master essential patterns

Engage their capacity to learn from memorizing isolated facts and biographical events

Engage emotional connections

Engage both conscious and unconscious processing

Engage both their ability to focus attention and learn from the peripheral context

Engage their ability to perceive both details and the larger view

3

The Development of Competence and Confidence Accompanied by Meaning or Purpose

Brain/Mind Learning Principle 11: *Complex learning is enhanced by challenge and inhibited by threat associated with helplessness and fatigue.*

 At the Core

For every human being on the planet, from birth 'til death, threat tied to fear and helplessness sabotages the most promising kind of learning, including the executive functions. Relaxed alertness is the ideal mental state for higher order functioning. Creating an environment that fosters this mental state must be a primary goal for teachers and educators.

Capacity: All students can learn more effectively in a supportive, empowering and challenging environment.

Self-distrust is the cause of most of our failure. In the assurance of strength there is strength, and, they are the weakest, however strong, who have no faith in themselves or their powers.

—Christopher Nevell Bovee, 1820–1904

HOW DO WE KNOW THIS?

The Unfortunate Impact of Too Much Stress

Stress is defined by the activation of the stress response, which releases specific hormones into the body and brain. Moderate amounts of these "stress" hormones can actually help learning, but in large amounts, either momentarily released or released over time, they will affect the brain, body, and immune system negatively (Sapolsky, 1998).

A great deal of stress is generated by fear accompanied by a sense of helplessness (not knowing what to do or how to react). It is common knowledge that the United States and most other modern nations face an epidemic of stress. It is not quite as well known that most children—and most students—are also highly stressed. The unfortunate corollary is that excessive stress actually short circuits the brain/mind and reduces the ability of people to engage their own higher order capacities. Recall that a sense of fear and helplessness sabotages the executive functions.

How Does This Happen?

Let us use a metaphor and compare the brain to an electric power grid. Electric power grids connect electric power stations across a very large area (several states or throughout a country). The grid is interconnected in such a way that power stations (known as nodes) "speak" to each other in order to keep the grid balanced. If there is too much power in one station, that node sends some of its power to other stations that can use the added energy. On the other hand, if one station needs a great deal of energy because of high demand, as during an emergency, for example, the other stations in the grid give some of their energy away and lower their own energy level in the process.

The brain works something like that. In a relaxed and alert individual, energy is available for many brain functions. Problems occur when human beings experience threat (fear accompanied by a sense of helplessness). When these conditions exist, the brain is designed to focus most of its energy on survival. Survival requires a quick, almost instantaneous response.

Just as in the electrical grid, this sudden surge of energy, required in order to respond to real or imagined threat, comes at a price. Some areas of the brain lose energy while those in charge of securing survival are charged. Areas in the brain that are minimized during threat include those that are not directly essential for survival and that process more slowly, such as areas that govern reflection, thinking and analysis, interpreting social nuance, and consciously analyzing a situation. These are abilities we have already identified as largely governed by the prefrontal cortex and the executive functions.

Survival can be in response to a physical threat or the result of a belief that something threatening is occurring. Either way, higher order functions are sacrificed.

LeDoux used the term "low road" (LeDoux, 1996). Caine and Caine used Les Hart's term, "downshifting" (Hart, 1978). The Caines defined downshifting as "the psychophysiological response to threat that is accompanied by a sense of helplessness or fatigue" (Caine & Caine, in press). Throughout this book we will be using the terms *low road* and *survival response* interchangeably. They refer to the same phenomenon.

Fatigue refers to the continuous buildup of stress hormones in the body. Sleep deprivation, overstimulation or continual arousal (constant change, even if it is "fun"), lack of exercise, and physical imbalances (due to lack of water or food, being very underweight or overweight, emotional exhaustion, and failing to take medication needed for proper functioning of the body) can all create stress. Over time, stress does not just compromise learning, it also compromises health. Once the body experiences an imbalance in the amount of stress hormones or is saturated with an overabundance of these chemicals, the survival response is more easily activated.

Mind States and the Ability to Learn

Although many researchers have studied and shed light on states of mind associated with stress, fear, and helplessness (LeDoux, 1996; McEwen, 2001; Sapolsky, 1998), one individual in particular, Bruce Perry, MD, PhD (2003b), has painted a picture that is immensely useful for educators. He identifies a continuum of five specific mind states, each of which affect the brain and the learner's ability to think and learn.

Daniel Siegel defined *mind state* in the preceding chapter as both a temporary and long-term condition that engages beliefs, feelings, and actions. Perry has investigated mind states that accompany the survival response. He has developed a continuum ranging from a mental state called *Calm*, to one of *Arousal*, to *Alarm*, to *Fear*, to *Terror*. Each of the mind states is defined by the following:

1. Which areas of the brain are predominantly active

2. What kinds of cognitive processing are available (how well or what kind of thinking can occur)

3. How the mind state affects the learner's sense of time or time horizons (a skill that involves the executive functions)

Mind State 1: Calm and Engaged

Perry's notion of calm is the "relaxed" aspect of what we call relaxed alertness. It is largely a consequence of feeling competent and confident. Only in the calm mind state does the learner access both the subcortex and neocortex (areas that include the executive functions). This is the state in which an individual can think in abstract ways (executive functions) and has a sense of time that includes the extended future (executive functions). When calmness is accompanied by the engagement of the learner in something of interest (purpose and meaning), then relaxed alertness occurs.

Perry's continuum, then, describes what happens to people as they move farther and farther from the optimum state for learning (relaxed alertness).

Mind State 2: Arousal

Most children and adults living in this century find themselves in the arousal state most of the time. In the arousal state the most active areas of the brain are the limbic area (emotions) and areas below the cortex. In the state of arousal an individual rarely thinks beyond concrete information based on right and wrong.

Mind State 3: Alarm

In the alarm state the brain's most active areas are the midbrain (sensory information) and limbic area (emotions). People in the alarm state are primarily sensing danger and are responding emotionally with anger or withdrawal. They are concerned with the next few minutes or, at the most, hours. Tomorrow or next week, let alone next year, are not concepts they can grasp.

Mind State 4: Fear

In the fear state the brain's most active areas are the brain stem (involuntary activities) and midbrain. Someone in the fear state is not thinking in the way most people define the term. In Perry's words these individuals are primarily "Reactive," which means that they are very much in a stimulus-response or automatic mode. They have very little choice over their reactions. Their sense of time is limited to seeing things in terms of minutes or seconds. You have probably worked with children in the Fear state. If you ask them to do something for tomorrow or remember the test on Friday, you will not be heard.

Mind State 5: Terror

In the terror state the individual is literally on "automatic." The brain's most active area is the brain stem; the autonomic nervous system is highly active. People in the terror mind state really cannot think in terms of how thinking is usually defined (figuring out how to do something, for example). They basically react and their reactions are reflexive and totally out of their control. They do not refer to a past or future—they have in fact lost all sense of time. You can recognize individuals in a state of Terror when you look into their eyes. The expression we have found most useful is "there is no one home."

A word about behavior. Not all behavior in these more survival-orientated states of mind leads to danger for others. Perry distinguishes between behaviors that are largely the result of aggressively acted out or hypervigilant responses, and more internal-fantasy–like responses that are dissociative. The hypervigilant students can be expected to become increasingly aggressive, as they shift along the continuum from arousal to terror. On the other hand, students who tend to internalize their responses move along the dissociative continuum and increasingly lose contact with reality. Educators often fail to recognize these students because they tend to be quiet and prefer to do the minimum, only what they are told, and to work hard at protecting their anonymity.

Look at Diagrams 3.1, 3.2, and 3.3, which illustrate these relationships.

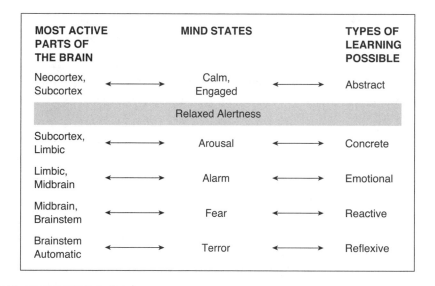

Diagram 3.1 The Effect of Mind States on Learning

SOURCE: Adapted from B. Perry, Pollard, Blakely, Baker, & Vigilante, 1995.

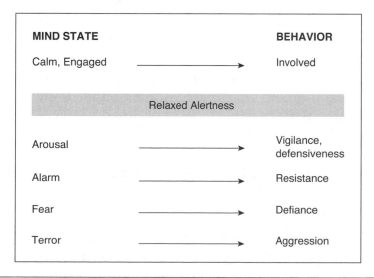

Diagram 3.2 How Students Behave Along the Hypervigilance Continuum

SOURCE: Adapted from B. Perry, Pollard, Blakely, Baker, & Vigilante, 1995.

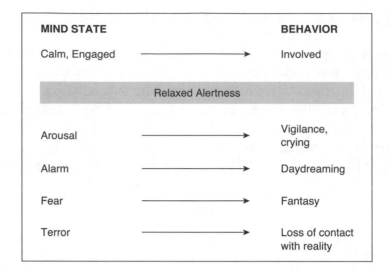

Diagram 3.3   How Students Behave Along the Dissociative Continuum
SOURCE: Adapted from B. Perry, Pollard, Blakely, Baker, & Vigilante, 1995.

Pause for a moment to think about the students you know. How useful are the above descriptions?

The bottom line is that optimum learning takes place when the learner is both relaxed and engaged, not alarmed, fearful, or in terror. Some arousal is also necessary, but not the constant sort of arousal experienced by so many children. Can you recognize the difference between those experiencing a temporary state and those who have taken on the survival response as a trait?

Individuals who are in the survival-oriented mind states, particularly those who function there most of the time, tend to need a great deal of concrete information and require lots of practice and rehearsal. They want clear descriptions, need more support and advice, and are frustrated by having to solve problems or come up with creative or hypothetical responses or solutions (abstractions). Using their executive functions for long-term planning, for example, is more difficult. So educators need to do everything they can to help students increase their sense of competence, confidence, and meaning or purpose, including a focus on what we call creative rehearsal (see Chapter 13).

PROCESSING THIS PRINCIPLE

Personal Connections

The best way to appreciate how the brain/mind can be compromised by threat associated with a sense of helplessness is to see and feel the phenomenon in oneself. We therefore invite you to explore the survival response in your own life by reflecting on a typical life situation.

Example: Public Speaking

The club or organization of which you are a member has just asked you to give a talk on your hobby. "Only ten or fifteen minutes," suggests the person inviting you to do this.

Reflect back. When is the last time something like this happened to you? Can you recall what happened to your thinking?

Commentary

Some people love and thrive on situations such as being asked to speak publicly. They experience an adrenaline rush and look forward to the event. They have inevitably done something like this in the past and feel a sense of competence and confidence when speaking to groups. This is also very likely something they look forward to doing.

Others move into a survival mind state. They may feel flattered but feel their heart pounding and their mouth getting dry. They nod their head and smile, but for a few minutes they can't think. If they move into the arousal state, then chances are they will almost immediately try to pin down concrete aspects of their talk; that need for facts will be driven by a powerful emotional urge for security. "What do you want me to say?" or "What are they expecting?" are common responses.

Individuals who are more into the alarm state will find that their reaction will be more emotional. Individuals at this point (along the dissociative continuum) experience a lot of self-talk as they berate themselves for agreeing to give the talk in the first place. They may even call themselves names for agreeing to do so.

In situations like this, most of us do not stay in a calm mind state. Most people would move into the arousal or alarm state. Even terror is not ruled out if this is the first time they have ever given a talk to a group of peers they see as powerful.

- *Have you ever had any of the feelings or responses just described?*
- *When was the last time you were asked to do something that led to your responding like this?*

Now think about how many students might feel when they are called to make a presentation at the front of the class.

- *To what extent do you think that their responses might be like those we all have when we move into a survival response?*
- *How might preparation and exposure to prior practice help students experience confidence and competence?*
- *How might personal meaning and purpose affect a student's emotional reaction?*
- *How might the response to such a request relate to relaxed alertness and/or affect students' ability to access their executive functions (make a plan and follow through)?*

All of us move into the survival mode when we feel helpless. Some individuals operate from the survival state as a way of life. Understanding your own range of reactions from calm to terror is essential before sharing your understanding with others.

Suggestions

Begin by observing yourself over the next few days. The goal is to catch and note the different mind states you experience. This can be difficult because one consequence of being in the survival response is a tendency to go into an automatic mode and lose awareness! It may help to keep a journal so you can trace your own patterns over time. It is also useful to spend a little time at the end of each day thinking back over how the day went. Sometimes our own responses become evident only in retrospect.

Here are some questions to help your observations:

- What clues did you have that allowed you to see that you were functioning at a survival level? Can you identify the specific mind state?
- What was it that caused you to move into that particular mind state?
- What did someone say or do?
- What did you interpret to be so threatening?
- How did you react (be as honest as possible)?

Going Deeper

You will find that you have your own unique way of acting when you experience the survival response. You will also discover that some others share your own general pattern, sometimes because of similar learning and personality styles. Most people describe the response as "not being themselves."

Recognizing a Common Short-Term
Survival Response: Perseveration

While there are many different emotional responses to threat and helplessness, one of the most prevalent—and useful to know about—is perseveration. When people perseverate they continually repeat the same thoughts or harp on the same situation, endlessly replaying the same words in their mind. Perseveration happens to almost everyone and it occurs so naturally that the individual may be totally unaware of doing it. For others the response is less verbal and more emotional, and they end up in a mood that they cannot shake.

When emotionally aroused, the brain triggers reactions from the autonomic nervous system and the endocrine system; the latter releases stress hormones into the blood stream, creating persistent arousal and reactivation of what ever thoughts are salient in the cognitive system. This arousal persists for several minutes and has an effect analogous to involuntary recycling of the stressful occurrence and the events leading up to it. (Bowers & Sivers, 1998, p. 631)

Perseveration interferes with learning and effective functioning because attention has been hijacked. Here are some everyday examples:

• *Receiving information that conflicts with what someone believes about himself or herself.* Francisco knows that he has been gaining a few pounds but he tells himself it is muscle. You, the teacher, jokingly suggest that he has been hitting the donut shop a little too often. He doesn't think that's funny even though he laughs along with you and his friends who overhear you. He feels hurt and depressed and later you observe him get angry at an innocent comment from a friend. Everyone may have forgotten your comment, but not Francisco. His thinking brain was hijacked by your comment, and he is either not thinking about much or is repeating angry thoughts to himself. Often when people don't feel good about themselves they will work at getting back to feeling the way they did before their beliefs were shattered. If they do not have the opportunity to process the situation effectively (talk it through in order to relieve the tension that was generated), they may "act up" or get into trouble.

• *Receiving information that contradicts what someone believes he or she needs or wants.* Kim feels he is ready to drive a car. His parents tell him that he is too young and doesn't have the ability or good judgment it takes to drive responsibly. Mentally, Kim defends himself to his parents over and over again. In class Kim is not paying attention, but is glum and uncooperative. You are puzzled and frustrated with him.

• *Receiving information that contradicts what someone knows and understands to be true intellectually or academically.* Karen is a history buff and prides herself on knowing U.S. history. As her teacher you're trying to make a point and say, "It's a good thing Kennedy followed Nixon to the White House." Karen is shocked. She goes over your comment again and again in her mind. She may finally get up enough courage to tell you that you are wrong. You minimize the event, not realizing that Karen has lost trust in you and may be less close or respectful in the future.

• *Information that questions an individual's moral or ethical beliefs.* Kelly's father is a Baptist minister and she has learned that Christ turned water into grape juice. Her best friend, whose religion is different, laughs at her. She asks her teacher what she believes and the teacher, not noticing how important this question is to Kelly, echoes her best friend by saying, "Jesus turned water into wine." Kelly doesn't talk or communicate with anyone at school about this. She is taking time out to decide who to believe, her father whom she loves and respects, her friend whose approval she wants, or her teacher who is also someone she respects. She is neither listening nor learning much in her classes.

- *Information that counters an individual's beliefs about his or her group (family, friends, club, race, or ethnicity).* Carlos is an avid football player and on the team. The team is not doing as well as in the past, but everyone is trying very hard. He overhears a comment by someone referring to the team as "those losers." It takes everything he can muster not to confront the guy and he is in no mood for his classes. He tries to work things out in his head. Teachers may find him truculent and sarcastic and may be shocked by his behavior.

Note that these reactions may have absolutely nothing to do with the person who observes these behaviors or who is on the receiving end of such truculence. The mind has been hijacked, and responses are those of someone who is struggling emotionally and mentally.

Here are suggestions for dealing with students in a short-term survival response (the period from a few minutes to a day ago) in classrooms where teachers are practicing Instructional Approaches 2 and 3:

- *Look for behavior that is out of character for your student.* An example: Miguel is ordinarily a great student but today he is driving you crazy. He is calling out to his friend across the room, fidgeting, and continually interrupting you and other students.

- *Analyze the situation.* See if you can begin to see all the behaviors as related instead of dealing with them one at a time.

- *Call the student aside (never deal with the issue in public).* Ask the student (Miguel, in this case) what is going on. Tell him honestly that he is upsetting you or driving you crazy. Be as honest as possible, and tell him that you have a need to understand why he is so different today (see "I" messages and active listening at end of Chapter 4).

- *Wait for a response.* Give the student a chance to figure out how much to trust you. If you've had a good relationship in the past and you have implemented the ideas in this section of the book, he will probably tell you what has happened. If your relationship is fragile, the conversation may stop here and you will have to let it go momentarily or call for a process meeting (see Chapter 5).

- *Stay neutral.* Remember that the chances are very good that whatever is going on with your student has nothing to do with you (although he may initially deny this). Perhaps your student's parents had a big fight, or have yelled at your student for being a "slob" after looking at his or her room. In high school, it may be a boyfriend or girlfriend problem. Simply listen until your student is finished. Don't judge and don't take sides.

- *Help the student identify and engage in actor-centered decision making by solving* his or her *problem.* Chapter 5 in this section introduces the "Acknowledge, Process, Act" procedure. The above example is an abbreviation: Invite the student to tell you what the problem is, briefly talk through the facts that created the problem, and never leave the situation without the student having come up with at least one possible action to take. Perseveration is like landing in a whirlpool. The person has to focus on the shoreline and head for it. This means that a fresh goal and direction are needed to resolve or refocus the original problem.

• *Thank the student* for trusting you and indicate that you trust in the student's ability to resolve the problem.

• *Ask the student what is needed from you.* Is time needed to write a letter? Be alone and think? See a counselor? Work on the problem in some way? Give the student time and/or space to do this and agree on a time limit. Remember that a student in the survival mode is not paying attention or learning much from you anyway. Your listening, respect, and support are usually all that is needed for the student to get back on track.

Advanced Skills

Help students become aware of the behaviors that tell them that they have moved into the survival response. Like adults, students have a repertoire of behaviors (similar every time). Some teachers have had success in helping students identify the very moment when they move into the survival response or soon after. They have given them permission to stop what they are doing and sit in a quiet space, wait for the teacher, and then go through the process above.

The goal is to remain in the state of relaxed alertness more consistently—to have it become a trait and to be able to recover more quickly when the low road has been taken. But the calm state cannot be faked or created by simply thinking one's way into it. The first step is to gain some control over one's reactions by observing when one suddenly slips into the low road. The second step is to develop the skills and enhance the qualities that make a difference. That is what this book, and particularly the first section on relaxed alertness, is all about.

We suggest that in your journal, with a learning partner, or in your learning circle, you discuss instances of perseveration that you have seen in others or experienced in your own mind. At the time, did the other person you referred to, or you yourself, know that you were caught up in this loop? How did it feel? How well were you able to complete your work?

Bridging to the Practical

A good place to begin is with techniques that directly lower stress levels. They can be used with students and modified for use in our own lives. Here are some suggestions:

• Play music softly during times when students are working silently on their own or entering or leaving class (classical music that is relaxing yet challenging to listen to is excellent, such as Baroque and sophisticated New Age). Administrators and counselors can use music in a similar way.

- Allow students time to visualize success and successful behaviors.
- Encourage people who are stressed to breathe deeply and more slowly (don't overdo this—stay at the level of brief, regular practice).
- Use brief exercises every day that have students practice giving full attention to what they are doing. A great time to do this is during "clean up" or during the last minutes of class when they have to get organized for what is ahead. Do these in total silence (don't demand perfection right away; let students get used to the idea).
- Have water available at all times and encourage children and adults to drink more of it.
- Encourage regular and moderate exercise focused on one's "personal best."
- Keep everyone away from toxic environmental materials.
- Help students understand they are profoundly influenced by the foods they choose to eat and programs they watch. One way to launch these discussions is with the phrase: "Whatever you do does something to you."

Take some time to select one or more of the above steps. Decide when and how to begin. Preferably work with a colleague or your learning circle. After your first action steps, come together with your colleagues to discuss findings.

TAKING IT INTO THE CLASSROOM

Let's look at how different teaching approaches might address this principle: Complex learning is enhanced by challenge and inhibited by threat associated with helplessness and fatigue.

Instructional Approach 1

This is the most traditional of the three approaches.

> This approach relies heavily on the teacher's authority.

Assignments and participation are largely controlled by the teacher. Motivation is inevitably vested in the teacher's power to grade, test, and evaluate. So Jenny has her rules posted in the front of the class. Students are reminded of them. Good students and good behavior are rewarded with extra credit, "free time," or even candy. Jenny has a great deal of responsibility.

What is missing? The teacher's power to evaluate and judge students' efforts as right or wrong creates a type of fear. That is why Alfie Kohn (1999) titled his book *Punished by Rewards.* Under these conditions students may memorize and do assignments. However, they will be unlikely to pursue creative and novel ideas, take risks, and engage in the type of actor-centered decision making that develops their executive functions. Motivation that comes from engagement in learning that has meaning and purpose, a core element of relaxed alertness, will be missing.

Opportunities for Instructional Approach 1 Teaching

Remember that the objective is to eliminate fear and helplessness.

1. Observe your students for signs of fear and helplessness and apply some of the strategies that we introduced in this chapter to deal with perseveration.

2. Reduce the use of rewards and punishments.

3. Introduce a little novelty into the classroom by having some brief but open-ended processes.

For example:

- Help students study something they need to study by designing a new way to do that (using games, creating mnemonics, etc.).
- Let students participate in a discussion about school or class events or rules that allows them to suggest meaningful changes that can be put into action.

Instructional Approach 2

There are options that take the curriculum from teacher-designed and -controlled activities to activities that include student ideas. There are "safe" spaces in the room, jointly created by teacher and students, where students can retreat to if upset or in need of a time-out. So Bill is beginning to share power by allowing his students to question some of the deadlines. He allows this as long as students take their responsibilities seriously and come up with different and respectful alternatives or suggestions. He has also decided that keeping learning at the level of right or wrong answers (veridical) is not very productive. It creates fear and helplessness in those who don't have the support at home or have a past history of failure. That is why he has also decided to use creative ways to approach assignments as long as the grading and evaluation process is spelled out ahead of time and everyone achieves the standards. He is looking for ways that students can work together effectively using better communication skills.

> At Instructional Approach 2 the teacher is still very much in charge but is beginning to share responsibilities with students.

Opportunities for Instructional Approach 2 Teaching

Practice the ordered sharing described as a foundational skill at the end of this chapter.

Instructional Approach 3

At this level, much of what is presented in the first section on relaxed alertness has become natural.

Survival responses are recognized and time is given for individuals to deal with those responses. The teacher helps students learn how to recognize their behavior when moving into survival and how it can be triggered. Collectively, teacher and students work on how to remain calm and engaged. Actor-centered, adaptive decision making is the norm, and executive functions are fully encouraged. So Carmen actually uses moments fraught with fear and helplessness as opportunities for learning and for using processes such as the ordered sharing skill described later in this chapter.

> The teacher shares power with students whenever legal issues or responsibilities permit.

Opportunities for Instructional Approach 3 Teaching

The growing edge for Instructional Approach 3 teachers is their own conduct, attitude, and being-ness. The challenge is to work to reduce their own stress, to bring balance into their lives, and to be centered, welcoming, and knowledgeable. One of many really good ways to begin is to use what business calls a 360-degree assessment—on yourself. Take a learning or personality style inventory so that you gain a better idea of your own strengths and weaknesses, but also use some sort of process that invites colleagues, friends, and those who are above and below you in the hierarchy to provide feedback. This will give you a much clearer view of how others see you, and that will be of enormous benefit in your classroom.

THE FIRST FOUNDATIONAL SKILL FOR RELAXED ALERTNESS: ORDERED SHARING

One of the most important skills to learn is how to genuinely listen to others. People need to be heard and feel heard; listening is therefore a foundational skill for learning and working together, and for generating relaxed alertness. Listening is indispensable for students and for adults, in the classroom and beyond. At the same time, it is really important to be able to say what needs to be said in a clear but nonconfrontational manner. It is also essential that there be an opportunity for students—and adults—to share what is on their mind without fearing ridicule, criticism, or judgment.

Our approach has been to develop a process that we call ordered sharing. We have borrowed from many traditions that use a version of circles to guide talking and listening. The essence of the procedure is to provide everyone with an equal opportunity to talk without competing for time and, simultaneously, develop a climate where each person who is speaking has the full attention of everyone else.

Ordered Sharing Procedures

Begin by having students in groups of five or six sit in a circle.

1. Introduce the Topic

Wait for silence.

Explain the following:

Teacher: "I will suggest a topic (see suggestions below). Please think about what you want to say. Anyone can begin." (Give time for students to think or ask questions.)

2. Ordered Sharing

Teacher continues: "Once someone has spoken, continue to the left, letting one person speak at a time. Take only about a minute to talk.

"Fully listen to the person talking, but do not respond in any way. Just listen. Go all the way around the circle without stopping."

(Give time for students to think or ask questions.)

3. Open Discussion and Reflection

Teacher continues: "When you are finished, you can talk freely. During this time share your thoughts but do not criticize anyone." (Give time for every group to finish, allowing for a 2- to 3-minute open discussion by each group.)

4. Teacher Leads a Group Reflection

Teacher: "What happened in your group? What did you notice?"

Remember: *Topic first . . . Ordered sharing . . . Discussion*

Possible Open-Ended Topics

- "What do you admire in other people?"
- "Who are your heroes and why?"
- "Discuss your favorite place in your town or neighborhood. Why is it your favorite?"
- "What streets do you take to get to school and why?"
- "Who would you like to be like and why?"
- "If you could do anything, what would you do on the weekend and why?"

A few helpful hints: The first time you use this process it will take 20 minutes to half an hour. After that, and depending on group size and how quickly students get organized, allow for about 15–20 minutes. Students should remain in initial groups for at least a month. The teacher and students can decide together when they feel it is time to reorganize groups.

Involve your students in an ordered sharing regularly or as often as possible. We suggest once a week when working with older students, and the beginning of the day for children in self-contained classrooms. Continue this until you have a clear sense that the practice has become a natural way for students to communicate.

Be sure that you can give these groups your full attention, not only to develop good group communication habits and skills, but also so you can get to know your students better. Remember, however, that you do not use this time to solve personal problems that may surface in the course of the ordered sharing. Use the suggestions for perseveration if you find you need to respond to a student's dilemma.

You also might want to brainstorm possible topics with your students, keeping in mind that individuals' relation to the question leads to their own truths. This is a powerful example of what Instructional Approach 2 or 3 teachers do in their classrooms. Adjust questions to address specific age groups and allow for more challenging questions to come to your mind. Ultimately, you want to focus on challenging issues emerging out of the curriculum and exploring such issues more deeply. As you listen, you can begin to see differences in culture or ethnicity emerge and can then develop new questions that elicit greater depth of understanding.

> Communication is deeply enhanced with ordered sharing. As people learn to listen respectfully to each other, what might have resulted in debates and arguments turns into discussion and dialogue.

Remember that during ordered sharing the teacher is a facilitator. You guide, listen, and observe yourself as well as the students in action. Once you have spent time to cover the procedure, resist the urge to explain further. Allow the students to struggle with the procedures and try them out, and then, during the reflection afterward, explore what happened and how to enhance the process. Make sure the discussion, questions, or confusion is worked on together in a spirit of mutual problem solving.

Look for these behaviors as you facilitate the process—solutions will emerge in the rest of this section:

- Are students defending their position? How/why are they doing this?
- Are they exploring alternatives? What evidence do you have?
- Are students listening to each other? How do you know?

From a Teacher's Journal

Our tutoring class required a great deal of interaction and discussion as we tried to develop effective skills for working with peers and with the elementary classes next door to our school. I had explained to the class that sometimes it is difficult to hear from everyone when we are in a discussion. I told the students about a technique that I had been taught. The students agreed to try out the method and see how it worked. So we pushed back our desks, divided into groups, and began an ordered sharing.

Interactions like the following were common:

"Brittany, not now," whispered Craig, "wait your turn." Brittany shrugged and mouthed "sorry" as the ordered sharing continued around the circle. Learning to wait until your turn and to not speak out when someone else was talking took time but was very important. It was also becoming evident that it was important to the students as well. They took charge of reminding each other not to interrupt. This carried over into our English and history classes. Students would take the initiative in order to make sure the process was honored and followed. Mark expressed it best at the end of the year. "We were heard and respected. There was time to really think and to own our thoughts. I really liked being listened to and to learn to listen."

Reality Check

We realize that all students and/or adults might not respond equally when a new process like this is introduced. *Remember that relationship and trust come first.* Be authentic, communicate, and empower others to become full participants in the process.

Using Ordered Sharing for Instructional Purposes

In Instructional Approach 3 classrooms, anyone can call for an ordered sharing in order to get everyone's input before starting a project or when things are not working. It can also be used to check quickly on what everyone is doing and their level of understanding. It is a great way to determine goals, check in on what has been discovered, or even have students share what they have been learning.

The power of ordered sharing lies in its ability to equalize the playing field. All students get the same, limited amount of time to express their thoughts. This prevents strong personalities from dominating and gives time for shy or hesitant students. *The objective is to create respect and to create a safe place where all can express themselves authentically.*

The ordered sharing procedure allows students to reflect on their behavior or ideas and on larger concepts, rather than having their responses and thinking overpowered by environmental conditions (such as peer pressure) or stimulus-response impulses. By listening to others, students have to make sense of ideas and behaviors different from their own. Students have the opportunity to discuss new theories and take time to reason things through. Truly listening to others and respecting their turn to speak helps students to keep quick and thoughtless emotional responses in check.

Remember that the prefrontal cortex houses the ability to develop longer time horizons, which are related to patience. Rather than focusing on one instant answer, this entire procedure invites students to put off instant judgment and trust in the collective answer that emerges. When this procedure is adopted as part of instruction, students make decisions that require them to be resourceful and know when to seek help from others and other sources. When led properly through open-ended questioning, students can develop the ability to think critically and creatively. This, in turn, can enhance reflection and metacognition.

THE TRANSFORMATIONAL ADMINISTRATOR AND THE PROCESS FOR MAKING IT REAL

Let us continue with the theme that students and staff should be treated alike. One way in which staff will begin to grasp the nature of Instructional Approach 3 is to see it in practice in the administrator. One suggestion is to begin using the processes mentioned in this chapter. How, for instance, can the environment be modified to reduce stress?

We have also found that ordered sharing is a superb process for helping staff in a school begin to really listen to each other (Caine & Caine, 1997). That is why our preferred way to guide professional development is to form process learning circles of adults (see guidelines in Resource C), with ordered sharing as the first phase.

After being exposed to the power of learning circles, some administrators have incorporated the method into their monthly staff meetings. In some cases, the administrator uses ordered sharing as an "opener" for the gatherings, establishing the dialogue around a non–school-related thought. Following that, the business of the day would be explored.

Here is a way for adults to use ordered sharing:

Step 1: Decide to use ordered sharing to open staff meetings.

Step 2: Have the staff sit in one or two circles, each with a process guide.

Step 3: Select (or invite the guide to select) a powerful proverb or saying, and use that for the thought to begin the ordered sharing.

Note that it is sometimes easier to form fully functioning process groups after the initial experience with ordered sharing in the way just described.

In tandem with the National Teaching Standards	Accomplished teachers establish a caring, stimulating, inclusive, and safe community for learning where students take intellectual risks and work independently and collaboratively.
	—Standard IV

All issues and steps covered in this chapter are in line with and support the National Teaching Standards. *It is not possible to create an effective community without reducing stress and creating a climate where people actually do listen to each other and feel safe enough to take risks.* Of course, the procedures introduced in this chapter will not do the job by themselves, but they are a very good first step.

Engage their individual style and uniqueness

Engage the physiology in learning

Engage social interactions

Reduce threat and enhance self-efficacy

If we want to create enriched environments that help students learn, then we need to include all of the following:

Engage their innate search for meaning

Acknowledge and engage developmental steps and shifts

Engage their capacity to recognize and master essential patterns

Engage their capacity to learn from memorizing isolated facts <u>and</u> biographical events

Engage emotional connections

Engage both conscious and unconscious processing

Engage both their ability to focus attention and learn from the peripheral context

Engage their ability to perceive both details and the larger view

How the Social Environment Contributes to Relaxed Alertness

Brain/Mind Learning Principle 2: *The brain/mind is social.*

 ## At the Core

Every individual on this planet comes complete with what Gopnik, Meltzoff, and Kuhl (1999) have called the "contact urge." Social relationships, with an emphasis on belonging, being recognized, listened to, and noticed, all contribute to a sense of relaxed alertness. Language, beliefs, our state of mind, and access to higher-order learning are deeply influenced and affected by the way we relate to others and how others relate to us. We cannot afford to ignore the impact of relationships and community on learning in and out of school.

Capacity: All students learn more effectively when their interests and ideas are engaged and honored.

Culture is one of the most precious things a company has, so you must work harder at it than anything else.

—*From* Nuts! Southwest Airlines'
Crazy Recipes for Business and Personal
Success *(1998), Kevin and Jackie Freiberg, p. 130*

HOW DO WE KNOW THIS?

Research from the neurosciences is documenting a remarkable dance between the neurons inside our brain, the responses of our body, and the social experiences we have with the world around us. The very relationships and interactions we have with others are capable of altering the way the synaptic connections of our brain cells grow and connect to other brain cells. Social interactions are capable of influencing the flow of chemicals that govern sleeping, eating, and mating and are related to stress, health, and disease (Detweiler, Rothman, Salovey, & Steward, 2000; Sapolsky, 1998). The implications are remarkable!

For instance, Paul MacLean (1978) was one of the first to warn that without appropriate social bonding, the human intellectual brain would be little more than a "heartless computer." Even executive functions that are not deeply connected to the limbic or emotional brain can lead to developing young people and adults who lack moral or ethical anchors. Without caring, compassion, or a capacity for empathy and love, children and adolescents are left alone and adrift. A healthy, social environment is therefore critical.

Survival Depends on Relationships

All human beings are born with a biological need to relate to others (Diamond & Hobson, 1998). Being in relationships has immense survival value because we could not feed ourselves, procreate the species, nor raise the young without help from others. This survival need is most easily recognized in infancy when the brain is growing and shaping itself at maximum speed. No infant could survive without others to care for it and, as most parents know, every baby comes biologically equipped with vocal chords that get it the attention it needs. As the infant grows, it learns how to survive within its community by acquiring language and other essential social skills. In adolescence, the drive of the species to procreate leads the adolescent on an urgent quest to mate. Human mating requires social skills and an ability to live within a social community. Adulthood is tied to survival as well, as adults seek to feed and provide for their families. This inevitably throws them into social relationships that require more sophisticated social skills. Finally, the aged need a social environment in order to manage the vulnerability of potential frailties.

> "We are an intensely social species, deeply dependent on one another for our very survival" (Gopnik et al., 1999, p. 23).

Throughout a lifetime, the brain/mind adapts and changes in response to engagement with others. Families, churches, towns, cities, countries, and world associations like the World Bank and the United Nations are only a few social configurations that have been established in order to respond to the human need for community.

Becoming Part of a Social Group by Observation and Imitation

Children and young adults learn by observing others. Surrounding learners with appropriate models is critical. For example, even one-month-old babies imitate facial expressions. Researchers have demonstrated this systematically by showing babies a person sticking out a tongue or opening his or her mouth. Babies' faces were videotaped while this was happening. The video-taped faces were then shown to someone else who had no idea what the baby had seen. The second person had to determine whether the baby was sticking out its tongue or opening its mouth—and did so accurately and predictably (Gopnik et al., 1999).

> "Imitation is an innate mechanism for learning from adults, a culture instinct" (Gopnik et al., 1999, p. 13).

Humans may have "mirror neurons." Neuroscientists are in the process of discovering the neurons that help individuals learn by simply observing others do something.

Detailing the Research

Leslie Brothers (1997) reports on neuropsychologist Giacomo Rizzolatti's research: "He demonstrated how certain neurons in monkeys responded both when they did a particular hand motion and when they merely observed some-one else do those same hand motions" (p. 79).

The continuing research on "mirror neurons" will show that we are all built to respond to and learn from what others in our environment do. No matter how much a person might like to think of himself or herself as a loner, everyone is designed to imitate and model others.

All learning is colored by social relationships and the groups of which one is a part. A child learns from its siblings, its parents, and its peers. Mothers of young infants learn from other mothers. People stepping into any world for the first time—medicine, stock-brokering, hospitals, road maintenance, outdoor adventure, tagging and marking graffiti, journalism, politics, border hopping—are all influenced by the habits and practices and language and values of those in the same arena.

In the absence of healthy emotional and social interactions and modeling by healthy adults on a consistent basis, children will largely "become" whatever their environment models. The surrounding environment may potentially include noncaring adults, violent characters on television, or aggressive peers (Bandura, 1973). What may be innocent entertainment for a child surrounded by healthy relationships and adults, can turn into a potential agent for a social and violent behavior in the hands of those who are lost and isolated (Perry, Pollard, Blakely, Baker, & Vigilante, 1995; Healy, 1998).

It is not difficult to see that children who feel disconnected, who experience isolation on the basis of being "different," bullied, or ridiculed, cannot access their best learning. This is exacerbated if the child's home life is less than ideal. We can also begin to understand that many students will do almost anything in order to "belong." Bruce Perry (2003a) and Richard Restak (1995) both suggest that students who have fewer social connections are much more likely to become addicted to drugs and alcohol.

Community and a Sense of Self

It is in community with others that one's genetic makeup interacts with parents, siblings, relatives, and strangers. These experiences powerfully affect how the brain and physiology become organized and tell children and even adults who they are. It is through interactions with others that individuals learn whether they are capable of doing something exceptionally well, whether they are likable, have a sense of humor, are especially creative in a given area, and so on. It is the community that helps shape individuals and convince them that they have contributions to make to the larger whole. It is when the family and broader community guide by way of example, restraint, caring, practice, and standards to be met that children become connected adults who relate to others with confidence and caring. This is how children learn that they belong.

> Lev Vygotsky (1978) suggested that even the ability for people to engage in internal dialogue—to think in their minds—is learned after experiencing external dialogue with others.

Reading Others and the Executive Functions

Developing our ability to "read" others, moderate emotional responses, and interact using social intelligence all depend on and develop the neocortex and executive functions.

Something else quite critical happens in the brain as the result of students' engaging in social interactions. Because social interactions occur in "real time," students must adapt to moment-to-moment signals from another and respond accordingly. One area in particular, the orbitofrontal cortex, is related to the ability to correctly assess external events and link them to appropriate action. The orbitofrontal cortex is part of the system that houses the executive functions.

> In other words, the orbitofrontal region is active in taking charge of unexpected internal and external conditions and creating new and flexible behavioral and cognitive responses instead of automatic reflexive ones (Siegel, 1999, p. 140).

The many intricacies involved in dealing with other peoples' ideas and perspectives, along with collective problem solving and challenges to one's own thinking, require students to develop areas of the brain located primarily in the prefrontal cortex.

"Response flexibility enables the mind to assess incoming stimuli or emotional states and then to modify external behaviors as well as internal reactions. Such an ability can be proposed as an important component of collaborative, contingent communication" (Siegel, 1999, p. 141).

This interaction between people can be very subtle and nonverbal. In their attempts to explain this connection, some scientists speak of a "mental state resonance" (Siegel, 1999). It occurs when individuals are aligned in a way that lets them feel understood at a deep level. This level is a type of a nonverbal attunement that Daniel Siegel, MD, calls "feeling felt." This same state assists therapists, good parenting, effective learning together, and exceptional teaching.

Healthy Relationships and the School Environment

The research leads to powerful conclusions. If the brain organizes itself to a significant extent on the basis of experience, then school and classroom experiences created by caring, respectful adults can play a major role in overriding old habits and creating new options for children. This is the positive side of plasticity (the ability of the brain to change itself in response to experience).

Through positive and ongoing interactions with significant adults over time, children and young adults can experience interactions in school that strengthen new and healthy pathways in the brain and affect how they act and interpret the world around them. Moreover, students with higher social skills do better academically. They tend to value school more and take school goals more seriously.

When students become socially capable, they are able to reflect on their own behavior and actions, have empathy for others, believe in their ability to change, be positive, and have a sense of humor. All of these are characteristics that protect children and adolescents from adopting destructive patterns that lead to failure in school and in life (Kokko & Pulkkinen, 2000). So, from the perspective of developing relaxed alertness, the following occurs:

- Healthy social interactions help children believe in themselves.
- Positive social interactions assist in the development of the executive functions.

Although infants and young children are extremely vulnerable, so are adolescents. They may be able to think abstractly and engage in complex planning. They may even be motivated to learn everything they can about a particular subject. But without interactions with emotionally healthy adults who are functioning in a healthy emotional community, much can go awry.

In today's schools we have seen too many examples of where bonding is lacking. The word *Columbine* has become synonymous with amoral adolescents. The students at the center of the tragedy were certainly competent and confident in some respects, and had the motivation to execute their plan of destruction, but they were totally unconnected to their community. Apparently, a teacher let the two boys rehearse the massacre on a video and then simply gave them a grade for their efforts without ever questioning them more deeply or communicating with their parents. If true, such a teacher had never internalized this critical Brain/Mind Learning Principle. We must also wonder about the parents, who apparently did not realize what was stored in the garage. Relationships among individuals who, by all rights, should care about each other yet who begin and end conversations only with "how was your day" answered by "fine," are a sign that something is terribly unconnected.

School as Apprentice Community

Creating a healthy social environment is difficult. Much more is required than mastery of some communication strategies. The adult members of the community need to be emotionally mature, and the community itself needs to function well. This means that, while at school, children are immersed in a healthy community within which they can develop and become socially capable. We like the term *apprentice community* as a descriptor of this environment.

Community in school is not just about everyone feeling good. It's about creating a network of self-regulated learners who support each other in the interest of learning. This means creating an environment of low threat and high standards that challenges everyone to master academic standards and develop their executive functions. Doing that includes developing behaviors that are guided by ideas, concepts, and plans rather than by automatic responses to environmental conditions. In a well-functioning, thinking community, behavior modification is often inappropriate and never enough. Students and staff need to be resourceful and know when to seek help from others and other sources. There will be a need to be flexible and able to shift our thinking in order to consider new information and input from others. Mistakes are not catastrophes but steps along the way to deeper understanding and mastery. There is time and opportunity to do better, become smarter, and see new connections. For adults or students it means there is almost always another day.

PROCESSING THIS PRINCIPLE

When put to the test, how many educators spend time on purposely creating an intelligent social community based on research and personal understanding? How many educators have shunted aside the time for social learning in favor of extra time to practice for the test or master purely academic standards despite a conviction that social relationships and learning go hand in hand?

Personal Connections

Most educators can remember a time when they felt totally disconnected from others. Student teachers often tell stories of feeling lost and alienated the first few days in "their" school. The teachers' lounge can be an inviting or desolate and lonely place, depending on the faculty and general sense of community. Those who have experienced these feelings can easily see that feeling isolated contributes to a mental state of arousal and alarm, if not fear.

Yet, if ever new teachers needed to access their memory banks and higher-order problem solving, it would have to be the first few days and weeks of facing students.

How welcome are the warmth and help that appear in the form of a faculty member or administrator who takes time to introduce himself or herself and is ready to talk things through and answer questions.

Ask yourself these questions and process with someone or bring this to your learning circle:

- Is there time for social interactions in your school and in your life, or is everyone too busy for this? List specifics that support your answer.
- Do people respect each other? How do you know this? List specific examples.
- Do people take time to actually listen to each other?
- To what extent does the physical environment support and encourage good relationships? (Take a critical look at the teachers' lounge or cafeteria as a first step.)

Going Deeper

Relationships that include authenticity, communication, and empowerment do for students what healthy attachment does for infants. They allow the individual to explore farther, take risks with new thinking and skills, and generally be challenged rather than intimidated by high standards and hard work.

> One of the best ways to enhance social relationships involves working on three critical qualities: *authenticity, clear communication, and empowerment.*

Authenticity

Authenticity means being genuine or as truthful as possible about beliefs and feelings. Being authentic means that people, including students and teachers, discuss real issues of concern to them as they occur or become relevant. Everyone is recognized and has their thinking and work acknowledged or critiqued in a respectful manner. As Barbara Larrivee (2005) states, "The opposite of authenticity is defensiveness. Authentic people, while not denying their fears, erect minimal barriers and have little to hide" (p. 13). She describes such individuals like this: "They communicate a powerful sense of inner authority. Being authentic means not depending on others for your sense of well-being, not having to appear in control, to look good, or refrain from rocking the boat." Authentic people experience being of value to the community. This may, however, require changes in how classes and schools and other places are organized.

Clear Communication

Clear communication includes sending, giving, or exchanging information or ideas and extends to the tone and manner in which people deal with each other. For many people, empathy and respect for others are not learned automatically. They emerge as people listen and talk with each other. The belief emerges that, "I can make this work because I understand those around me and they in turn listen to me."

Real conversation, however, takes time and a relaxed environment. Clear communication includes opportunities for silence and thinking. As difficult as it might be in classrooms and schools that are quite hectic and leave little time for reflection and conversation, we must introduce time to communicate. In addition to the school setting, knowing and seeing students outside the regular classroom can facilitate clear communication and often happens most naturally when teachers and students meet at sports events or social gatherings such as the grocery store, dances, exhibits, or community events.

Empowerment

Empowerment means to give power or receive power from another, indicated in part by showing real respect. Here the focus is on students' (and teachers') belief in their abilities together with a sense of entitlement to act. Empowered students and teachers have been given the chance to see themselves as continuous learners in both academic and social settings. They don't describe themselves or others as smart or not smart as if those are permanent aspects of a personality. The belief that tends to emerge is, "I choose to do this even if it turns out to be difficult. I support others in exploring their way of becoming fully competent." Teachers have provided enough opportunities for students to experience both failure and success in order to allow them to recognize learning as a process that takes time, includes trial and error, and continues to make students more knowledgeable and more able to master future challenges. They respect each other as individuals who can and will reach new levels of mastery both personally and academically.

Bridging to the Practical

Let's look at the following two scenarios. Answer the questions in your journal, with your process partner, or in your learning circle.

From a Teacher's Journal

Kenny

He was the rough kid in the 6th grade. I was told that Kenny was going to be placed in my room because he needed a male teacher. His record was well known. Anger, bullying, disrespect, low achiever, but nevertheless a bright young man. We've all been there when it comes to having a Kenny in our classroom. When he entered, he probably had the same goals of disrupting my classroom as he did in every other one that he had been bounced through. Granted, he was a tough kid, but he was a kid.

At first, my hopes were that because I was a "man teacher" Kenny would settle in and all would be right with the world. That reality lasted about 20 minutes. After he scoped out the conditions, his disruptive actions began. What to do?

Despite criticism from some of my colleagues, I had previously made the decision to spend my lunch breaks outside with the kids. A routine had been established that we always, come rain, snow, sleet, or hail, played tag football, with me as the permanent quarterback for both sides! During a game one late October afternoon, I noticed Kenny on the sidelines. He was never really welcomed into the game because his normal mode was to bully his way to get what he wanted. The kids who were playing didn't allow him on the field. The teams were astounded when I invited him to join us. They found him to be fast, nimble, and able to catch a football better than just about anyone else. Soon, he was the player everyone wanted on their team. He also became my occasional back-up quarterback. After that, the classroom disruptions essentially vanished. His grades improved and his negative reputation slowly disintegrated.

Take some time to reflect:

- How did Kenny originally communicate with others? How did they communicate with him? What changed in the manner of communication?
- In the scenario, when was Kenny being authentic? When was the teacher being authentic? When were the other students being authentic?
- In what ways was the teacher empowered? How was Kenny empowered? In what ways were the other students empowered?
- Can you see a relationship to competence, confidence, and intrinsic motivation?

From a Teacher's Journal

Four Students

Last spring, four upper elementary girls came rushing to the office after the end of the school day. They had just witnessed another student throwing junk on the playground. The girls were affronted to think that someone from their school would consider such an action! The girls asked to speak with the principal. They were asked to wait for a short while, and then the principal and the girls had a meeting. She asked them if they thought the other student should be punished and they said no. They were not trying to "report" the student. They were genuinely concerned with how to stop the practice. The principal thought for a moment, and then asked the secretary to come into the office. For a short while they all met and came up with a solution for the situation. The interesting point is that the school had changed so much for the better that this was the most serious issue that had to be handled that day, a far cry from the school's recent past.

Take time to reflect:

- How did the various parties communicate with each other?
- In what ways were they authentic?
- In what ways were they empowered?

TAKING IT INTO THE CLASSROOM

The objective is to build healthy social relationships by teaching students to be authentic, communicate better, and feel empowered. How this is done depends on the Instructional Approach being used.

Instructional Approach 1

Keep Control!   Instructional Approach 1 teachers rely heavily on their authority in order to maintain discipline and keep control. They believe this to be the best way to create the optimal environment for learning. So Jenny allows her students to take turns answering questions. When they raise their hands she acknowledges the student she chooses. This is how she keeps order in the classroom. Quiet and order must prevail if students are to do their work. She does not realize that this entire way of teaching controls the flow of information and keeps children from learning the social and negotiating skills that are integral to developing their executive functions.

Opportunities for Instructional Approach 1 Teaching

- Explore the use of group work and new ways for students to work together.
- Ask questions that invite the students' own thoughts and ideas for research.
- Incorporate student discussion when implementing class rules.
- Let students decide on some goals and/or timelines for some of the topics you must cover.

- Get to know your students as individuals outside of class time.
- Have students present their projects in informal groups first. Have the group select points and issues to be discussed by the entire class.
- Let students design the seating arrangement for a limited time.
- Create a survey that reflects what students are interested in learning about, and connect that information to the curriculum.

Instructional Approach 2

This teacher is beginning to look at ways to put the principle, "The brain/mind is social" into action with students. An example is Bill, a teacher who loves to create different ways for his students to interact. He uses groups, teams, role plays, and a diverse set of strategies to support learning. At the same time that Bill wants to empower his students, however, he is hesitant to let go of his sense of authority.

Empower Students!

Opportunities for Instructional Approach 2 Teaching

- After students have practiced ordered sharing, use it in small groups for a specific purpose, such as designing rubrics (spelling out criteria for grading or success).
- Process with students what did or did not work well in their project.
- Incorporate genuine open-ended questions generally and within assessment practices.
- Support students in any effort to express how they think or feel in a nonjudgmental way.
- Practice and implement the skills in this relaxed alertness section.
- Encourage peer coaching, student study groups, time for reflection, and dialogue using parts practiced in ordered sharing.
- Encourage a line of thought; for example, ask, "Can you say more about that?"
- Have the students pick some guidelines they want for the classroom or design rubrics for their projects.
- Give opportunities for students to gain experience in making choices.

Instructional Approach 3

Carmen is convinced that students are active meaning-makers. She challenges, questions, explores, cajoles, and demands that students bring their genuine thoughts and ideas into the open. She also expects to have her own views challenged and questioned. She sees that communication has much to do with learning that is deep as well as broad.

Seamlessness and Expertise!

The difference between beginning Instructional Approach 3 teachers and a teacher using advanced skills is in the seamlessness and expertise and the focus on developing the executive functions, including emotional maturity. Everything is negotiated and discussed in real time, not by a script, tight lesson plan, or other artificial constraints on learning.

Interactions are based on mutual respect that surpasses the more traditional roles and functions of the "teacher." This type of teaching is very dynamic, leading to a challenging exchange by learners on the edge of their abilities, knowledge, and intellectual understanding. Authentic teachers in this context simply are themselves—no artifice, no hiding behind roles. They respect themselves and respect others. They are continuous learners. They rely on processing their experiences and their own learning in an ongoing fashion (for a wonderful example of this kind of teaching in a traditional high school see Benesh, 1999).

Opportunities for Instructional Approach 3 Teaching

Collaboratively, teachers and students can

- take charge of their own learning by setting their own goals and taking part in the evaluation process,
- discuss what expertise looks like and how to achieve it,
- search for problem-solving strategies and master them,
- support each other in their passions and find ways to link curriculum to those passions,
- experiment with ways to help people learn from each other,
- develop new ways to listen to oneself, observe oneself in action, and reflect on one's own learning.

THE SECOND FOUNDATIONAL SKILL FOR RELAXED ALERTNESS: EFFECTIVE LISTENING AND "I" MESSAGES

Much of what educators want to do, including student research, tends to take some very basic skills for granted. It must be possible for students to identify their preferences, make intelligent choices, and work cooperatively with others. But for student communication to work, educators must be able to listen effectively. All students need to be listened to, and, like all of us, they love to be heard. Being genuinely heard increases a student's sense of self-worth. The problem is that many people assume that they know what others are thinking or what they mean, or they are so busy listening to themselves and planning what they are going to do and say that they don't hear the people with whom they are talking.

Renate's Story

My dissertation, written almost 30 years ago, focused on the effect that the teacher's use of "I" messages and active listening had on student self-concept and attitude toward school and teachers (Gordon, 1977).

Two very closely matched groups of teachers were included in the study. One group was trained in the use of "I" messages and active listening, which they would practice for 6 months with their students. The others acted as the control group and changed nothing in the way they had been communicating with students.

Six months later the students in classes where teachers used "I" messages and active listening had a significant positive change in self-esteem and attitude toward school and teachers. This research convinced me of something I believe to this day: When teachers change, students follow.

Effective Listening

The following section is for both review and mastery.

Effective listening is indispensable for good teaching.

The primary strategy suggested for Instructional Approach 1 is to increase "wait time" so as to give students more time and opportunity to think and respond. For Instructional Approaches 2 and 3 there is more.

1. Pay attention to the literal message

To avoid assuming that you know what is being said and to hear what students or staff actually say, take pains to clarify their words. Two techniques are *paraphrasing* and *summarizing.*

Paraphrasing is done when listeners repeat what they have heard in their own words. "What I heard you say is . . . . Is that right?"

Summarizing, a form of paraphrasing, reflects content and feeling after a longer sequence during a conversation. The listener can summarize at the end of the conversation or at intervals to clarify the speaker's thoughts (Bickmore, Goldthwait, & Looney, 1984). "So your main points are that . . . . Have I heard that right?"

2. Remain attentive and neutral

Your tone and presence contribute as much as your words. So do not interrupt, offer advice, or give suggestions. Maintain eye contact, show interest but avoid facial expressions that could indicate that you are making a judgment. Indicate with body posture that you are interested, but do not fake understanding. If something in the message is puzzling, then allow your eyes and demeanor to show that you are puzzled.

3. Use questions for clarification

Even the most articulate people sometimes do not say enough of what they mean. Use questions to find out in more depth what a student or staff member is really trying to say.

Ask specific questions for clarification: "Let me make sure that I understand. You did (such-and-such) and so you want (specific thing) to happen?"

Ask open-ended questions to elicit more general information: "What else happened?" "Can you tell me more?"

4. Go deeper as appropriate

All of the thoughts and feelings that people have are shaped by their beliefs and mental models. That means that all communication is full of assumptions and taken-for-granted ideas. Once you are comfortable with your ability to hear and understand the literal statements that staff and students make, start listening for their underlying assumptions, beliefs, and needs. These can be very personal, and sometimes the people with whom you are talking cannot or will not say what is really on their mind. But the key is still to listen. Many of the strategies and questions introduced in Part III of this book, Active Processing, will help. To begin with, the key is simply to ask yourself, "What is really being said? What does this person really want?" A way to help that person is to use, and encourage the use of, "I" messages.

"I" Messages to Clarify Your Message

Language is often confrontational and confusing. It is very easy to blame others by saying, "You made me do this" or "It's your fault." These are "you" messages. At the same time, it is possible to want something from others or to feel a particular way but never let it be known. The result is that even if others are willing to help a student or colleague, they may not know what to do or what is wanted. So the key is to use "I" messages and to help and encourage others to use "I" messages.

The essence of the situation is that you or someone needs to be listened to. Remember, the "I" message focuses on the speaker, not on the listener. It needs to state the speaker's feelings and what the speaker wants. It is not for placing blame. It is used so speakers can clearly articulate what they believe is happening and what they are experiencing. It allows for clear communication of feelings and needs and offers a way into solutions.

Traditionally there are four basic elements:

- I FEEL . . . (State your feeling for the situation)
- WHEN YOU . . . (State the specific behavior you reacted to)
- BECAUSE . . . (State the effect on your life)
- AND I WANT . . . (Say what you need or want to make the situation better for you)

Examples:

- I feel worried when you don't show up for our group meetings because I need you to contribute to the group project and I want everyone to do their fair share.

- I feel angry when I am teased by you because I try very hard not to do that and I want you to be more careful around me.
- I feel timid when someone new comes to our class because I am not sure what to say. I want to get better at meeting people.

There is a fifth element that makes "I" messages a useful tool to help individuals accept more responsibility for a given situation. That element is either to acknowledge personal responsibility for what is happening (when appropriate) and/or to indicate what action the speaker will take to help solve the problem. It is, after all, the speaker's problem. So either the statement should conclude with an action step, or the whole interaction should include a clear indication that the speaker takes some responsibility.

The fifth element:

- SO I WILL DO . . . (Something that you will contribute to make the situation work)

Examples:

- I feel worried when you don't show up for our group meetings, because I need you to contribute to the group project and I want everyone to do their fair share. *I am willing to call you a couple of times if you would like a reminder.*
- I feel angry when I am teased by you because I try very hard to not do that and I want you to be more careful around me. *If I do the same to you, please help me to see what I do, and I will stop.*

Hints for Practice

1. Share the elements with practice partners or the learning circle.

2. Select one or two examples of situations that are familiar to everyone. Formulate appropriate "I" messages, then role-play using them.

3. Discuss, role-play, or summarize the effects of "You" messages and how they differ from "I" messages.

   Example of an "I" message: I feel angry when you don't listen to me because I feel you don't respect my opinion and I want to be heard. In the future I'm going to ask you questions to check on whether I am being heard or not.

   Example of a "You" message: You think you are the only smart one here. Just who do you think you are?

4. Practice frequently in class or elsewhere. Then meet with your process partner or learning circle to discuss and reflect on the experience. Refine the process so that it suits your situation and needs.

Some aspects of this practice have been adapted from *Teacher Effectiveness Training* by Thomas Gordon (1977). Also see Bickmore et al. (1984).

When You Are Ready to Teach These Skills to Students

As Renate's research indicates, when educators become proficient in these skills, the overall climate improves and students automatically benefit. In addition, it is really useful to help students acquire these skills. The key is to be proficient and to practice the skills before setting out to teach them. In addition, each instructional approach will teach these skills differently.

When you are ready to teach your students, it can help to use the following questions:

- *What can happen when you or someone else does not listen?*
- *How do you feel when someone really listens to you? When they don't?*
- *When do you think it is most difficult to be a good listener? (Have students describe situations from their own experiences.)*

Reflection: Something to Think About

Take the time to consider the following questions about building relaxed alertness by using "I" messages and active listening.

- How do "I" messages and effective listening build authenticity for you and your students? Why?
- How do "I" messages and effective listening help communication? Why?
- How do "I" messages and effective listening empower you and your students? Why?

THE TRANSFORMATIONAL ADMINISTRATOR AND THE PROCESS FOR MAKING IT REAL

Just as in the classroom, a significant goal for the administrative leadership should be to concentrate on ways in which all educational professionals can continually strengthen their building or professional community. Though much has been written on the value of "team building," what we really want to emphasize is "community building." When strong professional communities are experienced within a school and/or district, the handling of conflicts and pressures is inevitably improved.

All three of these qualities—authenticity, communication, and empowerment—constitute elements for building positive social relationships and have tremendous ramifications for the adult interactions that take place within the school buildings and districts. As a direct result of the multitude of time constraints and demands placed on teachers and administrators by restrictions, Instructional Approach 1 educators can become consumed by survival behaviors and activities that do not allow them to understand how to practice and incorporate authenticity, communication techniques, and empowerment.

Reflection: Something to Think About

As teachers and administrators, look again at the descriptions presented for *Authenticity, Communication,* and *Empowerment.*

- How authentically do the professionals in your world act/react to the daily conditions in your school or district?
- Are the adults empowered?
- Is communication healthy and professional?

We suggest that you explore, individually and as a group, what you can do to nurture and support the qualities and skills we describe in this chapter for the adult interactions in your school and beyond.

In tandem with the National Teaching Standards	Accomplished teachers foster students' self-awareness, character, civic responsibility, and respect for diverse individuals and groups.

Although the principal focus of many schools is cognitive growth, teachers know that nurturing the social and emotional growth of students is often the key to motivating them to learn and to enhancing their overall development.

Teachers are concerned with their students' self-awareness and aspirations; with their development of character and civic responsibility; and with their respect for individual, cultural, religious, gender, ability, and ethnic differences.

—Standard VIII

All of the issues and steps covered in this chapter are in line with and support the national standards. More specifically, the use of "I" messages and effective listening can be of immense value for the adult community, and when used by the adults in their interactions with other adults create a climate that is more conducive to their use by students.

How Meaning Contributes to a State of Relaxed Alertness

Brain/Mind Learning Principle 3: *The search for meaning is innate.*

 At the Core

The need to make sense of things is characteristic of every human being from infancy to adulthood. It has been called the "explanatory drive" (Gopnik, Meltzoff, & Kuhl, 1999). Learning that is reducible to true-and-false is different from learning that engages actor-centered adaptive decision making. It is the search for meaning that organizes actor-centered questions and encourages the use of the executive functions. The search for meaning is enhanced by—and enhances—relaxed alertness. It drives actor-centered adaptive decision making.

Capacity: All students can learn more effectively when their interests and ideas are engaged and honored.

Everywhere one seeks to produce meaning, to make the world significant, to render it visible.

—Jean Baudrillard, French Sociologist, Cultural Critic, Theorist of Postmodernity, 1929– (www.egs.edu/faculty/jeanbaudrillard.html)

HOW DO WE KNOW THIS?

At the core of meaning is a sense of relatedness. When people finally make sense of new ideas or a new situation or new skills, the old connects with the new. When there is a sufficient depth of meaningfulness and relationship, it is as though they come to know something with their whole body and mind. There is a resonance. They get it "in their belly."

Here are some aspects of meaning:

Felt Meaning. This is a kind of recognition that engages thoughts, emotions, senses, and the entire body and goes beyond the physiology of the brain alone. That is why much of meaning is "felt" and why psychologist Eugene Gendlin (1982) coined the term "felt sense."

Novelty. Many different aspects of brain/mind functioning come together in the making of meaning. For instance, some parts of the brain respond to novelty—people (including very young infants) are surprised and alerted when the world does not act as they expected it to act. Novelty gets instant attention and engages the need to make sense of something.

Dissonance. Individuals in a situation where they have to decide between competing points of view that seem equally "true" can experience a great sense of discomfort or dissonance until the discomfort is resolved and things make sense again (Festinger, 1957). Regardless of the situation in which people find themselves—a new class, a new school, a new romance, a new country—they innately look for what is familiar and try to work out how things fit together and how to behave appropriately (for them). They search for a way to figure out what is needed or most meaningful for the situation. And as we show in the next chapter, all responses involve the ebb and flow of emotions. As Siegel says:

> "Generated by the value systems of the brain, these emotional activations pervade all mental functions and literally create meaning in life. In this way, we can say that emotion and meaning are treated by the same process" (Siegel, 1999, p. 159).

Valuing. Meaning has to do with what we have learned to value, including how we relate to ideas, situations, and other people. The way in which people relate to ideas and situations and other people always involves placing a value on the things we experience. Eating while in mommy's arms is "good," potty training is "bad." And as experiences are evaluated as "good," "bad," or "neutral," meaning is created, and new or incoming information both organizes and expands on basic beliefs or values.

This valuing system is connected to the emotions and is critical to determining what we will pay attention to, what we will avoid, and just what we will do with "learning" that is forced on us compared to pursuing what is interesting.

The valuing system, therefore, is very powerful. People pursue what they like, what they want to do more of or know more about, and what makes sense to them or serves them in some way. Finding a way to motivate students is far more important than having them participate in what is to them a meaningless curriculum.

This valuing system lies at the foundation of actor-centered, adaptive decision making. The "actor" is the learner, and the decision to learn something is based on what the learner needs to know, understand, or do. It is called adaptive because the learner is looking for a kind of best "fit" to the problem or question being asked or explored.

Meaningful Learning Is Intrinsically Rewarding

Many educators argue that students just need to trust that doing required assignments carries its own reward. The reasoning goes something like this: Students who succeed at tasks they may describe as meaningless or not useful will nevertheless benefit in the future. These educators point to examples like practicing the piano, using repetitive and meaningless exercises as the foundation for future mastery. But research doesn't support this. John Sloboda (in Ericson & Smith, 1991) describes how individuals who experienced extreme joy and connectedness to music at an early age were more likely to remain involved with music for the rest of their lives. He adds that no such "peak experiences" occurred in situations where students experienced external constraints or anxiety.

"A similar lesson emerges from a . . . study of leading American concert pianists by Sosniak (1989). None of those in her sample showed exceptional promise as a child, but in every case their early lessons were associated with fun and exploration, rather than with practical achievement" (Sloboda, in Ericson & Smith, 1991, p. 67).

Mastery

Meaning is essential for real mastery. Clearly there are skills and facts that need to be memorized, especially when doing so can provide some limited sense of competence and confidence. However, when skills and facts are taught in the course of solving more complex problems or the need to deal effectively with more realistic situations, the learning is richer. This is inevitably the case when learning engages the learner's ability to pursue a question or topic that the individual cares about. That is competence and confidence emerging out of meaning.

Meaningfulness Enhances Relaxed Alertness

The implication of the findings described above is that people of all ages feel more at home, more relaxed, and safer when what they are doing and what happens to them makes sense. Yet "making sense" is not a passive act or something that is handed to us. It includes an invitation to interact with what is novel, to resolve a contradiction, and to work hard to achieve something important to oneself. Teaching the curriculum in a way that requires students of all ages to make sense of what they are learning is an indispensable aspect of creating a climate of relaxed alertness. The reciprocal benefit is that when students are relaxed and alert, their brains and bodies are more fully engaged in their learning.

Revisiting the Executive Functions

Finally, when students are taught for meaning, it becomes quite natural to introduce processes that lead to the development of the executive functions because teaching for meaning is always actor centered. All of the following skills and capacities can be integrated into the teaching of any subject when meaningfulness matters and actor-centered adaptive decision making is emphasized. Such environments provide opportunities to do the following:

- Reason
- Assess risk
- Make sense of ideas and behavior
- Moderate emotions
- Make a plan and develop a timeline
- Ask for help and use resources
- Adapt goals based on new information or understandings along the journey
- Think critically and creatively
- Reflect and be self-critical
- Understand one's own approaches to learning
- See other peoples' points of view
- Anticipate potential problems and opportunities that affect outcomes and goals
- Access working memory and avoid distractions

Twenty-first–century children have little opportunity to develop these skills because they live in such an instant-information age. A meaningless curriculum will not allow them to experience the ownership and responsibility that develop the skills listed above.

PROCESSING THIS PRINCIPLE

Personal Connections

Think of something you do that you enjoy and find relatively meaningful (this may be a subject, hobby, or discipline you hold dear). *It should be something that you have done before.* Jot it down on a piece of paper.

Now reflect on it for a moment and then finish the following sentences:

- When I do this I feel _____
- While I am doing this I believe that _____
- My actions (what I actually do) can best be described as _____

Now think of something you do that has little meaning or purpose for you; something that you are forced to do but don't really want to (even if others say you "should" like it or that it is good for you.) *Again, it ought to be something that you have done before* (examples could include eating foods you don't like, mowing the lawn when the grass is too short to warrant it, or doing paperwork). Jot this down on a piece of paper. Again, finish the following sentences:

- When I do this I feel _____
- While I am doing this I believe that _____
- My actions (what I actually do) can best be described as _____

Hint: To be as authentic as possible, you may need to give yourself some quiet time for reflection.

Next ask yourself what the real difference is between the two conditions you have listed. For example:

- Under which conditions (meaningful or meaningless) did you feel most competent, confident, and intrinsically motivated?
- Under which of the above conditions did you feel less competent and confident?
- How did your feelings and beliefs influence your performance?
- How did your feelings and beliefs influence your emotional state?
- In this exercise we took you outside the school environment. Can you see the connection to school?
- What could happen to learning when most of the curriculum is never connected to students' prior experience or to what they value or want to know?
- How might students feel if teachers fail to help them arrive at a clear purpose for this new topic or subject, one that is related to what they value?
- How can students arrive at new understanding if they cannot question their personal experiences, beliefs, and conclusions?

Before you suggest that all adults have to do things they don't want to, check to see if there isn't something that gives meaning to even apparently meaningless tasks (you are protecting a valuable asset or saving face, proving a point or getting paid for your efforts).

When we teach in a way that allows students to connect, find purpose, and reach new understandings, we create the conditions that help students go beyond direct instruction and memorization. Students whose parents help them think ahead or students with well-developed executive functions may work hard because their future goals (going to college, becoming an athlete) have meaning for them. For most students, however, meaning tends to be more immediate and concrete—and needs to be connected to what they already know, understand, and value.

Going Deeper

Continue your exploration with your process partner or learning circle by discussing the material below.

It is useful to think of meaning as consisting of three basic elements: making connections, purpose, and understanding.

Making Connections

Making connections refers to seeing how new ideas, skills, and experiences are related either personally or academically to what we currently know or believe.

A teacher named Maria once asked one of us why, no matter what she did in her class, her high school students hated her course on literary analysis. We asked her whether she "did" literary analysis in her everyday life. She was dumbstruck. The thought had never occurred to her. She realized that if she didn't care about the subject and its only purpose was to fulfill a requirement set up by others, her students might not find much meaning either.

After some brainstorming and reflection about the purpose and value of her subject, Maria asked students to select a current movie for everyone to see outside of class. When everyone had seen the movie, she asked them questions that looked critically at the plot and the characters and that led to generating other questions that analyzed the movie. The discussion included lots of humor and aha's. Once students understood what it meant to analyze, she challenged them to explore their readings from different points of view, which ultimately resulted in students' feeling competent and confident in expressing their ideas. Literary analysis became fun and intellectually stimulating.

Notice how Maria connected her curriculum to something that was familiar to students: movies. Creating connections means that teachers provide experiences and opportunities for students to see relationships, associations, and logical links. Penetrating questions also allow for deeper associations to be made, and lead to higher academic standards.

Questions to ask students when attempting to make the curriculum meaningful:

- *How does that relate to what you know or understand?*
- *Where did you experience that?*
- *What follows next?*
- *Is that a logical path or conclusion?*

Notice the crossover from personal to academic connections. You really want both.

Purpose

Purpose relates to what a person values, cares about, and is interested in. Purpose and valuing have to do with where people are willing to put their time and energy. Questions like, "How does this relate to me?" "How does this connect to what I want to know?" "Do I care?" "Do I need this?" "What can I do with this?" may be bothersome in the traditionally controlled classroom, but they reflect the learner's search for meaning. One of the great benefits of engaging learners' own purposes is that they become more energized and motivated.

Almost nothing is more important to continuous learning than a student's inner drive to pursue and understand something. One of the changes that occurred in Maria's class, for instance, is that some students who were still more interested in movies than books nevertheless put energy into literary analysis because it helped them make more sense of how movies worked.

Understanding

Understanding happens when information is synthesized and new ideas and concepts are mastered in a way that allows for a shift in perception. This can rarely be guaranteed. Understanding emerges out of the kind of learning we are describing here and is frequently experienced as an *aha!* of insight. Brain/mind learning sees regular new insights by students as a critical outcome toward which every teacher should strive.

> The development of in-depth understanding goes beyond the use of words and symbols. The Root-Bernsteins (2000), who researched mental tools used by great scientists and great artists, showed that imaging or empathizing or gaining a visceral feel for what is being worked on is really important. They point out that Nobel Laureate Barbara McClintock spoke about a "feeling for the organism" (in her case, ears of corn). Einstein, they also say, repeatedly said that no scientist thinks in equations, and even he conducted mental experiments that involved visual images and muscular feelings.

Real understanding requires and leads to a shift in one's mental model. *Mental models are deeply held beliefs and assumptions about how the world works.* They are established through early experiences and can and will persist despite new learning that contradicts them.

Let's look at a couple of examples:

1. Gravity

Most adults have heard about gravity, have passed tests about gravity, and can carry on a conversation that includes references to gravity. But we have asked teachers all over the United States to draw a wine glass that contains red wine and to draw the glass at an angle to the ground. Inevitably one quarter to one third of adults draw the glass so that the line representing the wine is parallel to the lip of the glass (A, Diagram 5.1). The drawing reflects the mental model of 5-year-olds or those who have not shifted their understanding of gravity into their everyday world. The remainder correctly draw the surface of the wine parallel to the ground.

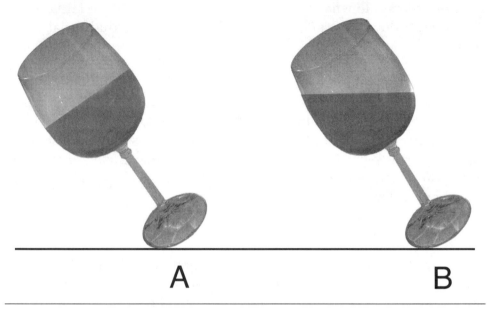

A   **B**

Diagram 5.1   Wine Glasses

2. The Seasons

Another famous example involves an exit interview of Harvard graduates (*A Private Universe*, 1992). They were asked what determined the seasons of the year. These were students who had taken courses in science and physics, yet many gave an answer that was intuitive rather than correct. They said that seasons were the result of Earth's distance from the sun, which shifted throughout the year. The correct answer is that the seasons are the result of the tilt of Earth's axis. Despite exams and research papers, many had not integrated the technical/scholastic knowledge into a new mental model.

Bridging to the Practical

Look at the following scenarios and answer the questions in your journal, with your process partner, or in your learning circle.

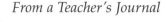

From a Teacher's Journal

Melanie

Melanie had a fabulous third-grade teacher who ignited a love for geography in her. Her teacher taught his students to go with him on imaginary journeys for which they had to prepare. In order to prepare for an imaginary journey, they identified different geographical features of a country by using topographical information, studying unique plants and animals they would encounter, finding out what language they would have to speak, what money they would need, what could be bought in the country, how people dressed and what they ate, believed, valued, and so forth. Sometimes they looked at works of art and at other artifacts unique to that country and culture. Many questions came from the students themselves, followed by research, discussion, and challenges to their beliefs and conclusions. Melanie continually urged her family to take trips whenever possible, and her family became used to her need to stop at historical markers or give everyone relevant historical facts about the places they visited. Now in high school, Melanie loves geography and ties new learning to her dream of becoming an international journalist.

George

George had no such first introduction to geography. Geography was nothing more than a subject he had to take in order to pass the tests and pass the course. He answered the questions at the back of the book and did other assignments, including a book report. He saw few connections between his own experiences and geography, and that is still true today. His family watches a lot of TV, enjoys sports, and works hard. Their own opportunities to travel are limited, and George relates primarily to his own neighborhood. He dreams of leaving someday but how or why remains unclear or has very little to do with what he learned in geography. This scenario holds true to some extent for all of his school subjects.

How do these two scenarios differ in terms of meaning?

Connections to Learning

- Which scenario allowed students to make the greatest number of associations between the required content and their own lives?
- Which scenario made it most possible for students to take actions in their own lives that connected with course content?
- Which student would be better able to apply what was learned to other courses and subject areas?

Purpose for Learning

- In which scenario did students have the most opportunity to spell out and follow their own intentions and goals (i.e., actor-centered questioning)?
- Which scenario sparked the most personal motivation and interest?
- Which scenario drew more on the student's executive functions?

Understanding

- Which scenario resulted in the greater expansion or shift in mental models (beliefs and assumptions about what was "true")?
- How might you know this is happening?
- Which students would be most comfortable planning a trip of their own that included time and distance considerations?
- Which student would be most likely to understand what is involved in being from another culture? As their teacher, how might you observe this?
- In which scenario did students have to think and explain how one thing depended on, involved, or followed another?
- How does all this relate to developing and using the executive functions?

TAKING IT INTO THE CLASSROOM

One of the major factors that marks the shift between instructional approaches is the way in which each deals with meaning.

Instructional Approach 1

Much of traditional teaching is based on the belief that skills and information have value because they ultimately add up so that students can pass the tests and get the grades that will allow them to pursue higher education and the highly regarded professions. Meaning is inevitably seen from the parents' and teachers' point of view and represents the knowledge and information required by the formal (state or district) curriculum. So Jenny, an Instructional Approach 1 teacher, uses daily lesson plans, unit plans, and semester overviews, all constructed from the point of transmitting essential knowledge to the students. Since understanding always requires more than didactic (lecturing/telling) instruction, most of Jenny's teaching leaves understanding to chance, ignores students' purposes, and generally does little to help students create connections to their own lives. Many opportunities for actor-centered adaptive decision making are lost.

Opportunities for Instructional Approach 1 Teaching

After creating relaxed alertness in the classroom . . .

- Ask students for their opinion on a topic or concept and discuss with them what the topic might mean. Find out what they think the purpose of studying the topic is.
- Check for true understanding by seeing if students can come up with what something means in their own words.
- See where additional connections with the curriculum can be made, and help students make their own connections by allowing them to choose how to do an assignment.

Instructional Approach 2

Instructional Approach 2 teachers do think about meaningful lessons for students. They tend to look for techniques, prepared lessons, or strategies that make lessons more engaging. Bill, for example, wants to help students understand distance, so he has his students measure how high or far they can jump in terms of meters and feet. His belief is that the experience will make the concept of measurement more meaningful. This could work for students who love jumping or sports, but it may well leave the rest of the students with a meaningless experience.

This is because real meaning is personal and actor centered. The experience itself must be developed with student input, input that relates to their own questions.

Opportunities for Instructional Approach 2 Teaching

- Help students find their own questions and connections by providing opportunities and time for them to explore the subject matter.
- Let students make choices whenever possible.
- Understanding comes with "felt meaning," so deepen the experience by comparing and contrasting aspects of a topic to students' own experiences, and by enriching classes with stories, books, art, and metaphors.

From a Teacher's Journal

Jacob

Jacob was the person who taught me to value student questions. We had worked hard to develop a good classroom climate, and when Jacob first came into our class he fell in love with the atmosphere and sense of community. Then he started to challenge me. Jacob had a really inquiring mind. I guided him and we set boundaries within which we would ask questions about everything that I said, and before long, Jacob was requesting that the class members be able to pick their own topics and/or interest areas and do presentations. We, teacher and class, worked it out together because we had been learning skills like planning, working together, reflecting, and more through the year, but suddenly they became real (remember the "revolution of rising expectations"). The year was a struggle and a joy. It was also the first time we ended our year with a fourth-grade celebration tea where parents were invited and students in small groups shared their projects as a culminating activity to demonstrate the skills they had developed over the course of the year.

Instructional Approach 3

The Instructional Approach 3 teacher is capable of giving genuine choices to students and yet ensures that they learn essential facts and skills called for by the formal curriculum. In order to do this, such teachers can use "in the moment" questions and experiences in the classroom to connect to the formal curriculum. This process is very different from using teaching strategies or materials "packaged" by someone else. Carmen knows that at any moment an unexpected event may occur in her class that she could use to teach some aspect of the curriculum, from the need for correct spelling to deepening insight.

Opportunities for Instructional Approach 3 Teaching

- Take more time to explore your own growth based on what is happening in the classroom.
- Spend more time examining your relationship to what you are teaching.
- Play with bigger ideas and concepts in order to increase the range of connections between what you are teaching and other subject areas.

THE THIRD FOUNDATIONAL SKILL FOR RELAXED ALERTNESS: PROCESS MEETINGS

If teachers want students to master the essentials of the discipline while engaging in higher-order thinking, then the students must have the opportunities to ask and work on questions that engage and challenge them. Meaningful learning requires a community where connections of all types are continuously explored in an orderly way. Practicing the search for meaning in the community results in greater student competence.

Process meetings provide unique opportunities for making personal choices, clarifying a purpose, and developing more complex understandings of issues and questions. Process meetings provide a natural forum in which students share responsibility by addressing and resolving issues that are a part of any learning community. In fact, what are often referred to as class meetings are much more powerful and effective when they are set up as process meetings.

Process Meetings: Steps to Take

This expands on ordered sharing and incorporates the use of "I" messages and effective listening. You may want to rehearse this process several times to work out any "bugs" and let students feel comfortable with the procedures.

Step 1. We suggest a time period of approximately 10–20 minutes for younger students and 30–45 minutes for older students. You will need to be guided by your own judgment and by your students.

Step 2. The students should be seated in a circle so all can see and hear each other.

Step 3. Open the meeting with a topic that you or the students have suggested.

Step 4. Help make sure that the topic has meaning for almost everyone. Since class meetings tend to deal with dilemmas, this is not difficult to do.

Step 5. Help students clarify personal connections to the topic. Ordered sharing can be an effective way to begin, allowing everyone to share their opinions and be required to listen to others.

Step 6. Challenge students to deepen their learning perspectives, and help them identify and articulate problems and solutions.

Step 7. Check as needed to see how things are going. *Procedure checks* refer to periodic calls to remember the procedural agreements, such as time limits, topic focus, and effective listening. *Process checks* are periodic calls to reflect on any apparent or real disturbances or glitches dealing with individual and group agreements, assumptions, or beliefs. Examples include a lack of participation, dominance by one person, or a sense that people are holding back from saying what needs to be brought into the open.

Step 8. Summarize and reflect on the process and/or the outcome of the meeting. This provides an excellent time for students to review their understanding of themselves and the process.

Setting time limits for the meetings helps keep everyone on task. Like ordered sharing, process meetings can be called as needed. They are requested by students or the teacher and relate to a clear purpose.

Here is an example of a process meeting:

From a Teacher's Journal

José

We had previously set up our timeline for our project, our groups, etc. when José mentioned that we needed to look over how everyone would be assessed. José was sure that the class would have some good ideas based on our previous writing of rubrics for other projects. We called a process meeting and after getting into our circle, José began with his request. Students took a moment to compose their thoughts, followed by a quick ordered sharing on where everyone stood on the issue. The class agreed that because of the complexity of this writing (a persuasive essay) and the need for practice, we should make an overall rubric and have several benchmarks along the way that would be part of the assessment. The process and discussion deepened as we looked into the components that fit with the English standards as well as our own purposes in mastering this style of writing. There were times when the discussion became quite heated over potential problems, but going back to an ordered sharing and our commitment to working through dilemmas helped. José would remind us of how much time we had, and the class extended that in order to complete the rubric. When we had worked out what we thought was needed, we agreed to revisit the rubric in a week. We took a few moments to reflect on how we had worked as a group, as individuals in the group, and on the process. José shared how good he felt about having a leadership role.

Can you see the steps for the process meeting as they were outlined? Take the time in your learning circle to look at individual aspects.

- How could you incorporate this to work with students on an upcoming class project?
- Would you need to add or change anything?

Process meetings can introduce and strengthen the following:

1. Practicing the use of "I" messages and effective listening.

   Example: Let me see if I understood you. I heard you say that . . .

2. Practicing insightful, creative, and critical thinking (executive functions).

   Example: What might be another way to look at that?

3. Practicing how to set goals, engage in respectful interaction, and promote teamwork (executive functions).

   Example: We have agreed to work as a team. What steps do we need at this time to get back on track?

4. Developing social and emotional capacities and control by identifying with the thinking and actions of others (executive functions).

   Example: What did you think they believed when that happened? What did you assume to be true for him or her at that moment?

5. Developing personally by fostering social skills such as reducing shyness.

   Example: We work best when all of us have shared our ideas. Is there anyone who has not given an opinion?

6. Enhancing aspects of character education such as being trustworthy and fair.

   Example: What did you experience in your group that helped you feel that everyone was being fair? Trustworthy?

7. Reducing anonymity and promoting feelings of acceptance and being worthwhile.

   Example: It helps me be clear on what is important when we each share our thoughts. How about an ordered sharing to make sure we are on the same page?

8. Building a trusting and caring relationship between teacher and student and among students themselves.

   Example: I hear what you are saying. How can I help?

9. Creating a sense of community by increasing class cohesiveness.

   Example: Since we have agreed to make our decisions by consensus, how does everyone feel about this decision?

10. Practicing relevancy where students talk about subjects that interest, affect, or concern them.

    Example: How can we connect that to our current discussion?

As can be seen from the classroom process meeting example, there are guidelines, but they are flexible and allow for many possibilities. For one thing, the guidelines are negotiated or are open to discussion except for instances where legal or safety issues are concerned. Either way, it is critical that students are involved in the process as much as possible.

The teacher plays a major role as facilitator for the discussion. When first introducing the class process meeting, the teacher needs to review procedures, pose questions, monitor participation, and conclude the session. Later, most of these tasks can be monitored by designated students. In Instructional Approach 3 classrooms, the entire process is often initiated and handled by the students.

If students are to talk about what is meaningful to them, then the teacher must avoid making premature judgments. One way to do this is to allow a few seconds after a student is finished talking before doing or saying anything. This models for students' good listening skills and emphasizes the importance of reflection.

Other Purposes

Process meetings can be used for deciding on guidelines to follow and clarifying standards. The goal should be to help students relate to them personally. A process meeting is also useful whenever the teacher wants to work with the students to examine and think about the program or deal with frustrations with an assignment. The following two examples show how an elementary class and a middle school class used their process meetings.

From an Elementary Teacher's Journal

Amy

In a burst of frustration Amy sputtered, "Our group wants to have a process meeting. We need more time on the project." After consulting with other group facilitators, I arranged for the class to have a meeting before the end of the period. Each group was delving into research on the earth science area they had found the most interesting. As the class moved into a circle I could see relief on students' faces. They were glad the issue was being addressed. Several concerned voices were raised as we explored the topic. Knowing our timeline, we looked at alternatives. We came to the conclusion that if we could add one more week to the research portion of the project, and if some of the preparation for the presentation would be done outside of class, we could do it. A side benefit was that several groups exchanged resources as they had found information that other groups needed. Thus, we increased cooperation between groups and enriched each other's projects.

From a Middle School Teacher's Journal

Arbor Day

Part of our agreed goal as a tutoring/peer mediation class was to find ways we could be of service to our school and community. We were discussing Arbor Day in our process meeting. Some of the students thought our school could use more trees. After several students shared how they felt about the idea, they decided that they wanted to organize a fundraiser for this purpose. Committees were formed on the basis of what was needed. Regular work did not suffer because we agreed on how much time we could give to the project and still complete other responsibilities.

Since we had consensus, everyone was involved on one level or another as we contacted the district maintenance department to learn about what trees we could plant. We consulted with our custodian to see where we could plant and the local nursery to see what trees were available and at what price. Groups went to homeroom classes, explained our project, and left posters and collection cans.

We ended up with two trees and a planter box of flowering shrubs that we planted together. The students felt they had done a real service for the school.

THE TRANSFORMATIONAL ADMINISTRATOR AND THE PROCESS FOR MAKING IT REAL

> Most educators feel a calling to work with schools and students. Much of the frustration experienced on the job has to do with a loss of purpose. One of the best ways to reinvigorate the staff is to rekindle the sense of purpose.

We suggest that the place for administrators to begin is with themselves. Take the time for personal reflection, to talk with a colleague, to participate in a powerful conference, or to take some other action that is nourishing and refreshing.

Next, explore ways to help the staff rekindle their passion. In our experience, properly facilitated learning circles serve well because they are both relaxing and energizing and create a sane oasis in a very hurried and complex world. Learning circles also provide intellectual and professional challenge. In addition, the issues of purpose, meaning, and connection can be raised as topics to be explored in a learning circle. Further steps include finding creative ways to schedule events and shape instructional and work time so that staff members have more personal time.

The central point is that supporting the staff's personal search for meaning is not a last step with least priority, but a first step with a very high priority. The reason is that everything people do is organized in terms of what they find meaningful.

In tandem with the National Teaching Standards

Accomplished teachers understand that students come to the classroom with differing experiences and backgrounds, and they design activities that encourage students to enter a common discussion.

Students need a healthy, stimulating, and supportive work environment that welcomes the open expression of ideas and encourages the search for greater understanding and knowledge.

—Standard V: Learning Environment

All issues and steps covered in this chapter are in line with and support the national standards. The chapter guides teachers in the development of student understanding and provides tools that help students deal realistically with situations that arise and need resolution. At the same time, the processes in the chapter help develop the learning climate of relaxed alertness that makes higher-order thinking and functioning possible.

Engage their individual style and uniqueness

Engage the physiology in learning

Reduce threat and enhance self-efficacy

Engage social interactions

Acknowledge and engage developmental steps and shifts

Engage their innate search for meaning

Engage their capacity to learn from memorizing isolated facts _and_ biographical events

If we want to create enriched environments that help students learn, then we need to include all of the following:

Engage their capacity to recognize and master essential patterns

Engage both conscious and unconscious processing

Engage emotional connections

Engage both their ability to focus attention and learn from the peripheral context

Engage their ability to perceive both details and the larger view

Emotions and Patterning

Brain/Mind Learning Principle 5: *Emotions are critical to patterning.*

 ## At the Core

Emotions are central to human life. They are a part of every thought, decision, and response. Powerful learning is enhanced by rich emotional experiences guided and moderated by the executive functions. Relaxed alertness can be facilitated by educators who fully grasp the relationship between the role of various emotions and learning.

Capacity: All students can learn more effectively when appropriate emotions are elicited by their experiences.

HOW DO WE KNOW THIS?

Perhaps the single greatest gift the neurosciences are giving educators is confirmation that emotions and learning cannot be separated. Brain research is helping educators begin to feel validated when they insist that teaching is never simple. It also helps them understand why the most painstakingly precise research on practice all too often cannot be transferred to a new classroom setting full of unique human beings, each with unique relationships, assumptions, beliefs, reactions, and mental models, all of which are tied to emotions.

Where Are Emotions Housed in the Brain?

The attempt to link emotions to how the brain and physiology function is a complex process. At least four worlds are crossed—the molecular, the cellular, the psychological, and the behavioral.

To begin with, neuroscientists such as Antonio Damasio (1999, 2003) and Candace Pert (1997) confirm that every thought and action is accompanied by emotion. Although the amygdala in the center of the brain is often referred to as the center of emotions because it is so deeply involved with threat and fear, emotions of any kind engage many areas of the brain and a cacophony of chemicals and other physical interactions. For instance, many muscles are involved in emotional reactions, and the immune system, which guards against many diseases, is affected (Detweiler, Rothman, Salovey, & Steward, 2000).

Some really exciting work confirms the wide reach of emotional reactions. As we have seen, neurons are the cells in the brain that transmit the signals essential for human functioning. Chemicals called *neurotransmitters* carry signals across the gaps—*synapses*—between neurons, and make thought, mood, and emotion possible. In the 1980s, Candace Pert and her colleagues (Pert, 1997) discovered that those same neurotransmitters are part of a class of chemicals (also called *ligands*) found throughout the body, including the immune system. Every emotion a person feels is accompanied by a cascade of ligands that affects the way cells organize themselves. This is why she called ligands "molecules of emotion" and why we say that emotions are a part of every thought, decision, and response.

Emotions as a Weather System

The best way to understand emotions is to compare them to a weather system. Emotions, like the weather, are rarely made up of one thing. Clouds gather together and along with other factors, like particles in the air and atmospheric pressure, they produce rain. It is possible to understand in general terms what causes certain types of weather just as it is possible to understand in general terms what will result in certain kinds of emotions. Like the weather, emotions do not occur on a whim but rather because certain conditions exist. That does not mean, however, that emotional reactions are always predictable. They are not.

Emotions are lawful.

The Range of Emotions

The basic emotions are hardwired into every human system, and each plays a biological role. Scientists do not completely agree with each other on how many different types of emotion there are, however. There are even different ways of looking at basic or universal emotions (see, for example, Ekman & Davidson, 1994).

For practical purposes, we will simply make the distinction between negative and positive emotions. For instance, we introduced the notion of perseveration in Chapter 2. Perseveration is a short-term survival response that occurs when a personal belief (what one believes to be true of others or of the world generally) or belief about oneself (what one believes about one's own actions or reasoning) is challenged. Such challenges inevitably lead to an emotional reaction (Bowers & Sivers, 1998).

It is very important to understand that emotions themselves are not good or bad. Negative emotions are basically painful, and positive emotions are basically pleasurable, but all play important roles.

Positive Emotions

We deal with the primary negative emotion—fear—in Chapter 3, but positive emotions and their effects must also be understood. Some positive emotions have been linked to optimum health and well-being (Fredrickson, 2000). Specific emotions such as joy, awe, gratitude, and compassion have also been explored (Robbins, 2003).

Martin Seligman (1998; Gillham, 2000) is one of the most important researchers of positive emotions. He researched hope and optimism and the important role both play in health and well-being. Seligman argues that just trying to teach self-esteem is sending precisely the wrong message to adults and children because it often ignores the role that doing well in school, at work, or in other areas of life plays in feeling positive and optimistic.

His argument underlies the point we repeatedly make about the state of relaxed alertness that develops as the result of successful learning and performance, and the sense of accomplishment that comes with mastery.

The optimal state of mind for meaningful learning rests on an emotional foundation, and the best foundation includes competence and confidence.

Positive Affect: The Emotional Climate That Enhances the Executive Functions

A very important contributing factor along the way is a pleasant environment for learning, a climate that promotes *positive affect*. Positive affect occurs when there is a mild increase in positive feelings brought about by common, everyday events. These feelings include moments of contentment and joy, interspersed with hard work accompanied by intrinsic motivation (Ashby, Isen, & Turken, 1999).

Psychologists have known for years that individuals learning in such environments

- have better working memory,
- have better episodic memory (memory for events),
- see more options for solving problems,
- are more flexible in their thinking,
- are more competent in dealing with social relationships (helpfulness and sociability),
- have greater verbal fluency (give more innovative examples),
- have better decision-making abilities.

Notice the overlap between these increased capacities and the executive functions!

Neuroscientists are confirming that something as seemingly simple as learning in a pleasant environment can actually have an effect on the brain. They have traced the paths of some neurotransmitters that influence learning and have shown that when we enjoy learning while in a pleasant environment, the neurotransmitter dopamine is stimulated in just the right amount by our pleasant feelings. That, in turn, stimulates the right amount of another neurotransmitter, acetylcholine, that directly stimulates the hippocampus, the major center for new learning (Ashby et al., 1999).

What, then, contributes to positive affect? Research highlights factors that are right at the heart of relaxed alertness.

- One factor is choice, and the freedom to pursue work of personal interest, a central aspect of actor-centered decision making.
- Another factor is having opportunities to choose and change contexts, including being able to work alone, in pairs, or in groups as needed.
- Yet another is being relaxed or in what Csikszentmihalyi (1993) calls the "flow" state.

PROCESSING THIS PRINCIPLE

Personal Connections

Can you relate to the following incident?

One of us recently spoke with a young man who lamented the fact that he disliked writing and yet recognized that if things had been different, he would have become something besides an electrician. Knowing what we do for a living, he asked almost hesitantly what the current thinking is on left-handedness. We said that these days we don't deal with it as anything unusual and that current thinking suggests that left-handed learners not be singled out in any way. As we continued to talk he told us that he traces his weakness in writing to the early years in school when writing with his left hand, he would inevitably drag his hand over his writing. He said that all his words ended up smudged, particularly since everyone was writing with pencils at the time. He did not like the way his writing looked and neither did the teacher. Over time he became discouraged and ashamed of his work. This young man is very intelligent and the head of a company that has 17 employees. There is no doubt that he could have excelled in writing. What stopped him was an emotional experience.

The teacher or teachers who criticized his writing had no intention of determining or influencing his life's path but nevertheless inadvertently did so. This is precisely how emotional memory works—a particular emotion is experienced and associated with an act or behavior. The body "learns" how to respond automatically to given conditions. This type of learning can happen all at once, but it usually takes a number of associations or associated events that are consistently the same over time.

> Teachers may *not* realize they are teaching when they affect the emotions of students, but in fact they are. Teaching of this nature may be even more powerful in determining some students' futures than mastering aspects of the curriculum.

Try to recall a particular course you took some time ago, like drawing or singing. Select one that you began with a great deal of enthusiasm, only to decide over time that this was not something you wanted to pursue.

- Can you recall what led to your "change of heart"?
- When you recall the fact that you didn't continue, what emotion surfaces?
- What would have made a difference? What would have kept you learning?

Now take a moment to reflect on joyful, exciting, and fulfilling experiences that you have had while learning something. Note that they may be so obvious that they have been taken for granted.

- Do you have a hobby or an interest that you delight in mastering? What happens in your body and mind when you feel delighted?
- Is there something that you are so confident about that you can persevere, expecting success, even when things are not working

out? Describe that feeling of optimism. How do you know that things will work out?

- Have there been moments when you simply felt awestruck—perhaps looking up at the stars or listening to great music? What shifted in your body, mind, and thoughts?

Going Deeper

How Emotions Shape Self-Image and Identity

Over time, consistent experiences literally become a part of the person.

Instead of being a passing phenomenon, some emotions "fuse" in the brain with interpretations that come to represent a consistent worldview. Brain cells combine into neural networks that fire together in consistent patterns. Thus, strong and repeated emotional reactions become a part of the physiology (Perry, 1996). Emotions, therefore, are deeply engaged in the development of a sense of self and are bound up in a person's beliefs.

Revisiting Perseveration

A threat to a person's organized sense of self has emotional repercussions. Adults need to know that when a belief about oneself has been disturbed or contradicted, perseveration follows. Here is a classroom example:

Christen walks into your class late. She has done this before, and lately other students seem to be doing the same. You are having a particularly trying day and have simply had it. You tell Christen that you are tired of her always being late to class. Christen, on the other hand, believes herself to be a conscientious and responsible student. She tries to be on time but her science class always seems to run over, especially since they have been preparing for the science fair. She quietly goes to her seat but does not hear anything you say for the next few minutes because she is very angry.

By now you can recognize perseveration and realize that Christen is perseverating on what you said. This means that your comments are reverberating in her head. With her silence she is both telling you how wrong you are and defending her actions. Your comments caused a "tear" in her sense of self and she must repair it before she can attend to anything else. Unless she has a chance to deal with her feelings, your relationship with her could be in jeopardy.

When strong emotions are not processed or dealt with, teachers will notice the following emotional behaviors that signal that a sense of self has been violated in some way:

Suppressing: Pretending not to feel anything

Rebelling: Acting out in order to irritate or annoy another

Bullying: Wanting to overtly hurt or minimize another because one's own self is perceived as inadequate

Undermining:	Making a joke or using sarcasm or subterfuge to undermine someone else's authority or privilege
Ignoring:	Failing to recognize or deal with the problem or situation
Ostracizing:	Removing the person or persons someone believes to be responsible by excluding them from contact, by damaging their reputation, or minimizing them personally in some way
Retaliating:	Getting back at someone even if what was done was not intentional
Intimidating:	Similar to bullying but using more devious means (threatening words, for example) that go beyond physical means
Marking:	Destroying property or leaving one's physical mark in some way (graffiti)

Most of the above also tell adults that these students are not in relationship with others. They have stopped caring about themselves and their community. This doesn't excuse the behavior, but it may open the door to their receiving help. This does not apply to students who have proven that they are dangerous. Be sure you know the difference!

The central point . . .

. . . is that students' emotional states profoundly influence their learning, and educators need to come to terms with this fact and learn how to work with emotions—theirs and their students'.

Bridging to the Practical

Educators must be emotionally mature and able to deal with the normal range of emotions students are likely to experience and express in school. Our suggestion is to begin with two basic objectives.

• The first is to work toward having students experience some of the positive emotions on a regular basis. This occurs much more naturally with Instructional Approaches 2 and 3, but the basic goal should be for every educator.

• The second is to develop the skill and capacity to work with students in any emotional state. Remember the goal of building competence, confidence, and meaning or purpose for developing resilience against negative emotions.

How to Introduce Three Positive Emotions: Joy, Enthusiasm, Awe

Joy

Joy tends to be connected to play (Panksepp, 1998). In childhood, joy is closely connected to roughhousing and in adults to sports. At Instructional

Approach 1, fun (a precursor to joy) is experienced when creative games are used that also result in successful memorization.

From a Teacher's Journal

One of us used to play a game called "A Cat in the Hat" with students who were in survival mode most of the time. Students were given specific definitions that needed to be memorized. Next they were given time to work with each other and use a number of memorizing strategies. When everyone was ready, the teacher presented a hat with bits of paper, each of which had a question requiring the recall of a definition. A student would reach into the hat, read the question, and have a first turn at recalling the definition accurately. If he or she wasn't able to, the teacher chose from the many hands that had sprung up. Everyone got at least three chances to show what they had learned. In the process of the game they also heard the definitions over and over again, which helped memorization.

Games, of course, range along a continuum. So, on the one hand, the game itself can become more and more complex and incorporate more and more elements of the curriculum to be memorized. On the other hand, teachers using Instructional Approach 3 can work with students to develop very complex projects and self-directed roles that become intrinsically joyful. We introduce some ideas about this in the next two sections of the book.

Enthusiasm

Enthusiasm is generated when students are presented with novelty and find creative ways to explore or to connect with the new and novel.

A great way to begin is by presenting students with a puzzle or model of something new to them. Karl regularly takes a "Segway" into schools as a result of his work with the Convergence Education Foundation (www.cef-trek.org). The Segway is a marvelous two-wheel "computerized" machine for traveling or maneuvering in large buildings or on sidewalks, with an ingenious solution to maintaining balance and changing directions. Students and adults alike want to know how it works, want to ride it, and want to figure out what they can do with it. Tying math and science to experiencing the Segway is easy.

Awe

Awe is generated when students see or experience something that inspires them. Watching Karl maneuver the Segway as if it were an extension of his body creates a sense of awe in many people. Watching any expert at work or seeing examples of mastery can be very inspiring.

> At its core, awe is associated with a sense of wonder and engages the search for meaning. It is much more likely to occur and be nurtured in Instructional Approach 3 environments.

In the next section we describe ways to create such experiences. We call them *Global Experiences.* They represent the first foundational skill for *Orchestrated Immersion in Complex Experience* and create powerful emotional connections to learning.

Dealing With What Actually Happens

Educators have to accept the fact that they are not therapists, and yet, because cognition and emotion are so entangled, they have to develop skills to help students deal with their emotions. Some of these skills involve helping students gain self-awareness and personal understanding. These skills can be adequately taught, however, only by people who are already somewhat aware and skilled themselves. This is why we encourage you to master the concepts and practices in your learning circles before bringing them into the classroom.

First, remind yourself that in almost all instances students are engaging in automatic emotional responses they themselves don't understand. Being totally respectful is a big key to progress. Small children, especially, may need their feelings recognized and need a signal that they are "safe" before giving you an explanation for their behaviors. Don't be surprised if they need time to think.

Second, you want to access reasoning capability. This is particularly true for adolescents. You can also divert students temporarily with a question that doesn't immediately address the problem in order to get them out of their emotional or survival state before addressing a problem directly. Effective listening and paraphrasing are essential if you want students to gain insight and understanding about their own reactions.

Third, remember that feeling competent and confident amounts to the best insurance for emotional stability. When the self is under attack, it is best to help students remember the things they do well. Remind them of positive things you have observed about them, but make these relevant and be truthful and sincere.

Fourth, empowering students to rely on and challenge themselves in order to succeed and to see themselves as competent and confident learners should be the general policy of all teachers and administrators. It will do much to avoid emotional encounters and will diffuse emotional reactions.

Invite, Allow, Encourage: An Approach to Creating an Environment That Prevents Emotional Problems

Teachers need to recognize emotional interactions as significant and meaningful opportunities for learning. Here is a powerful initial way to begin helping students deal with emotional issues—Invite, Allow, Encourage students at every opportunity (Barzakov, 1986).

Invite

To invite means that we ask students what they think or want to do before we tell them what they need to know or do.

Allow

To allow is to give students an opportunity to struggle on their own before we make a suggestion or tell them what we think would be helpful to them. The struggle should allow opportunities to think, reason, and understand something about their own beliefs and options.

Encourage

To encourage is to express an innate belief in their capacity to come up with an idea or project and succeed, and to perform to their highest ability.

TAKING IT INTO THE CLASSROOM

It is useful to view emotional issues through the lens of the instructional approaches because one of the characteristics of an instructional approach is that it influences how an individual first perceives a situation—and that perception (based on a mental model) governs the ways in which emotions are handled in the classroom.

Instructional Approach 1

Most Instructional Approach 1 teaching expects students to control their emotions so that essential learning can take place. That is why most Instructional Approach 1 teachers have rules posted along with a list of punishments for any violation. When teachers see mastery of the curriculum linked to memorization governed by practice and rehearsal resulting in high test scores as their primary goal, emotions tend to interfere. These are some of the reasons why emotions are rarely addressed in traditional education except when they cause a disruption. So Jenny controls her classroom. She is fully in charge and prides herself on the orderly way her students behave. The principal is pleased with Jenny, as is her community. From an Instructional Approach 1 perspective, Jenny is doing exactly what she should be doing in order for children to learn.

What no one notices as significant is that if Jenny leaves the room, or students have a substitute for a day, chaos reigns. Students don't know what to do without Jenny controlling them. Her excessive control deprives students of the opportunity to gain self-control. Most critical, from our point of view, is that students from Jenny's class can't survive in an environment that requires self-discipline—managing their own emotional reactions guided by higher-order reasoning and decision making.

Opportunities for Instructional Approach 1 Teaching

- Have students help set time limits for a particular class activity.
- Have students share creative ideas on how to memorize some material that needs to be mastered and work on putting those ideas into practice. This will help students feel their ideas are valued and respected.

- Have students reflect on a real-life incident and explore how they could have handled things differently.

Instructional Approach 2

In the Instructional Approach 2 classroom, students have much more opportunity to interact openly and freely in multiple configurations (groups, dyads, as experts, etc.). This signals a shift in control and trust.

The Instructional Approach 2 classroom adds specific procedures that shift some control from the teacher to the community. Teachers are still in charge and always remain so. Their professional training and legal responsibilities remain clear. But given those, the teacher and students begin to require that everyone work with one another.

So Bill has worked hard on creating community by having everyone practice effective listening and "I" messages and using ordered sharing whenever possible. He has encouraged students to use the parts of ordered sharing that allow them to talk one at a time whenever they don't feel heard or they want to hear what others think. Students have learned how to call for these procedures even when not engaged in formal circles. Bill is also teaching more meaningfully (engaging meaning from the student's point of view) and having more authentic interactions with his students.

The problem for Bill is that this way of teaching can bring many emotional questions and issues to the surface. He needs to know how to identify and deal with emotional reactions that are a part of the type of learning that takes place in a more open and fluid environment.

Opportunities for Instructional Approach 2 Teaching

- Through modeling, share with students your own steps in thinking through a problem or dealing with an emotional situation.
- Be genuine in your emotions, without going into detail. Let students know where you are coming from. Use "I" messages and effective listening yourself.
- Learn how to resolve problems using the suggestions in this chapter.

Instructional Approach 3

When students in the Instructional Approach 3 classroom are asked to identify and research topics they have chosen, and when such research includes working with others, setting priorities, coming to consensus, dividing tasks, and taking responsibility and credit for individual contributions, many emotional issues can surface.

Carmen has become a believer in process, which helps when dealing with emotional issues that pop up from time to time. Carmen knows how important it is for students to know that they will be heard and that emotional issues will be addressed. She sees such opportunities as critical to engaging higher-order problem solving and therefore regards each opportunity to process an emotional issue as an opportunity for powerful learning. Instructional Approach 3 teachers are also working continuously on themselves.

Opportunities for Instructional Approach 3 Teaching

- Because understanding emotions is so important, take the opportunity to reflect, define, and engage in better understanding of your own emotions.
- In your process group with fellow teachers, focus on deepening trust and openness.

THE FOURTH FOUNDATIONAL SKILL FOR RELAXED ALERTNESS: RESOLVING CONFLICT

Sometimes people keep emotional reactions to themselves. This can result in little or no communication, leading to confusion for others. At other times, students find themselves in open conflict that they really don't understand. Being able to help students (and others) work through conflicts is an immensely important foundational skill. Bringing conflict into the open, clarifying it, and then resolving it successfully, however, requires a strong sense of community and trust built up over time.

Acknowledge-Process-Act-Review

In order to implement these steps, the community must already be at a point where everyone is somewhat invested in the success and well-being of others. "I" messages are used and effective listening has become natural. This also means that there is mutual respect and a belief that skills ("I" messages, effective listening, ordered sharing, and process meetings) exist that allow everyone to deal with difficult issues.

Step 1—Acknowledge: *Identify an issue as clearly as possible.*

Someone, teacher or student, recognizes and calls attention to an issue. Using "I" messages, students express frustrations or confusion: "I think we have a problem" or "I am feeling confused, frustrated, angry" and so on. Individuals, being as clear as possible, express exactly what they think the issue is. It is important to focus on actual events, the sequence of those events, and/or actual observations that can be corroborated. The student may also express the agreements, beliefs, and ideals he or she believed were being violated.

The teacher needs to stay nonjudgmental by sticking to data and facts and asking for clarification:

"Can you tell me precisely what you are describing?"

"What actually happened or is happening?"

Observers can help identify or quantify the problem.

Step 2—Process: *Seek to clarify the basic issues and the facts by using democratic processes, applying reasoning and logic, and clarifying rights and responsibilities.*

The teacher reminds students to use self-reflection, effective listening, "I" messages, and aspects of ordered sharing (one person at a time without interruption). Everything is done in order to arrive personally or collectively at a point where everyone shares a common understanding of what took place and led up to the emotionally charged reaction or situation. This should be relatively impersonal, without blame or judgment.

Here are some questions and strategies that the entire class, individual groups, or individuals can use to avoid or clear up misunderstandings.

- What did you (we) expect to happen?
- What actually happened?
- What led to the dispute?
- How did things escalate?
- How is this similar to anything that we have experienced in the past?

Step 3—Act: *Shed light on future actions.*

What will the parties agree to DO in order to handle this more effectively in the future? Focus on responsibility, opportunity to change, choice, and commitment. Develop or revise the plan of action as needed. Note that action usually involves some change in behavior, and that those new behaviors need to be practiced and monitored in some consistent way. Make this part of the agreement.

This process requires and relies on higher-order thinking and decision making (executive functions). Reasoning, metacognition, logic, and reflection are continually honed as students learn about their own beliefs and behaviors, defend their assumptions, and take time to reflect on alternative scenarios and ways of thinking. When done well, this process can be used to deal with many ethnic and cultural differences and some "hot topics" such as sexual behaviors. Sometimes, however, when things get out of hand, it may be necessary to have a process meeting to solidify the community, and sometimes the issues are too complex to resolve by even this process. Remember, also, that teachers do have ultimate responsibility, may have to cast a deciding vote, and may need to search out professional advice.

Step 4—Review progress

Using this process helps to review what transpired so that you can learn from and improve upon what happened. Here are some useful review questions for both the teacher and students.

- What specifically happened to get the group to acknowledge the problem?
- What steps were taken to process the problem?
- What steps were taken to process the solution?
- How did the class respond?
- Did the situation help the class and the students in conflict to defuse their emotions?
- How would this manner of handling the situation help maintain an atmosphere of relaxed alertness?
- In your view, was the class empowered? Have the students in conflict been empowered? How has this helped rebuild the community?

Helpful Hints

Although we have described this process almost as a formula, it is more than that.

1. Your emotional tone will have a major impact on how the process works. Being matter of fact is much better than being angry or hostile, and being matter of fact and caring is much better than just being neutral. That is why educators need to consistently work on themselves and develop personal competence and confidence in their ability to deal with emotional issues and conflict.

2. Taking action requires more than making a promise to act. Yet threatening students with punishment if they do not act will usually (but not in extreme cases) defeat the purpose of the process. One suggestion is to help individual students think of ways to reward themselves once some action has been taken.

3. There are some issues that are too complex or intense for the process just described to work. For instance, we believe that this process should not be used when students are abusing drugs or alcohol. Part of any process is recognizing its limitations and knowing when and how to ask for help. The purpose of Acknowledge-Process-Act-Review is for students to think more deeply and become capable of developing emotional maturity. If you do get lost in the emotional dynamics and can't keep things at the level of problem solving, seek help. There are a number of programs available that deal with conflict, including peer mediation, that you might find useful.

4. Sometimes the way the process is described has an impact. You may want to refer to it as negotiation rather than as resolving conflict.

The Fist of Five

Reaching agreement—such as through consensus, where all parties can accept a solution as workable—sometimes requires a lot of time. One way to speed up the process is to use a simple check that helps everyone see if they are approaching agreement or if they need to address concerns that are not being voiced. It is called the "fist of five." When a possible agreement has been reached, the group leader calls for a vote. Students raise a different amount of appropriate fingers to signal how they feel about the idea.

> Five Fingers—Wow, this is a great idea.
> Four Fingers—This is a good idea.
> Three Fingers—I am OK with this but not overjoyed.
> Two Fingers—I can accept it, but I have some reservations.
> One Finger—I can live with it, but I have real questions about it.
> Fist—No, I don't accept it, but I have another possible answer.

SOURCE: Adapted from California Teachers Association Leadership Training, 1989.

This procedure works with adults as well and provides a quick check on how things are going. It should not, however, take the place of the processing that leads to greater insights and understanding. Sometimes it helps remind participants that in consensus building everyone accepts his or her own responsibility for making the solution a viable one. Make it a practice to check whether those raising three or fewer fingers were satisfied with the solution and could truly "live with it." Asking questions or acknowledging concerns helps everyone feel that their reactions are validated.

Chain of Escalating Conflict

Probably the hardest thing about resolving differences without violence is maintaining the spirit that any problem can be resolved if individuals so desire. It also requires that everyone keeps a lookout for the first indicators of a potential problem. One way we can assist ourselves and our students in recognizing the signs of conflict is to process an actual conflict as if it were a chain (adapted from the Community Board Program, 1987a, 1987b, and Loescher, 1986).

Start at the point of conflict and backtrack each step that happened. It may be useful to draw it on a board, one link at a time. Then take the time to discuss how each link could have been broken before a chain was created that resulted in the conflict. Make sure the group can answer the following:

- What was the original conflict?
- Which were the acts that escalated the conflict?
- What could have been done to "break" the chain?

This will help with acknowledging a problem, processing the causes and possible solutions, and acting to change the way difficult situations could be handled in the future.

THE TRANSFORMATIONAL ADMINISTRATOR AND THE PROCESS FOR MAKING IT REAL

To help students develop emotional competence, adults need to have emotional competence. All the behaviors seen in students are also played out in adults. In recent years the issue has received a great deal of attention and has come to be thought of in terms of emotional intelligence (Goleman, 1997). A great deal of information and guidance is now available on the subject.

> Our preferred approach is to use the learning circle because it can work as a superb vehicle for learning to deal with one's emotional life and for exploring issues. Some procedures, such as the regular practice of ordered sharing, can lead to an automatic increase in emotional competence. Other procedures can be introduced and explored as the group desires.

Here lies a major challenge for administrators because, of course, administrators can support their staffs only if they too are emotionally competent. Administrators need to find ways to participate with the staff and yet maintain their own focus. Do not participate in and accept sarcasm in the school, lounge, or administration building, or allow yourself to focus on complaints and criticism. Remind yourself and others of their strengths.

We believe that educators became educators for a powerful and noble reason: to better the lives and potential of students in their communities. There was and is tremendous emotion behind each educator's decision to pursue this field. The pressures from politicians, media, parents, and each other have caused so many to lose sight of those noble reasons. In many respects, our positive emotions have been squelched by these pressures.

- As a leader, are you taking positive actions to build a positive future for education?
- How is your leadership affecting your staff?
- Are you encouraging everyone to contribute positive energy and action to the learning environment?

Reflection: Something to Think About

From what you have read, how do you see yourself including this information in your work with your students and staff? What have you noticed about your awareness of your own emotional states? What can you do to promote adaptive decision making in your classrooms and school that can result in a better ability to handle emotions and develop students' use of their executive functions?

In tandem with the National Teaching Standards

Teachers make students their partners in establishing and maintaining a community of learners.

—Standard IV

The skills and concepts dealt with in this chapter all contribute to an increased partnership for establishing and maintaining a community of learners. Educators connect more completely with students, and students with each other. Fuller participation and sharing of responsibility occur. A more authentic and empowered community results. In such communities, students learn to communicate and interact socially with both adults and peers. They also develop emotional intelligence. We call such an environment an apprentice community.

This completes the first section. By yourself or in your learning circles, take time to review what you have learned:

- What is relaxed alertness?
- How is relaxed alertness essential to developing the executive functions?
- What types of environment lead to developing the executive functions?
- What are you doing differently now that you have read this far? What skills have you practiced? What skills have your students practiced?
- What will you need to do in order to continually create an environment of relaxed alertness?
- Can you describe a relaxed alertness community? Students?

PART II

Orchestrated Immersion in Complex Experience

Introduction to Immersion in Complex Experience

Creating an enriched environment for learning

 At the Core

In the first section of the book, we focused on developing the optimal climate and state of mind in the learner and teacher. A shorthand label is "apprentice community." Now we move more directly into instruction. In this chapter we lay some foundations and introduce a model for teaching in Instructional Approaches 2 and 3. Then, in the rest of the section, we expand and unpack the various elements of that model.

We begin with the notion of an enriched environment, one that provides the greatest opportunities for remembering specific facts and skills while also encouraging and nurturing the development and use of the executive functions.

HOW DO WE KNOW THIS?

Some of the earliest research was begun 30 years ago by pioneers such as Marion Diamond, PhD (1988). Current researchers such as Bill Greenough,

PhD, at the University of Illinois continue to expand on Diamond's original findings and research that compared the brains of experimental animals from impoverished and enriched environments.

The differences between the two environments are profound. Animals in impoverished environments were kept in a cage, away from other animals. Even contact with humans was limited. Food and water were available, but there were only minor opportunities for play and exploration. This environment led to reduced connections between neurons in the brain.

In the enriched environment, animals had the company of other animals, played with toys, and freely explored items that were changed frequently. Animals living in enriched environments showed an increase in synaptic connections (connections between neurons) and improved their ability to perform complex tasks, such as learning their way around a new maze.

Although the original research focused largely on rats (because their brains structurally resemble those of humans), the implications for the research have now been extended to humans (Huttenlocher, 2002). Greenough's research (Greenough, Black, & Wallace, 1987) suggests that "enriched" environments should be stimulating, complex, and challenging, with elements of novelty and variety. He also found that rats like to socialize.

Rumbaugh and Washburn (cited in Lyon & Krasnegor, 1999, pp. 201–202) report on their work with chimpanzees, which spans 25 years. Their conclusions suggest that brain development appears to be optimized in chimpanzees under three conditions that mirror the three elements of this book:

1. They should be reared in a stable, supportive social context [relaxed alertness].

2. They should be immersed in a challenging environment as their "lifestyle," not just for an hour a day. The environment should address the animals' developmental needs with opportunities to "control" both its resources and activities [immersion].

3. In addition, the environment should be structured so that the consequences of behavior or feedback are immediate, reliable, and relevant [active processing].

Although many teachers feel uncomfortable using work based on experiments with animals, such research is extremely important. Educators tend not to have the opportunity for controlled and long-term studies of this type. Animals, particularly chimpanzees, are also extremely close to humans genetically and share many characteristics with us.

Rumbaugh and Washburn (1999) tell us that all chimpanzees reared in this way improved their ability to pay attention, to work with members of their social group, to improve memory, and to work "tenaciously on tasks/problems" (cited in Lyon & Krasnegor, 1999, p. 202).

Immersion of the Learner in Complex Experience

We use the terms *enriched* and *complex* interchangeably when referring to the best environments for human learning.

There needs to be novelty, variety, instant feedback, and opportunity for student choices, and experiences need to be driven by actor-centered questions and to result in multiple exposures to the same or similar facts and information over time. Many attempts have been made to describe these sorts of environments. Project-based learning (Hassard, 1999), experiential learning (Luckner & Nadler, 1997), self-regulated learning (Boekaerts, 1996; Perry, 1998; Zimmerman & Martinez-Pons, 1990), integrated thematic instruction (Kovalik & Olsen, 1997), and learner-centered teaching are a few examples.

> In order to place students in adequately complex or enriched environments, teachers need to immerse students in complex experiences in which the curriculum and standards are naturally embedded.

The key is for students to be "immersed" in rich and complex environments as a way of life, not just for an hour a day per subject. An occasional project serves as a beginning, but the ideal is an environment in which projects, research, and multiple relationships are ongoing and are the norm, not the exception. This is an expansion of the notion of an *apprentice community* (Caine & Caine, 1997). Thus, much of the workings of the real world play themselves out in a manageable and appropriate way. The teacher and school are responsible for ensuring that the various aspects of the environment are present. That is why we describe immersion as "orchestrated" primarily by the teacher but with continual student input.

Just having an experience, however, does not guarantee adequate learning.

This is why immersion needs to be supplemented by teacher-led processes to make sure that students learn what they need to learn. These include effective questioning, summarizing, and multiple opportunities for students to learn essential facts and skills as well as engage in higher-order thinking and problem solving. We call this *Active Processing*; Part III of this book deals extensively with active processing.

Expanding the Nature of Immersion

In this section of the book we describe, and help educators create, immersion-based teaching environments. To do this, chapters will be organized using a number of specific Brain/Mind Learning Principles. As in the previous section, they tell us that

- all learning engages the physiology,
- learning is developmental,
- the brain/mind processes parts and wholes simultaneously,
- the search for meaning occurs through patterning.

These specific principles were chosen because they inform us powerfully about how to use an understanding of human learning to orchestrate the best teaching. It is important to remember, however, that ultimately it takes all of the capacities and implementation of all the Brain/Mind Principles to create an enriched environment.

PROCESSING THIS PRINCIPLE

Personal Connections

The First Immersion: Our Native Language

Most people cannot remember how they mastered one of the most critical skills for life—how to speak their native language. Yet learning to speak one's native language provides the purest example of immersion in complex experience. Although it seems as though all human beings are designed to acquire language naturally, the conditions that support language acquisition offer a wonderful illustration of what effective immersion looks like.

In general, and with respect to language, even infants feel competent, confident, and interested. Motivation is compounded by the longing to belong and the explanatory drive that we introduced in the previous section.

Questions to ask yourself about how you acquired your native language:

- *From what age were you exposed to language? And in how many different ways?*
- *Was there ever any doubt (do you think) that you would learn how to speak?*
- *Do you think that you were free to babble and experiment in your own way?*
- *Do you think you ever received guidance and feedback about how to speak properly?*
- *To what extent do you think you just "picked up language"?*

Going Deeper

There are some very useful ways to categorize factors that contribute to language acquisition and orchestrated immersion generally:

- A context that teaches
- Modeling and guidance
- Complexity

Let's look at these three factors as they guide the acquisition of language.

A Context That Teaches

Almost like the air around us, what we need to learn is present everywhere.

Parents, relatives, and strangers all speak to infants, about them, and to each other. Infants very likely also overhear speaking on the radio or television and hear words that are a part of songs. All this makes up the context (environment and culture). Day by day, infants learn a little more about speaking as they hear sounds and practice those that are interesting or important to them.

In addition to acquiring language from their parents, infants mimic and copy what others are doing. Sometimes the modeling is so automatic that infants seem almost to learn by "osmosis" (Claxton, 1997). This is how they pick up their accent and the structure of their particular language. At other times there is guided repetition and feedback, generally sensed as playful, interesting, and challenging. In addition, either they surpass the number of vocabulary words of their peers or are left behind, depending on how often their parents (and others) speak directly to them in the course of the day (Sternberg & Grigorenko, 2001).

Modeling and Guidance

The use of language is continually modeled.

The pattern of development is shaped by the babies' culture (context). For example, Korean children tend to acquire verbs before nouns, whereas Western children tend to acquire nouns before verbs (Gopnik, Meltzoff, & Kuhl, 1999).

Language is multilayered. For instance, there is a cadence and a rhythm to every language in addition to vocabulary and syntax. There are very simple and very complex ways of speaking. Vocabulary and other aspects of speech tend to vary according to occupation, culture, and other factors. There are differences in the ways children and adults speak to each other and with each other. Infants are immersed in many of these overlapping layers, which are shaped by other events such as mealtimes and playing games.

Complexity

Infants are exposed to multiple levels of complexity.

Not everything is exactly like learning a language, and brains do change with age. The concept of immersion is valid, however, because it is based on the fact that powerful learning involves multiple experiences that challenge learners and relate to what interests learners personally. Immersion therefore includes the layering or "weaving together" of information and essential skills. This is done by way of multiple experiences that include practice and application, such as the continuous and ongoing exchange of thoughts and information with others, novelty generated by questions that intrigue learners, and individual and collective research that requires critical thinking, analysis, and problem solving (executive functions). Through these processes, students learn to master the "languages" of mathematics, history, writing, art, science, and other disciplines.

Revisiting the Foundations of Orchestration

It can be seen from what we have just said that appropriate experiences for students need to be more than just a random set of activities and events. When teachers set out to immerse students in complex experience, those experiences need to be orchestrated. Regardless of the curriculum requirements (preschool through adult learners), the three generic elements described above all need to shape the experiences that educators set up for students in whatever the curriculum requires. The generic fundamentals for immersion in complex experience are the following:

1. A context rich in resources of all kinds

2. Modeling and guidance, with lived examples of expert work

3. Complexity that exposes students to, and requires their participation in, both basic and sophisticated performance

A Word About Standards

These generic elements are always framed in terms of standards because brain/mind teaching begins with standards. The standards may be formal and spelled out by the state or district, or the teacher may spell them out ahead of time based on students' highest content knowledge. Regardless of where they originate, the teacher must be clear about the standards for immersion.

> The guiding question should always be, "What will students have mastered when they are finished with this experience?"

Bridging to the Practical

Let's look, for a moment, at two different scenarios in order to gain a felt meaning for what immersion and the absence of immersion might look like in instruction. We contrast two approaches to teaching the same standards, which involve understanding elements of commerce and economics. Students are to master essential concepts by examining the operation of a restaurant. Core concepts include the definition of *entrepreneur*, the notion of profit, and key elements of a market economy in which many decisions are made by businesses for themselves.

Scenario 1

The teacher's method is to follow the textbook and supplement the text with lectures. Students are provided with a list of additional reading. The teacher will cover a lot of ground. Issues range from discussing the types of restaurant that might be suitable for a particular locality and whether they cater to the "high end" or "low end" of the market. They include the economics of the use of space and time, how menus and various dishes are selected, and decisions about how much to order to satisfy needs without wasting too much food through spoilage. The teacher may go into some issues in some depth. Concepts are defined, principles are analyzed, facts are memorized, and students are then tested to see if the standards have been met.

Let's look for the three fundamentals of orchestration.

Where do you see the following?

1. A context rich in resources of all kinds

2. Modeling and guidance, with lived examples of expert work

3. Complexity that exposes students to both basic and sophisticated performance

Here are some additional questions that focus on immersion:

- To what extent would you expect students to buy into the topic?
- Was actor-centered decision making elicited?
- How many opportunities do you see for students to use their senses and to experience novelty, surprise, challenge, and relationship?
- To what extent did the students observe and learn from experts?
- How many layers of experience were students exposed to?

Scenario 2

The teacher is guided by the same standards, but in this scenario students actually investigate a restaurant because they have expressed an interest in a particular type of cooking and food. Not everyone agreed in the beginning about which restaurant to visit, so students who wanted this particular restaurant had to present and defend their choice.

Once at the restaurant, students have opportunities to look around wherever they like and to follow or "shadow" employees in every job from chef to manager. At times they are to stand back and observe a procedure or sequence, at times to do things or try things out. Upon return to the school, videos, texts, and resources are made available to students in the classroom, where they meet regularly to share their progress and experiences back in their classroom.

The teacher subsequently works with students to help them reflect and report on their experiences. She asks questions such as, "What elements of an economy did you see operating in this restaurant?" "Who made decisions?" "What role did profit play?" "What relationship did you see between how this restaurant is run and commercial success?" "Seventy-five percent of restaurants in our city do not last more than three years. On the basis of your experience, can you explain this?" and so forth. The teacher is in charge of taking essential facts and skills and other curriculum elements and embedding them on a continuing basis in the students' restaurant experience, group discussions, and periodic summaries.

Once again, let's look for the three fundamentals of orchestration. Where do you see the following?

1. A context rich in resources of all kinds

2. Modeling and guidance, with lived examples of expert work

3. Complexity that exposes students to both basic and sophisticated performance

Here are the same questions presented with the first scenario of what students might learn from this approach:

- To what extent would you expect students to buy into the topic?
- Was actor-centered decision making elicited?
- How many opportunities do you see for students to use their senses and to experience novelty, surprise, challenge, and relationship?
- To what extent did the students observe and learn from experts?
- How many layers of experience were students exposed to?

Note that this example is *not* intended only for career and technical education. We are talking about immersion in complex experience for the purpose of developing high academic standards in any context. Teachers can create or take advantage of any physical sites where the elements of motivation, context, modeling, and complexity are present or available.

TAKING IT INTO THE CLASSROOM

Diagram 7.1 shows the overall model that we use to guide the development of Instructional Approach 3. You will see that all three elements are represented: relaxed alertness, orchestrated immersion, and active processing.

Diagram 7.1 Guided Experience Model

As we have already acknowledged, it is not always possible to give students a real-world experience. The objective, therefore, will be to introduce all the necessary elements from a real-world experience into the classroom.

Guided Experience Cycle

The illustration above represents a model that facilitates Instructional Approaches 2 and 3. We call it the guided experience model. The specifics always shift and change, but the described elements will be present regardless of subject-matter focus or discipline (see Resources D and E).

Before you begin

Know your subject well, and be sure that you know the essential facts, concepts, and skills to be mastered and that you have internalized the standards.

Classroom Climate

It is critical to remember that the model will work only if the teacher and students have established the basis of an authentic community and the sort of climate advocated in Part I of this book.

Phase 1: Global Experience

A superb way to introduce a new topic or body of material is to create what we call a global experience. This is a relatively engaging event that involves the students in multiple ways, helps get them really interested, and begins to convey a feeling or felt meaning for the subject. Global experiences are discussed in depth in Chapter 8.

Phase 2: Student Choices and Questions

At the end of the global experience, students are given opportunities to talk about what interested them and to ask actor-centered questions. The teacher uses this session to help focus the students' questions to assure that the standards will be addressed in their subsequent research. We describe how this is done in Chapter 9.

Phase 3: Deep Exploration Through Research and Projects

The primary way to "teach," then, is to support students as they research their questions. This will be an ongoing process, involving individual and group work using multiple resources supported by the teacher through questions and suggestions. Resources might include access to experts, the World Wide Web, and libraries. The teacher will use open-ended questions, guiding comments and direct instruction when needed in order to consolidate essential knowledge and skills. The teacher will constantly keep an eye on student progress. The exploration phase helps students continuously improve, refine, and process what they are learning. The teacher's role during Phase 3 is to actively process student work in an ongoing fashion, keeping high standards, critical skills, and disciplinary knowledge and rubrics in mind. It is the teacher's responsibility to see that all students master basic knowledge in the field despite divergent research and/or projects.

Phase 4: Consolidation and Final Assessment

Although assessment is ongoing throughout active processing, it is in this fourth phase that various modes of assessment may be used as a culminating activity. For example, understanding is demonstrated through authentic assessment of all types, including projects, posters, or designing a grant application to further develop or justify a project (Wiggins, 1993). Students can design and take exams covering critical elements. The teacher can engage students in oral and written exams. Oral exams could include "mock courts" or interviews requiring students to recall and use essential information, concepts, and logical and systematic thinking. This would help students further process the experiences and material at the same time that they demonstrate they can use acquired knowledge in new and spontaneous situations. Note that as the model is mastered, students will begin to perform better on standardized tests, even though such tests will be a secondary consideration with this approach. For a step-by-step instructional guide, see Resource D.

An Example for Grades 4–5: Biology

Delaware Standard Six: Life Processes . . . Structure/Function Relationship
   1. Living things have structures that function to help them reproduce, grow, and survive in different kinds of places.

As the teacher, you have decided to approach this standard by teaching about insects.

Global Experience

You want to engage students in the topic from the start. You have come across the Disney movie *MicroCosmos* (Barratier, Mallet, & Perrin, 1996), which depicts insects in their respective environments doing insect things like washing themselves, swinging, working, eating, and the like. The insects are beautiful and fascinating. The video takes the audience from above the clouds down into the world hidden in everyday grass. You show the first 15 minutes of the video while students watch in silence punctuated by their sounds of interest and excitement.

Generating Actor-Centered Questions

When the video ends there is momentary silence. As the teacher, you ask students to recall any particular insect that they found interesting and want to know more about. Wait for them to respond. At this point you are looking for signs of their interest or enthusiasm. Some students won't know the name of the insect they like. You can reveal the name, get on the Web as a class, ask students to get on the Web, look in the encyclopedia, or use other resources on insects to find the appropriate name. You suggest that they "adopt their insect" and learn as much about it as possible.

As a class you now generate some additional questions. These should come from the students. Your job is to gently guide their questions so that the standards and basic facts and processes will automatically be a part of what they want to know about insects (actor-centered adaptive questions that engage decision making).

- How long do insects live (and what about *your* insect)?
- How do they die (and what is the greatest danger to *your* insect)?
- What insect is this insect's closest relative in the insect world (and what is *your* insect's family)?
- How do they get around (and does *your* insect fly, crawl, swing)?
- How fast do they move (and how fast does *your* insect move)?

Notice that all of these questions are likely to be generated by the students themselves and that all of them can be related back to the standards.

Research

Record and sort these questions, then ask questions about possible resources the students plan to use, how much time they will need to work on gathering initial information, whether they will work in groups or alone, and the like. Students who pick the same insect can form a research pair or group.

As you proceed, you need to continually process student findings (use processing questions from the next section) and make sure that students deal with the issues spelled out in the standards. Group sharing of information can be done through ordered sharing, and there can even be opportunities for individual students or groups to record their progress openly for the entire class to track. If there is a standard that needs to be addressed directly, a mini-lesson can be introduced for the class.

Consolidation and Final Assessment

Allow students to document what they discover about their insect and insects in general. Posters, written summaries, or photographic "albums" are only some of the ideas they may choose from.

Even if you return to the text and a written test, the students are more willing to participate because they now have a personal connection to the world of insects.

A Developmental Path to Improved Teaching

Improving teaching takes time and depends on the skills you have already developed. The path may begin at Instructional Approach 1 for most teachers and move to Instructional Approach 2 over time. The model above culminates in Instructional Approach 3 teaching.

Throughout this section, therefore, we provide suggestions for teachers to push themselves to their own next level and to develop more complex skills at their own pace. For example, the first step for Instructional Approach 1 teachers is simply to develop more creative and exciting ways to make presentations. These can be very powerful and can serve to better stimulate and engage students, and so provide a next step on the path toward implementing the model. Instructional Approach 2 teachers need to focus on creating powerful global experiences and inviting student questions.

In addition, we strongly encourage teachers to look for golden opportunities to connect the world to student learning. Take advantage of a road crew repaving a street near the school. Realign the schedule to coincide with the school district maintenance team present in the building repairing a leaky pipe or a broken window. Use the upcoming bond issue to invite the school district business manager into the classroom to explore the financial conditions that have brought the vote before the parents and community. Local, real issues at play immediately around the learners and within the immediate environment accent the curriculum. Explore the problems, decisions, and solutions that these people are addressing. Working adults are modeling actor-centered decision making!

> Consequently, when we capture these opportunities for learning, no two years of curriculum are alike. Instructional Approach 2 and 3 teachers are at the ready, eyes always searching for ways to bring the real world into the classroom. *They are working in the moment,* searching for real ways to embed the standards and curriculum.

THE TRANSFORMATIONAL ADMINISTRATOR AND THE PROCESS FOR MAKING IT REAL

Here we enter more directly into the realm of instruction. The challenge for learning circles is to work on the ideas and processes. Participants use each other for support and feedback. The three elements (context and resources, modeling, and complexity) offer great topics for discussion over a period of regular staff meetings as well. Invite the staff to reflect on how they are using them in their classrooms.

> An ordered sharing could be your format, giving each teacher a chance to share his or her success and—if the community is sufficiently strong—struggles with colleagues in a positive way.

If they have not already done so, teachers could embark on some peer coaching and develop ways to assist each other toward more proficiency.

Our model can also become a vehicle for integrating all of the inservices and trainings that are used. The more that specific skills and processes can be seen to fit together, the more they reinforce each other and accelerate professional development.

The transformational administrator can support the process in other ways. Sometimes a classroom visit can be invaluable; for instance, in helping teachers see which aspects of powerful teaching they may be implementing without being conscious of doing so.

At least as important is working toward a climate where the three elements are lived in the everyday working lives of adults outside the classroom. In what ways are issues introduced so that they can be motivating? If a classroom teaches, so can the school. One of the best indirect ways to support higher standards is for the adults in the school to naturally use materials, ideas, and processes from the curriculum in their own work and discussions. This happens naturally with reading and simple math, but there are many more opportunities for adults to live and help students experience what is being taught. We invite you to explore ways to bring this point to life in your school.

In tandem with the National Teaching Standards	Accomplished teachers select, adapt, create, and use rich and varied resources.
	They look beyond the textbooks in their classrooms and consider how a variety of materials and people might be employed to deepen conceptual understanding.

—Standard III: Instructional Resources

The approach described here is in accordance with the National Teaching Standards. The model helps teachers vary instructional resources and materials and to bring the rich and complex nature of the curriculum to life. In addition, the approach is in accordance with the standards that suggest that teachers "not rely on a single method of assessing students, because behavior is influenced by the setting in which it occurs. They know that students have skills that will not emerge in certain settings or during the course of a single assignment." An immersion-filled classroom will reduce the number of discipline issues per day, increase the number of engaged learners, and increase exciting energy! Students' choices in providing you feedback will further empower them, a condition that supports relaxed alertness.

Seeing the Parts and Experiencing Wholeness

Brain/Mind Learning Principle 6: *The brain/mind processes parts and wholes simultaneously.*

 At the Core

The brain/mind is designed to make sense of the world. The world that surrounds any one of us at a given time contains an infinite amount of information. Making sense of experience requires both a big picture and paying attention to the individual parts. Teaching needs to begin with an experience for students that provides exposure to the overall nature of the subject. This is somewhat like going to a concert or hearing an instrument played before beginning to learn how to play it. The experience of the whole provides a story, a model, or a fascinating example of what can be achieved. The details or "parts" are taught as students pursue their urge to create or understand something of larger significance to them.

Capacity: All students can learn more effectively when their experience gives them a sense of the whole that links the details (facts and information).

A human being is part of the whole, called by us "universe," a part limited in time and space. He experiences himself, his thoughts and feelings as something separate from the rest—a kind of optical delusion of his consciousness. This delusion is a kind of prison for us, restricting us to our personal decisions and to affection for a few persons nearest to us. Our task must be to free ourselves from this prison by widening our circle of compassion to embrace all living creatures and the whole of nature in its beauty.

—Albert Einstein

HOW DO WE KNOW THIS?

It should be expected that the brain and mind are designed to deal with the difference between parts and wholes. In fact, the way in which human beings "construct" reality has been a central issue in psychology for a long time.

In the late 19th century, a form of psychology was developed that still has powerful messages. It was called Gestalt psychology, the word *gestalt* roughly meaning "the whole." A more modern version is called *perceptual psychology*. Both Gestalt psychology and perceptual psychology tell us that we continually choose what to focus on (what is in "figure") given the sea ("ground") of information that always surrounds anything. They investigate the rules that determine what we look at and how we organize perception so it means something.

The brain itself is also organized so that different parts are to some extent responsible for different functions, and yet the parts all act together in order to respond to life experience.

> The executive functions are a case in point. A central feature of the executive functions is that separate capacities and skills are integrated for the purpose of making effective actor-centered, adaptive decisions in the moment. Short- and long-term memory, time horizons, motivation, and a host of other factors are all being integrated simultaneously, with many regions of the brain being accessed.

There are also many ways of connecting stimuli into patterns that consist of parts and natural wholes. Language itself is a wonderful example. Every language has its own vocabulary, grammar, and syntax that combine in the larger unity that we call language. Language comes together in the moment to represent whole ideas or to express feelings and beliefs that are inevitably more complex than the words themselves.

Many psychologists argue that the entire brain/mind itself is organized into a whole "self" that is the foundation of what each of us calls "I" (Llinas, 2002). The nature of this "I" is very illusive. You can test this for yourself. On a piece of paper, jot down things that you identify about yourself. You'll very likely begin with items like "I am a parent," "I am an educator," and "I am a male (or female)." No one single description will describe you totally. Try as you may, you won't be able to find a way to describe the "whole" of you.

PROCESSING THIS PRINCIPLE

Personal Connections

Parts and wholes are always present. Your hand is in a room, which is in a building, which is in a neighborhood, a city, a country, on a planet, and so on. At the same time your hand has skin, cells, atoms, and subatomic particles.

Take a moment to look outside your window. Imagine that you are talking on the phone to a friend and that you want to describe what you are looking at. Chances are that you will name one thing or group of things at a time such as trees, sky, houses, or grass (if you are in a town or a city). This need and ability to describe and identify the parts separately is amazing, given that we live in a world where everything is connected and always exists together in relationship to other things.

> Everything is always a part of something bigger and can also be reduced to minute particles.

No matter how hard you try, you cannot give your friend a complete sense of what you are looking at. It is almost impossible to describe the "whole" without reverting to words that are a part of a total experience. Continue to look outside:

- What else do you see?
- How does it feel?
- What sounds do you hear?
- How are your senses affected?
- What does your present mood add?

Now add more detail and answer each question again. Are there any limits to the detail you can add? All of the details go into creating your experience, but even if you itemized them all, they would not create the "wholeness" of your experience.

No matter how hard you try, you cannot provide an exact or complete picture using explanations. Only an experience can give that sense of the whole.

Ideas Are Wholes With Parts

The above is not just an exercise to tease the mind. Moving between a big idea or a whole and the parts that make up that big idea is critical to learning anything in depth. Much science is based on direct observation and analysis of the parts. Scientists look at something and want to know what it is made of. Scientists see the real world in operation and ask, "How does it work?" "What makes that happen?" and "How does one arrive there?" Much of the time, scientists break the whole into its component parts and find an almost infinite amount of facts and information about the physical world in which we live. Other scientists deal with relationships and the multiple ways in which things are interconnected. Even in the world of brain research we find these two approaches—there are those who examine different isolated functions and brain regions, while many are also curious about the brain/mind as a unified system.

A sense of interconnectedness is frequently best conveyed through the arts where it becomes possible to experience things that we cannot always describe, even to ourselves. Many people resort to poetry or painting in order to capture the wholeness of an experience. Here is an example:

Spider Web

As the sunlight streaks across my carpet I look

to the window and see the gossamer threads of your web.

How many millenniums have you spun

holding the secret of life in your strands,

letting all see the interconnectedness,

showing us our oneness?

From the dew diamonds dancing on your filaments in the meadow

to dark, dank corners of caves woven full of traps for unsuspecting

insects,

You have spun and spun, sharing this inner knowing,

each day beginning again, giving the world full understanding

if it will notice . . .

we are all a part of your web of life, we are one.

Ah spider, my broom stays at rest for this day, letting those

gossamer threads tell their truth . . .

Spin on oh prophet, share your good tidings,

Spin.

—Carol McClintic

How does this differ from a standard classroom description of a spider?

Music, paintings, stories, poetry, and sculpture draw us into the more interconnected "wholeness" of experience. These experiences can provide new insights into aspects of life or expand on current understanding. A sense of wholeness can also be synonymous with a sense of wonder or awe. Being in nature can create feelings of an interconnectedness or wholeness that some sense as spiritual, because those who experience them say that they become a part of a totally interconnected fabric. This is what many native cultures and millions of individuals value deeply. It is important to appreciate the difference between fragments and the whole because that is central to meaningful learning.

Going Deeper

Traditional education focuses heavily on having students learn the parts. Knowing the parts is very important to feeling competent and confident, yet without a clear sense of how parts are connected, meaning is lost and much potential learning is wasted. Questions like, "What can I do with this?" "Why does that happen?" "How will that help me do what I want to do?" and "How is this connected to that?" are gateways to learning that go unused.

> When wholeness is gone, meaning is gone. In fact, when wholeness and connectedness are dismissed, a student's personal questions become irrelevant and powerful learning is undermined.

Brain/Mind Learning Begins With the Whole

Let us look at different aspects of the core curriculum in terms of parts and wholes.

Reading traditionally involves associating sounds with marks on a page or blackboard. However, unless students experience the sheer pleasure of stories, and are invited to bring meaning to a text, their intrinsic motivation for reading and the ability to read for understanding may not develop. This is particularly true for a generation growing up on "visual" stories provided by television and movies whose stories do not require a lot of preparation and hard work to experience.

Mathematics traditionally depends on recognizing numbers and learning how to add, subtract, divide, or multiply those numbers. What may be left out is the role played by mathematics in the real world and a grasp of the underlying concepts that are crucial to more sophisticated mathematical thinking. Basic operations should be accompanied by a sense of the magic that helps students measure or analyze something they want to build (actor-centered decision making). Mathematics needs to generate and inspire questions that can lead to more systematic thinking. Students need to see mathematics as a way of describing the physical world. This automatically engages the executive functions.

History is traditionally based on recognizing important dates and places instead of generating questions that link individuals and events to the students' present world.

Frequently, physics, biology, and chemistry, some of the very fields that beg students to ask questions about their physical world, do not relate to their actual experiences. For example:

- Do you remember your high school chemistry class?
- How about all of those formulas you were required to memorize?
- Did you ever wonder where they came from?

Formulas do not emerge out of thin air. When scientists are confronted by a puzzle or question, they do some research, return to their puzzle, learn more, discover a new way to look at their puzzle, and so on. Formulas are the result of exploring interesting—often relevant—problems.

Bridging to the Practical

The kind of learning we propose relies on providing students with some type of experience that openly invites actor-centered questions and decision making. There is, therefore, a profound difference between veridical knowledge and information that can easily be reduced to "right" and "wrong" answers that are determined by others, and actor-centered adaptive knowledge, which results when learners engage their own unique search for answers.

> There are many ways of organizing information and activities that work to introduce an experience, giving a larger sense of the subject or topic and leading to actor-centered questions. Stories and projects are two methods that can be used at every level from pre-kindergarten to postgraduate studies.

Stories

We naturally perceive and relate to stories. Children acquire a sense of narrative when they are very young. In part, this is a consequence of the autobiographical memory system that registers one's own life story. The power and fascination of stories continues throughout life. Thus, almost every detailed item in the news is in story form.

Think about it. Early humans developed stories to pass on religious, historical, scientific, and cultural knowledge. Subsequent generations added new versions and developed extensive ways to express the meaning these stories communicated. During nostalgic times we often recount moments of the saga of our own self-narrative. There is a sense of wholeness, connectedness, and meaning that is conveyed in a story that would otherwise be only irrelevant fragments of experience.

We therefore invite you to explore the use of stories and to develop your own storytelling skills. There is a notable difference in the engagement of students (at any age) between when a story is told to introduce a subject or topic and when facts are simply presented. Moreover, when a story illustrates a larger truth that can be examined through subsequent activity, it serves as a way to connect the curriculum to a larger purpose or to foreshadow what can be done with what students are about to learn.

Explore some of the ways in which stories infuse your life:

- Discuss the extent to which items in the news are framed in terms of a story.
- Brainstorm ways to bring more stories into anything that you teach.
- Search for relevant stories that introduce or expand on your curriculum. These can be found everywhere: in newspapers, on the Internet, in both fiction and nonfiction books, and in the stories people tell. For a great way to begin, you might want to look at *Teaching as Story Telling* by Kieran Egan (1986).
- Jokes and cartoons that tell a story and make a point are also excellent.

Projects

A project has a purpose that naturally organizes people's attention and efforts. Setting up a business, designing the layout for a brochure, installing a computer network, designing and maintaining a garden, creating a new Web site—these are all projects. They are also all wholes that contain parts. In fact, with both stories and projects, note that we begin with a sense of the whole even though there are many specifics that still need to be addressed. That is how the brain/mind likes to function. It is designed to identify details as it engages larger purposes that make sense.

Examine some projects in which you have been engaged recently.

- How were you motivated?
- What questions did you have?
- What decisions did you have to make?
- How did you organize your time?
- What sorts of parts (skills, vocabulary, data) did you have to master?
- To what extent can you bring or have you brought projects into the classroom?

TAKING IT INTO THE CLASSROOM

Although every subject and every discipline is best understood when the parts "fit into" a whole, there's more, because each whole is also a part of something bigger. For example, a story is a whole that interconnects characters, plot, and setting, but every story is also part of a wider field of literature. And that, in turn, is part of a larger culture. This chapter focuses on what we call *global experiences*. They are the first foundational skill for this section. Global experiences were introduced in Chapter 7 as orchestrated events that engage students in multiple ways and lead to actor-centered questions.

One of the crucial differences between the three instructional approaches is the way in which they deal with parts and wholes. Let's look at the three instructional approaches through the teaching of the Bill of

Rights. This topic can be taught with different degrees of sophistication at different grade levels, but the basic differences between the instructional approaches remain.

Instructional Approach 1 Teaching

The teacher uses passages from the Bill of Rights supplemented by a text and lectures. There will be some historical background, some discussion about concepts such as "free speech," and students will do almost all their work alone at their individual desks. There will possibly be a paper to write and standardized tests in which students are asked to identify right or wrong answers to questions concerning the Bill of Rights.

Note that the Bill of Rights is treated as a separate topic, unrelated, say, to how the classroom works or what is happening in the community. There is no link to literature or the arts that relates to events of the time, other than textbook references. The odds are that there will be no reference to other topics previously dealt with in this class on social studies. In short, the topic is treated as a stand-alone topic in a stand-alone subject area.

There is almost no chance for students to gain a "felt meaning" for the various rights and liberties spelled out in the document.

Opportunities for Instructional Approach 1 Teaching

Give your course a broader context by connecting any topic that is being taught to some other topic that came before, and to some other topic that will follow. In addition, introduce some human element through the arts, including stories, paintings, and copies of authentic documents, to help students gain a sense of the larger context that helps to make a topic more useful and important to students.

Instructional Approach 2 Teaching

In this approach, much more is done to enliven the topic and to connect it to other areas of life. This is done by way of preliminary global experiences.

Teachers read stories or have students read stories that are relevant. Parts of documentaries or movies may be shown. Students will have opportunities to work together and possibly even draft their own suggested amendments to the Bill of Rights. The history of the Constitution will be referred to and current-day events may be discussed.

The teacher will work very hard to connect the individual topic (a part) to other topics (a larger whole) and to the lives of the students (also a larger whole).

Individual students (parts of the class) will work together in groups (a larger whole). The totality of experiences will provide a much richer understanding for students, irrespective of what type of assessment is used.

Opportunities for Instructional Approach 2 Teaching

Give students opportunities to select what aspect of the topic to research based upon real student interests. Where enactments are possible, provide opportunities for student-selected and -led enactments. Allow students to bring in relevant information and possibly guests selected by students. Let the topic flow beyond the specific confines of a narrowly defined curriculum. Here, the "whole" that is being expanded serves to engage the students' interests and involvement.

Instructional Approach 3 Teaching

Instructional Approach 3 uses more sophisticated global experiences and in-the-moment real events to set the stage for the topic. Many stories in the daily news, ranging from disputes about the death penalty to who owns the media, can serve as a foundation from which to launch a discussion. That means that the topic will not be dealt with in a prescribed sequence, but will expand out from the global experience in the directions taken by the students' actor-centered questions. The standards will be incorporated naturally, primarily because the key concepts and ideas in the Bill of Rights can be applied to almost any specific issue or question.

Note here that working with the whole is dynamic rather than static. The whole doesn't just mean that more material is covered. It means that the coverage occurs in a way that involves students personally and emotionally, and the overall fabric of the topic is woven in as research selected by individual students comes together. Note, also, that the executive functions are more readily engaged in a demanding and mature way when a topic is taught and learned in this dynamic way.

Opportunities for Instructional Approach 3 Teaching

Expand the students' voice in creating global experiences that launch topics. Help the students hone their questioning skills so they can "unpack" a topic and examine each other's reasoning. Both of these make the whole topic and experience more alive so that different interests and questions make sense. In addition, when students see and make connections to other topics or subject areas, allow some time for those new and unplanned connections to be discussed. This practice becomes a natural way of integrating the curriculum (one of the hallmarks of teaching the parts through the whole).

THE FIRST FOUNDATIONAL SKILL FOR ORCHESTRATED IMMERSION: DESIGNING TEACHER-ORCHESTRATED, GLOBAL EXPERIENCES

Global experiences are defined as physiologically rich beginning events that evoke an impression of the "whole" subject to be explored and engage the students in several simultaneous ways. They help students get a feel, or felt meaning, for the subject or topic (Caine & Caine, in press, define felt meaning as "an unarticulated sense of relationship that culminates in the 'aha!' of insight"). Global experiences are also intended to stir interest and curiosity and to elicit actor-centered student questions.

> A global experience is a novel situation that links initial learning to the student and to life.

A global experience may include the following:

- Enticing stories
- Innovative presentations
- Simulations
- Moral or ethical dilemmas
- Projects
- Video clips
- Artifacts whose very existence invites questions
- Art
- Music
- Poetry
- An exercise in personal insight
- An ordered sharing

Example

Standard—The student will recognize the Civil War as a major test of America's founding principles.
    Minnesota Curriculum Standards (working draft, Sept. 2003)
    Grade 7—U.S. History—Era 4: Civil War and Reconstruction, 1850s–1870s

---

The teaching team began with the words "torn asunder" boldly displayed on the whiteboard as the classes came into the room. After the students were settled, the teachers began by sharing some poetry dealing with separation. The students then thought of an experience where they had had a sense of being "torn asunder." This was introduced with the caution to stay with an experience that was not too emotionally deep. They created a sensory poem of their experience, followed by an art form to display the poetry. With soft music playing in the background, the teachers moved about the room in support of the students while teachers also wrote (modeled) and took part in the art experience.

When the students were finished, the teachers each shared diary entries from soldiers of the period. The entries made the experiences of the soldiers more real. A short clip from the movie *Gettysburg* was then viewed with the sound turned off. A recording of Charlotte Church singing "Pie Jesu" (Church, 1998) played softly in the background. The teachers placed overheads on a projector that gave statistics about the battle and briefly told what happened to the soldiers who wrote the diaries. When the presentation was over, there was silence. After a short while, the teachers asked the students, "What questions do you have?" The responses were overwhelming! The students were moved, curious, indignant, enthralled. Their questions (see page 144) formed the basis for the learning and teaching that followed. Students divided into research groups to pursue their questions. Information was gathered and continually processed by the teacher in order to make certain that the standards were met. The class project was to create a timeline for the entire Civil War period that included essential events and data. Individual research groups created articles, visual summaries, and presentations on information they uncovered.

1. Note that the essential foundation was having a good sense of community in the class. The atmosphere, the teachers' relationships with students, and the teachers' knowledge of standards and subject matter were all critical to the success of the process.

2. Remember that the global experience is meant to engage the learners in exploring their own genuine questions. It is important not to lecture or inundate students with facts or information during this time. It is the students' questions that will ultimately lead to meeting the standards.

General Hints

Here are some hints for developing global experiences:

1. *Select material and develop ideas.* You might like to use the design wheel in Resource F as an aid in developing your global experiences.

2. *Set a very loose time limit of about 15–25 minutes for initial, in-class experiences.* You are not trying to cover every aspect of a topic. The goal is to have a sufficiently "global" and integrated experience to give students a feel for the topic and to inspire questions. As you develop expertise or go beyond the classroom, you may need more time.

3. *Engage the arts in some way.* We suggest that you usually combine at least three modalities, such as words, pictures, and music; or language, illustration, and activity. The objective is to fully engage students, and words alone are rarely enough unless you are a superb storyteller. Even then, setting out to engage several senses at the same time is really important.

4. *Include emotional tone.* Dissonance, tension, and disagreement are aspects of life. So are joy, intrigue, fascination, and charm, but these reactions should emanate from the global experience without disrupting the relationships in the classroom. Do not leap into global experiences that engage strong emotions without practice and, ideally, some training. If your

global experience causes students to move into survival response (go into alarm, fear, or terror), you may find yourself unprepared for their reactions, and your effort will be wasted, at best.

5. *Select items that convey the essence of your theme.* Wholeness does not require completeness. You will be able to introduce only a small amount of material, so it should illustrate the overall theme, present several of the critical issues, and generate a sense of enthusiasm.

6. *Develop a sense of timing and drama.* Teachers are actors too! There are ways to introduce material that increase the effect. We suggest that teachers work with each other, calling on those who are skilled in relevant areas for help.

7. *Allow ideas to flow.* The easiest way to design a global experience is to brainstorm with others and play with ideas and possibilities. More will come than you need, but that wealth enables you to select the material that will really work.

8. *Keep it simple.* There can be enormous temptation to be overly dramatic or complex. It is not necessary. It can be a lot of fun to create and design these experiences, but the purpose is to engage students—not overwhelm them. So begin gently and keep it simple.

THE TRANSFORMATIONAL ADMINISTRATOR AND THE PROCESS FOR MAKING IT REAL

What fun it would be if you became an integral part of the global experience itself. Imagine the looks on the students' faces if you were the one who came into the room dressed in Civil War attire! As you wandered through the building as the character you have researched, your message to the rest of the school would be that you were fully endorsing the learning. Perhaps your character is that of a general who has many leadership responsibilities to the regiment. This level of participation communicates authentic beliefs that this type of education is valued and encouraged in your school. This is not everyone's cup of tea, but if you are even remotely motivated to partic-ipate in this manner, we want to encourage you to do so. Are you making yourself available to your teachers in these supportive ways?

Again, we encourage you to enhance collaboration between and among teachers. Although subjects and disciplines are separate in some ways, they also interpenetrate each other. *As teachers work together and, perhaps, visit each other's classrooms or develop global experiences in tandem, the students naturally begin to become aware of connections in the curriculum and, sometimes, of under-lying big ideas that are embedded in every subject.* We suggest encouraging the intellectual development of the staff so that an exciting climate starts to pervade the school as a whole. This is powerful, indirect support for high academic standards for the students—at *all* grade levels.

In tandem with the National Teaching Standards

Accomplished teachers understand that substantive learning rarely occurs when students are presented large amounts of seemingly unrelated information or when students memorize facts divorced from major themes, concepts, or principles.

—Standard V: Meaningful Learning

The connections these teachers make between schoolwork and the larger community help students understand and apply principles of justice, freedom, liberty, and responsibility.

—Standard VIII: Social Development

This standard speaks directly to the need to integrate parts and wholes because it calls for information to be related to other information and connected in multiple ways. It also calls for those relationships to be dynamic so that students can "explore" and "confront" important material.

Engage their individual style and uniqueness

Engage the physiology in learning

Engage social interactions

Reduce threat and enhance self-efficacy

Engage their innate search for meaning

Acknowledge and engage developmental steps and shifts

Engage their capacity to recognize and master essential patterns

Engage their capacity to learn from memorizing isolated facts and biographical events

Engage emotional connections

Engage both conscious and unconscious processing

Engage both their ability to focus attention and learn from the peripheral context

Engage their ability to perceive both details and the larger view

If we want to create enriched environments that help students learn, then we need to include all of the following:

Engaging the Physiology in Learning

Brain/Mind Learning Principle 1: *All learning engages the physiology.*

 At the Core

Every learner is a physical universe. Physical movement and engagement of the body and senses are essential for learning. Less well understood is that the physiology is engaged in decision making and in the exercise of executive functions. One reason so much traditional teaching involves students sitting in their assigned seats is the belief that the brain is somehow separate from the body and that the body is not very involved in learning. The research on plasticity as well as brain research in general tell us that the body and mind are totally interconnected. When a person is appropriately engaged in a complex experience, including decisions about what to respond to and how to adapt, multiple body/brain/mind systems are integrated, focused and working together naturally. Educators must begin to understand what this principle is saying and how to translate this information into practice.

Capacity: All students learn more effectively when involved in experiences that naturally call on the use of their senses.

A sound mind in a sound body; if the former be the glory of the latter, the latter is indispensable to the former.

—Tryon Edwards

HOW DO WE KNOW THIS?

From feeling the warm sand under one's toes to feeling one's hair being shifted by the wind, the human being is a physical organism. Every one of us experiences the world through our senses, and it is through our senses that we learn.

Though we often think only in terms of seeing, hearing, touching, tasting, and smelling as the senses that determine how we experience the world, they actually constitute only the very basics.

Awareness

For those who can tell the temperature by how their skin feels, or who wake up in the middle of the night and automatically know what time it is, or who wake up every morning at the same time without an alarm clock, something more is happening. It is as if they have additional senses. Awareness is literally an expanded sense that can be developed purposely through meditation or biofeedback, for example, or through specific techniques.

Entrainment

Another kind of sense is mostly unconscious. It explains why women who work together for 40 hours or more a week tend to synchronize their menstrual cycles. Pheromones are indicated as the culprit. Pheromones are molecules that come off the surface of the skin and are absorbed through the nose. Pheromones can pass on traces of sexual arousal and also of stress to those in the immediate vicinity. If you've ever wondered why your entire class appears to become agitated when your least favorite "stressor" walks in the door, your answer may lie here.

The neuroscientist Antonio Damasio (1994) spells out interconnectedness quite explicitly:
"1. The human brain and the rest of the body constitute an indissociable organism. . . . 2. The organism interacts with the environment as an ensemble: the interaction is neither of the body alone nor of the brain alone" (pp. xvi–xvii).

All learning begins with our senses, but human beings do not learn through just one sense at a time. Brain/mind learning and teaching require more complex understanding. In fact, body, brain, and mind are deeply interconnected. This is very important for educators to grasp. It means that for a person to fully understand something, to get the felt meaning that we introduce in Chapter 5, many aspects of the human being need to be involved. The senses will be engaged. Emotions will be involved. The social context will have an impact. The physical environment will literally be absorbed. The intellect will be working. In other words, learning, particularly for meaning, engages the entire physiology and mind together.

Using Experience in Teaching

Not all experience is useful experience, and not all experience engages the body, brain, and mind in ways that support dynamic learning. A noisy, disruptive classroom provides students with "experience," but probably not the one the teacher had in mind.

Thus, Instructional Approaches 2 and 3 are both an art and a skill. It is a matter of designing, orchestrating, and facilitating experiences in such a way that an almost infinite number of a student's capacities and skills are called upon as high standards are addressed.

Another implication is also important: Educators are not providing a child with just information and skills—educators and the contexts they provide are potentially participating in the wiring and restructuring of a child's body/brain. That is why it is imperative to ensure that all learning engages the physiology, and why educators need to work with the physiology in multiple ways to teach for high standards.

PROCESSING THIS PRINCIPLE

Personal Connections

Take a moment to reflect on any subject area or skill that you have mastered fairly well, to the point where you can use it effectively in the real world. It may be investments and your stock portfolio. It may be an instrument that you play. It may be the way you successfully counsel and advise people on how to deal with crises and grief. It may be your success in bringing up your kids, or your ease of use of the World Wide Web, or your ability to travel to new places without major problems.

Now reflect on the number of physical experiences that contributed to your successful learning and discuss these with a process partner or in your learning circle. You might also look for the things that are so obvious they are easily taken for granted. For example, to master your skill, did you:

Read about information or events in journals or newspapers?

Have discussions with friends over coffee or a meal?

Observe experts and possibly work with and learn from them?

Try things out in different ways?

Put yourself in situations where the whole context related to this subject or skill?

Join relevant clubs or groups?

Go through emotional highs and lows, ranging (perhaps) from frustration and anxiety through enjoyment to fulfillment?

Can you see how these experiences contributed to your expertise? Shouldn't students have such experiences when learning math, science, or literature? How could this be done?

Going Deeper

Let us look in a little more detail at one aspect of physical experience that effects learning: the physical environment.

Have you ever visited your old elementary school and encountered that familiar "school smell"? Did that smell bring back an impression or even conscious memories? This is one example of how your brain was registering and partially recording the entire environment through your senses even though you were unaware of this (more on this unconscious kind of learning in Part III). During that brief moment did you experience anxiety, joy, sadness, or nostalgia? Your body was literally "picking up" these feelings when you were a student in school even though you may not have been aware of the fact.

> The entire structure, organization, and social and emotional climate all constitute the "flavor" of the physical environment that influences what is ultimately learned and that helps to shape the ways in which decisions are made. These constitute memories we take into new learning environments and experiences.

Working With Physical Space

One way to address how students learn from their context is to honor special places and their functions as a way of creating order that flows and is quietly respectful. Once spaces and/or appropriate use of time have been identified, create physical symbols and materials that honor the purpose of the space. For example, you may want to include the following:

- Plants that fit (not too many and not in the way of traffic)
- Seating that can shift with every function but can always be returned to an orderly structure
- Room to spread out (can be done even in small spaces by leaving a "free zone")
- Places for gathering and places to be alone
- Soft classical or other music that does not carry a popular melody or create a particular mood (save that type of mood music for specific purposes)
- Artwork (varies with student age from more fantasy in early years to thought-provoking art and realistic diagrams and photos later)

This is how an elementary school teacher describes what she does:

From a Teacher's Journal

Once my students and I are clear on what we want to accomplish, they are free to decide on how best to approach the task. They can work in groups or alone, move about the room, use carpet samples to sit on, sit in the sofa area, sit outside, rearrange desks, or sit at our extra tables. We have established these routines as a classroom community after discussions about how we learn best and how we can learn to use our own style without infringing on the learning of others. We also have approval from our principal, who supports our removing our shoes while we are working. This is for those of us who are comfortable doing so. These little details help our need to move around even as we focus on the work at hand. I was delighted to find that the more I did these things, the less time I spent keeping students on task.

Remember that brain/mind learning is natural, so this is only a recommendation. You may want to begin with the list offered here, but it is also important that you learn to play and to change things as needed.

Working With Organizational Space

There is a great difference in how elementary schools and secondary schools are organized.

Elementary Schools

The intact classroom is an ideal environment for the early grades. We suggest that educators experiment with rotating teachers who have special skills or subject-area expertise so that all children can benefit from being exposed to the highest academic knowledge within a school. Partnering and occasionally "swapping" an expert math teacher with an expert reading teacher can benefit students and teachers alike. This can also allow students and the classroom teacher to have access to a different gender adult or specialist whenever a project requires it.

Secondary Schools

It should already be clear that traditional schools based on 15-minute homerooms and 50-minute classes are not compatible with what we are recommending in this book. As Part I, "Relaxed Alertness," points out, students need to be in an environment where they are known and where ordered sharing and dealing with emotional issues is possible. Today's massive high schools present an immense challenge. This is truly like trying to fit a round peg in a square hole.

Research on smaller schools and classes provides the best evidence for breaking these huge factory-like structures into smaller communities (Finn, Gerber, Achilles, & Boyd-Zaharias, 2001; Nye, Hedges, & Konstantopoulos, 2003). We suggest that one of the first orders of business for any large middle or high school is to participate in a restructuring plan that makes secondary schools more like a college campus. These more readily provide environments that foster a positive effect (Chapter 6). Or students can be organized into smaller "schools" or "houses" where they are known and where they get to participate more or less directly in decision-making processes that also make them accountable. Once again, we suggest that teachers, as well as students, be rotated in order to make expertise more available as students do research and engage in learning that crosses disciplines. Although students in high school can be housed in "schools" that specialize in a specific discipline, we suggest all students have opportunities for learning that engages or integrates a wide array of subjects.

At the very least, flexible scheduling, such as larger time blocks, teaching subjects every other day, and taking certain days for larger projects, should be investigated. Schools should research, and if possible personally investigate, places that have implemented such changes. Findings should be presented to the entire faculty and spend time on deciding why the changes are warranted and how best to implement them. Including the larger community (i.e., parents and business) is critical.

Bridging to the Practical

In traditional teaching, much of the interconnectedness of the brain, mind, and body is essentially ignored. The only way to adequately engage multiple capacities of the brain so that they support and reinforce each other as they are designed to do is by involving students in complex experience. Complex experiences call attention, perception, dynamic memory, motivation, emotion, relationships, and the entire body into play as the learner engages in moment-by-moment applications and decisions. Here are some ways to shift teaching in order to engage the physiology in learning:

Instructional Approach 1 and 2 Teaching

Provide hands-on experiences that have students touch, measure, assess, assemble, or take apart something to be learned.

This is why many teachers use manipulatives to teach basic math and why field trips are so valuable. Many aspects of the curriculum can be modeled. Whales can be drawn on the floor, castles can be made out of cardboard, models of molecules can be made with toy building materials. Here are other strategies to try:

- Connect words or vocabulary to physical action, like catching a ball in different ways.
- Use other movements that facilitate memory such as rhythm, song, or music.

- Use movement to generate energy or help with pacing of energy during intense periods or projects (take time out for breaks).
- Have students represent information in different ways from drawing to rephrasing to making sculptures or presentations that make the information more real and meaningful for them.

Instructional Approach 2 and 3 Teaching

1. *Encourage the use of kinesthetic metaphors in which students dance, walk, or move in such a way that they physically express and experience aspects of a concept, idea, or basic pattern.* Here, the art is to help students "become" or take the place of something about which they are learning. For example, we once saw a science teacher who was talking about the structure of DNA and the smaller molecules that made up the larger molecule. He had each of his students become one of the four molecular bases (adenine, guanine, etc.). He then choreographed a dance so that the students linked and joined hands so as to form a double helix with its bonds on the floor of the classroom.

From a Teacher's Journal

There we were, immersed in place value and it was obvious that quite a few of the students were not understanding the concept. So, each person took a 3 × 5 card that had written on it what part of a sum of a billion they wanted to represent. Everyone began to line up. Many became a number. Some became indicators (dots and commas) and joined the group in order to clarify specific amounts (commas squatted on the floor).

We had a person step out of the line and the remainder of the students called off resulting changes in value. Students called out numbers as those in the line switched places or the line added new people who had cards that added additional zeroes. Everyone was having great fun becoming a place value and soon we had the concept internalized.

2. *Even imagination calls on past sensory experiences.* One of the most powerful of all tools is the student's imagination. The art is to help them imagine what they are learning about. This can be done with stories that describe actual situations. Even complex ideas in mathematics and science can be brought alive by reading about the life and times of those who made fundamental discoveries. Imagination can be strengthened by inviting students to act out aspects of what they are discussing. As the teaching becomes more transformational, more student choice and control are invited. For instance, students can begin to select what is to be investigated in this way. They can take charge of creating the situation that is going to aid the imagination.

From a Teacher's Journal

We were discussing the slave ships that brought slaves from Africa after we had concluded reading "The Drinking Gourd." The students could not conceive of how cramped the ships were so we measured the approximate space, moved the desks to become the ship's hold, and then lay on the floor next to each other to understand how little space there was.

We talked about the lack of sanitation, fresh air, food, being able to move, privacy, shackles, and sleeping. To a fourth grader, the shock of the conditions raised questions followed by discussions that launched us on the path to discovering more about slavery and the results of that practice.

It helped students understand people like Harriet Tubman and her profound desire for freedom. Students were excited to learn and needed little encouragement to discover everything they could about the time period because the body/mind connection was so compelling.

Initial Learning

When students are being introduced to totally new concepts or procedures (we will call this *initial learning*), they should be given opportunities to use their senses, emotions, movement, and repetition as much as possible. That is one of the purposes of the global experience.

Advanced Learning

Advanced learning builds on what is already known. Once the foundation for learning has been established in the physiology, the nature of "physiological" becomes more subtle. All of us have learned through a lecture or by simply listening to a piece of music that we later recognized. Obviously our senses were engaged in the listening experience, but not to the same degree as in hands-on practice. Instead of laying a foundation (initial learning), we were adding new knowledge, using what had been previously learned or mastered. When we learn something that adds to what we have already mastered, we engage or expand on "maps" already present in the brain. Advanced learning requires a more comprehensive focus on questions such as why, how, when, where, what, and who, which make deeper connections for the learner.

Of course, what is "initial" and what is "advanced" depends on the context and what students already know. It is equally clear that there will often be an overlap. The point is that efforts should be made to structure new concepts physiologically, even in the later years of school.

TAKING IT INTO THE CLASSROOM

Here is an example of how the different instructional approaches might work with the physiological basis of learning when some specific standards are being addressed.

An eleventh grade life science benchmark dealing with the classification of biological organisms based on how organisms are related.

—*South Carolina Life Science II.3.b*

Instructional Approach 1

This teacher would use the textbook, worksheets, videos, and lecture. Students would engage in little or no movement or interaction, and would receive very little sensory stimulation.

Opportunities for Instructional Approach 1 Teaching

One of the best actions to take is to make presentations of information more dynamic, artistic, and lively. Some suggestions:

1. *Use more technology.* PowerPoint slide shows, particularly ones that include dramatic photographs and even video clips, engage audiences of all types. Also, use videos and the Internet. The key is to avoid letting the media take over. Don't just play a video, for instance—select key segments and use them to illustrate the material that you want to cover.

2. *Work with a colleague from a different subject area.* We have seen powerful presentations where a history teacher invited an art teacher to come in and simply show paintings and works of art from the period the history teacher was covering.

3. *Learn to tell stories.* Students of every age love stories. You might read a book or take a course or work with a friend to develop your skill. Begin simply. Work with material that you really enjoy. Remember the point of the story and the punch line. Adapt the stories to your standards.

4. *Brainstorm with colleagues.* Many of your friends and colleagues will have found masterful ways to present information that they have not shared, possibly because they thought no one else would be interested. The ideas and techniques are there for the asking by those who work together.

Instructional Approach 2

This teacher would begin by seeking a complex experience in which students can get physically involved, possibly by locating a nearby aquatic system (river, pond, lake, or ocean) where organisms can be collected for review and study. Students would then be asked to sort and organize the collections into groupings as determined by the students in the class, using the textbook and other resources. Student-generated graphs, reports, presentations, or posters might follow as an assessment tool.

There is physical movement and full involvement of body and senses as students examine the organisms in their natural habitat. This teacher still determines the direction of the learning but does release some control to the learners by allowing them to decide the categories and how they present their discoveries.

Opportunities for Instructional Approach 2 Teaching

> One of the most important steps to take is to increase the amount of interactivity and decision making in the classroom. Even though an Instructional Approach 2 teacher is still in charge of what is happening, students love being authentically involved.

1. *Improve the art of asking questions.* Encourage questions that focus on technical/scholastic knowledge that addresses the who, what, where, how, why, and so forth. Several ways of asking questions are dealt with later in this book. The art is to learn which questions make the essential connections and then how to keep the conversation flowing and alive. This actually requires mastery of listening as well as of questioning.

2. *Learn how to invite student questions authentically.* This can be a challenge because students have to feel free to ask their own questions. As you move around the classroom and work with small groups, listening to student discussions, you will be provided with clues that help you ask questions that will strengthen their technical/scholastic knowledge.

3. *Generate opportunities for students to be creative and to contribute.* There are often stories in the press that are wonderful sources of information for a course or class. Rather than a teacher being in charge of all of this, give students opportunities to bring in material and even run discussions on the topics in question.

Instructional Approach 3

The students suggest that a river trip needs to be planned following a visit by a local aquatic biologist. The interaction with the expert prompts the realization that a local watershed has been a point of study by the Department of Natural Resources. Through mutual agreement, the students create teams of "biological scientists" who understand their task of examining one of the following: structural adaptations, physiology, nutritional strategies, biochemical similarities, genetic similarities, embryological similarities, and methods of reproduction (technical/scholastic knowledge). Their findings could be reported in the format of their choosing to the rest of their "scientific team" and the local experts at the Department of Natural Resources. Timelines, checkpoints, evaluative rubrics, and procedures would be negotiated between the scientific teams and the teacher. The Instructional Approach 3 teacher might even join one of the teams as a member.

Again, there is large-scale physical movement and use of the senses in conducting the investigation over quite long periods of time. Note that more complex elements can also be added. Individual students can choose which organisms to examine and which roles to play in the entire process.

Even though the teacher sometimes provides the initial experience, because the students work to develop their own research, multiple experiences occur. Essentially, a domino effect of exciting learning takes place.

> All the while, the effective teacher continuously weaves standards and benchmarks into the newly arising learning opportunities. This approach engages the individual's use of the executive functions because many more real-world (actor-centered) decisions have to be made.

Opportunities for Instructional Approach 3 Teaching

1. *Work on timing and self-assessment.* Practice observing how much students can handle, and experiment with the rhythm of your questions and the clarity with which you make suggestions.

2. *Work on balancing simplicity with complexity.* Instructional Approach 3 teachers can be overwhelming and incorporate too much in a disjointed way. Practice using times of silence and developing a sense of aesthetics and balance in the design of the classroom environment.

THE SECOND FOUNDATIONAL SKILL FOR ORCHESTRATED IMMERSION: GUIDING ACTOR-CENTERED LEARNING

From a Teacher's Journal

An inner-city school we work with was in the early days of exploring waterways and water quality when the teaching team decided that a great global experience for the students would be to take them on an adventure that involved the *Appledore,* an educational sailing vessel on Saginaw Bay, Michigan. As a part of the total learning package, the school staff connected with local environmental engineers from General Motors who became not only local experts, but ultimately became closely attached to the learning family at the school.

While sailing under a drawbridge, a sight that the vast majority of the students had never seen before, a very quiet young man approached one of the GM engineers on the deck. The young learner asked the engineer if he could share something he was thinking about. "Certainly, what's on your mind?" The young fifth-grade student said, "I wonder how they pour concrete under water. Can you help me with this?" The engineer was amazed at the level of the question. He had no idea that the fifth grader processed at those "depths." The engineer sat with the student as they passed by the bridge, explaining what was below and what the civil engineers had to do in order to accomplish the task of establishing the concrete pillars underwater. Another moment. Another opportunity.

Here, this young mind was taking small bits of information he had and began to look for the larger picture. The event was a global experience. With a good relationship as a foundation, the student felt relaxed and alert. And so his interest, wonder, and curiosity flourished and led to asking an actor-centered question.

Remember that a central goal, in addition to helping students acquire some feel for the topic, is to elicit students' own questions. This goes to the core of Instructional Approach 3. The challenge for the teacher is to interest students and to perceive individual and collective student interests, and then to "ride the wave" of that interest as a basis for helping students learn what needs to be learned.

Let's return to the global experience introduced in the preceding chapter and look at actor-centered questions that emerged. It had to do with the Civil War. Following the global experience, the teachers simply asked the students, "What questions do you have?" and the responses were overwhelming. "Why did they fight?" "Why did the soldiers walk into enemy gun fire?" "Were women *really* fighting and why did no one know?" and so on. These propelled students into research.

Setting Research and Learning in Motion

The objective is for students to investigate the questions that interest them *and* in so doing to cover essential standards. That requires a teacher to master five elements: *asking questions, knowing the standards, developing student teams, guiding use of resources,* and *helping students with time management.*

Ask Questions to Elicit Questions

The big challenge for teachers is to refrain from telling students what they need to study. Rather, follow the global experience with a general question such as, "What interested you?" As the students ask, you (or a student) can make a record of the questions on a chart or a board. The next step is to find out how many people are interested in each of the questions. Some students may be interested in everything, so you would want to find out where their greatest interest lies. This can be done by tabulating numbers using the chart or board on which the questions are recorded. Remember to honor *their* questions; that will keep them fully engaged and enthusiastic and keep their interest flowing.

Connect Student Questions to the Standards

Instructional Approach 3 requires a teacher to have a very good grasp of the standards and to be fully proficient in the subject that is being taught. Because student questions will come from many unexpected directions, a teacher will need to be both very spontaneous and constantly on the lookout for places in which to introduce the standards.

Each of the questions asked after the Civil War global experience can be connected to standards very easily, ranging from reasons and causes of the Civil War to social issues revealed in the roles of men and women.

> The more familiar a teacher is with the material, the easier it is simply to wait for and recognize the appropriate opportunity to introduce or emphasize something relevant.

Place Students in Teams

Sometimes students will choose to work on their own question alone, but often they will work in teams. The central task will be to group students who have similar interests or whose questions overlap. One way to do this is simply to ask, "Who else is interested in such-and-such a topic?" and then to ask the students to work with each other to clarify their research question. Sometimes the teacher will need to find ways to make topics and questions link, and that will depend on the teacher's knowledge of the material. For example, two of the questions above—"Why did soldiers walk into enemy gunfire?" and "Were women really fighting and why did no one know?"—both relate to the culture of the time and to values and beliefs.

Reminder: The mere fact of having overlapping interests does not mean that students will actually listen to each other. In our experience, the use of ordered sharings, process meetings, and procedures for the resolution of conflicts, all introduced in the last section, provide an essential foundation for good student teamwork.

Guide Students Toward Resources

The amount of guidance needed depends on how much students already know about resources and their use. If the students have not done much research before, we suggest that their first use of a global experience be quite simple and that your primary purpose is to introduce students to the art of research. This might entail asking them to formulate one simple question and then directing them to one or two simple resources such as an encyclopedia or a Web site. You can then start expanding the depth of the question and the range of resources available. With this in mind, after conducting a global experience, help students recognize and identify multiple ways to access information using search engines, texts, documents, and experts in the field. Help them distinguish between expert sources and opinions.

Possible questions:

- What do you need in the way of information?
- Could an online search help?
- Is there an expert you could contact?
- How could this be documented?
- What evidence do you have? Is it enough to satisfy an expert?

Time Management

One vital skill that requires use of the executive functions relates to planning. A way to help students is to introduce self-management and priority-setting questions into the actual work they do. The objective is to help students set goals, plan, and then implement their plans. This involves intermediate goals, timelines, and assessment of outcomes and consequences. The key lies in the appropriate use of questions.

Possible questions:

- What deadline have you set for yourself?
- When do you think you will be finished? (Elementary)
- How did you prioritize?
- How much time do you think you'll need? (Elementary)
- What did you decide to do first? (Elementary)
- How did you divide the essential steps?
- Do you still think that was a good idea? (Elementary)
- What sequence have you decided to follow?
- What order did you decide to follow? (Elementary)
- What do you predict will happen if you do that?
- Where do you want to be on the project one week from today?
- How will your present actions and decisions help or hinder you?

From a Teacher's Journal

We were opening a small new middle school with only 600 students in Grades 7 and 8. I had introduced process meetings from the beginning in our English class. Many of these students said that they felt they were alone since the school's population had been pulled from various locations and tracks and thus most of the student body was unfamiliar with each other and many students had to leave long-standing friendships behind. Because of their ages, these adolescents were feeling really isolated. So I asked them, "How can you get to know each other?" There was a wonderful abundance of suggestions such as conducting interviews, writing a newspaper, designing questionnaires, polls, making graphs and posters, holding activities that the student council could sponsor, and introducing people over the intercom at morning announcements. Because of time and considerations of expertise, I suggested that we break into groups and come up with two or three things we could actually complete as a class. After the groups had decided, we reconvened as a whole and looked at the suggestions, determined what we could agree on, and then formed committees to do the tasks. The students who were collecting data for a survey decided they needed more information on how to create graphs and sought out assistance from the math department. Another group that was designing welcome posters asked for more supplies from the art teacher than we had available in our room and so he joined us during his break to see how he could help. The office joined in with data and with introducing themselves, as one group of students took on that area as an important part of the physical community and layout. They even designed a map of important places to know when first coming to school. The students were discovering ways to improve their relationships. When the projects were completed, we processed how the event had worked as well as how we felt about our relationships. I asked such questions as, "What did you like about how your group worked?" "What would you want to improve?" "Have you a better sense of community and belonging? Why?" "What might be our next step to improve relations?" This opportunity led to a stronger school and class community and all because I asked a question instead of providing answers.

THE TRANSFORMATIONAL ADMINISTRATOR AND THE PROCESS FOR MAKING IT REAL

With your teaching staff, look for ways the physiology is being engaged throughout your school.

Help and encourage your staff to zero in on specific activities that get students up, out of their seats, and moving about the classroom and outside as they are engaging the curriculum. Your intent is to allow for maximum sensory input involving sound, taste, smell, sight, and touch.

Think about how the physiology of the staff is engaged in their work outside the classroom. Sometimes, of course, there may be too many demands on them. How can their health and comfort and enjoyment be increased? Sometimes it is a matter of creating more rhythm and an even pace in the day-to-day environment so that staff rush less and have more peace of mind. Surprisingly, sometimes very small changes (such as gaining control over the air conditioning) can lead to major benefits.

More generally, it may be appropriate to start an ongoing conversation among staff members about how to work collectively to introduce more lived experience into the learning and teaching process. For instance, new partnerships between people who teach subjects that are not ordinarily connected can be very fruitful for all concerned.

This conversation is also facilitated by good learning circles.

In tandem with the National Teaching Standards

Accomplished teachers require students to confront, explore, and understand important and challenging concepts, topics, and issues and to improve skills in purposeful ways.

Teachers develop meaningful learning experiences in a variety of ways, such as designing activities that allow students to work as writers, scientists, historians, and artists, and they model some of the working habits of these professions. Teachers pose realistic and compelling dilemmas with which students can struggle, while helping students frame, pose, and explore their own questions.

—Standard V

The issues and steps covered in this chapter are in line with and support the national standards. The procedures we have introduced provide ways to engage students and to link curriculum to their interests and lives while still maintaining high standards.

10

Engage the Learner's Capacity to Recognize and Master Essential Patterns

Brain/Mind Learning Principle 4: *The search for meaning occurs through patterning.*

 At the Core

All human beings are driven by a need to identify, name, and organize the configuration of elements—or patterns—that make up their known world. *Patterning* refers to the meaningful organization and categorization of information. All decision making is based on the patterns that a person perceives and the choices that are made about where to focus. The brain is designed to perceive and generate patterns and resists having meaningless patterns imposed on it. Education is about increasing the patterns students can use, recognize, and communicate. As the ability to see and work with patterns expands, the executive functions are enhanced.

Capacity: All students increase learning when new patterns are linked to what they already understand.

HOW DO WE KNOW THIS?

In a way, the brain is both artist and scientist, attempting to discern and understand patterns as they occur, giving expression to unique and creative patterns of its own. Piaget (1976) was spelling out the same general principle when he distinguished between *assimilation*, by which he meant the way in which whatever is perceived is made to "fit" into a person's worldview, and *accommodation*, by which he meant that a person's worldview or internal world needs to adapt to what is perceived.

Everyone is biologically equipped at birth with many basic capacities for perception. These include the ability to detect lines and edges and curves and movement, light and dark, up and down, basic smells and tastes, loud and soft, and a basic sense of numbers. Infants are intrinsically attuned to voices, faces, and people. With experience, the basic elements that are perceived naturally (they are sometimes called natural categories) combine and gel into more complex categories (such as forests, computers, houses, and cars) and ways of behaving.

> In many ways, the approach of infants and young children mirrors the way that scientists work. Because of the similarity between how scientists and infants search for patterns, researchers Gopnik, Meltzoff, and Kuhl (1999) call infants "scientists in the crib." So there is some profound decision making going on naturally at a very early age.

Whenever individuals try to figure out what something means, they search for patterns that make sense to them. Making sense of something is not the same thing as memorizing rules in math or the dates of various wars.

One essential key for helping students in their search for meaningful connections is to point out that every subject in the curriculum is basically a tool (using its own language or perspective) for organizing and describing some patterns in the real world.

From the Concrete to the Abstract

One of the most powerful and important growing edges in pattern perception is the shift from the concrete to the abstract. Piaget formulated this more or less universal path of growth as the shift from the world of the concrete (sensorimotor, preoperational, and concrete operational) to the world of the abstract (formal operations). In fact, one of the keys to developing the executive functions is linked to the ability to use abstract thinking.

Human beings have the capacity to organize information in terms of physical "things" and in terms of relationships (how things connect), which they do through the use of concepts and ideas. They can also represent things symbolically, letting a symbol stand for an idea or object.

Once learners begin to think at the level of concepts and symbols, they begin to understand that the curriculum is actually interconnected to represent human experience. For example, some curriculum focuses on the story of humans through time (the essence of history), some focuses on where people have been and where they are located in space (the essence of geography), and some on how human beings communicate (language and the language arts). Thus, the core curriculum is an ongoing organization of patterns of collective experience in any culture.

The problem of helping students see interconnected patterns is daunting because most school learning splits the curriculum into separate subjects that appear to have little in common with each other. This often means that material is memorized and focused so narrowly that the larger patterns are lost. When this happens, students can't answer questions that go beyond the assigned work, such as: "How does war affect people?" (literature, history, sociology), "How do swallows know where to fly in the fall?" (biology, geography), and "What does it take to reseed a rain forest?" (ecology, botany, geography).

When mathematics is not relevant in history, history is rarely dealt with through literature, and science has little to do with health and making healthy personal decisions, then the specific information or discrete patterns that students learn to master really can't help them make sense of their world or apply what they have learned very readily.

Before we can really help students research their own questions, and before teachers can formulate or allow actor-centered questions to drive student research, the concept of patterns has to be better understood.

PROCESSING THIS PRINCIPLE

Personal Connections

Look around you.

- Which patterns can you identify by name? (examples: chair, cat, window, table, rug).
- Can you group some of the things you are looking at into inclusive patterns (categories) and name them? (examples: furniture, pets, exits, floor coverings).
- How else can you think about the things around you? (examples: home, office, laboratory, classroom).

Next, take a walk down any street and look for items that just seem to be naturally connected. For instance,

- Is there a difference between the way leaves seem to be connected to each other when they are on a tree and when they are lying on the ground?

- What is the difference between your perception of plants in garden beds and plants in fields or weeds in the cracks in a sidewalk?
- Compare a single shop to the cluster of shops and stores that you see in a mall.
- What is the difference between a group of people wandering in the streets and the crowd flowing out of a football stadium at the end of a game?

One can carry the same process to any situation and can "look" in both concrete and abstract ways. The basic result is always the same—the brain/mind makes sense of things by perceiving patterns.

Going Deeper

Clearly there are many different types of patterns and ways of patterning. We need an approach that makes sense of what is known and that is useful to educators.

Although educators all agree that students need to learn and understand myriad facts and skills that make up the academic curriculum, one of the biggest problems facing those who want to raise standards is that the key to high performance is never limited to concrete patterns. Ultimately, we do need to know more details, recognize distinguishing characteristics, and master the specifics of a given thing.

> Knowing facts is never enough. Scientists, for instance,
> *"look beyond the surfaces of the world and try to infer its deepest patterns. We look for the underlying, hidden causes of events. We try to figure out the nature of things."*
>
> —Gopnik et al. (1999, p. 85)

Higher-order thinking, problem solving, and exercising of the executive functions require that information be dealt with at a mental or conceptual level that very often touches on the emotions. That means that high standards always depend on more than a mastery of facts or specific skills reducible to right and wrong. So how do students internalize a sense of compassion, interconnectedness, beauty, intelligence, symbolism, expertise, honesty, morality, or empathy?

A useful pathway into types of patterns is to explore the differences between *categories*, *concepts*, and *metaphors*.

Categories

The concrete everyday world is always organized in terms of natural or basic categories. According to Lakoff and Johnson (1999), every living system categorizes. They point out that even an amoeba must categorize things into food and not-food. All people use basic categories to make sense of and move around in a concrete reality that consists of people and vehicles, birds, clouds, and cities. This is the level at which everyday learning first begins to happen. While there are many differences based on culture and context, all human beings learn to navigate through their own concrete everyday world without needing much thought analysis of what they see, feel, taste, and touch.

Illustration: "Chain"

Let's look at the word *chain* from the perspective of a basic category. A person would focus on what a chain looks like and feels like, and define its purpose and function. That would lead to an understanding of what it means to chain a bicycle to a tree. Any connections made to the word *chain* at this level would be factual (veridical), even though chains vary in size, weight, design, and color. It is possible to

- identify a chain;
- buy, sell, or build a chain;
- measure a chain;
- design a chain.

Concepts

There is another kind of depth of understanding that can be reached when we move beyond "things" to "concepts." This is a move into the realm of the abstract because a concept is a way of mentally organizing physical objects.

As a concept, the word *chain* refers to the *idea* of a chain. The word *chain* could be used to describe things that have some of the characteristics of a chain. Examples include the food chain, feeling chained to a person or idea or behavior, a chain of events, or a chain of escalating conflict.

Conceptual understanding allows students to see how an idea organizes information. "What is the concept of a city?" "How are cities organized?" "What does it mean to be a town?" and "When is a city not a city?"

> Concepts can't be touched or be physically manipulated, yet they are essential for understanding and thinking.

All deeper understanding requires a grasp of the essential concepts of a subject or discipline. Some examples are the notions of "government" and "rule of law," the idea of "war and peace," and the essence of a hypothesis and of evidence. These can be used by students only when they "get" the concept. Think also about mathematics and the use of "negative numbers" or "infinities." If students don't understand these as inclusive concepts that stand for an idea, it will be very difficult for them to think mathematically or advance beyond the level of simply doing problems to making effective decisions.

Metaphors

Metaphors are used in order to shift a frame of reference by using one concept to explain something else. For example, the Caines used the metaphor "city in the mind" to explain the major functions of the brain in *Making Connections* (1994). New knowledge is often introduced using metaphors and analogies. Thus, a door can stand for a gateway or path symbolizing movement from one world to another. Knowledge can become a "door" to success, and the concept of equal protection can be symbolized by the scales of justice. One way in which metaphors work is by abstracting some of the qualities of a concept and using them in a new context.

A central quality of a chain is linking. One could begin to explain an ecological system by saying that all the elements in the system are linked together. All the interacting chains create a "web" of relationships. That web of relationships is not a physical web like a spider web but rather a multidimensional, interconnected whole that stands for a broader concept like ecology or the "web of life."

Interestingly, although every human being naturally uses all three levels—categories, concepts, and metaphors—many people cannot actually think about and understand the three levels. For example, we have seen many teachers try to teach concepts without seeing that a concept is essentially an idea and not a fact. Teachers have to think in more abstract ways to raise standards. Recent reports from both within the United States (NCATE, 2003) and from countries whose students perform very well on international comparisons of math and reading show that teachers whose students perform well teach for conceptual understanding (National Center for Education Statistics, 2000). Educators must put these three ways of thinking into their professional bag of skills if they are truly intent on teaching students to use more of their brain.

Bridging to the Practical

Let's apply the distinctions explained above to an aspect of the curriculum to see how understanding is expanded at each level. The example is teaching about division.

Concrete

The focus would be on recognizing the need to do division and then on memorizing and mastering the specific process for doing so. How to actually solve a division problem would be explained and modeled by the teacher. We have encountered many teachers who test for understanding by giving students problems to solve on a timed test. This may demonstrate that students can physically do math problems, but it does not test for understanding the concept of, for example, division.

Conceptual

The additional focus would be on having the students get the concept of division so that they understand what it is they are being asked to do. Teacher and students would need to address such questions as the following:

- What does it mean to divide things into parts?
- How is division related to multiplication?

Metaphorical

An extension of the focus would be on having the students see a broader range of meanings beyond the basic concept. Teacher and student might explore what is meant by "divisive language" or by "a divided community or nation."

Notice that at this level the term *division* crosses disciplines and broader connections can be made. This is a critical aspect of teaching that allows for curriculum integration. Also, notice that both conceptual and metaphorical thinking may necessitate reflection or critical analysis on the part of the student, thus requiring more time.

A Quick Reflective Exercise

Explore the term *literacy* in the following ways:

- How would you describe literacy in concrete terms? Give a few examples.
- How would you describe literacy conceptually? Give a few examples.
- In metaphorical terms, what might literacy become? Give a few examples.

A reminder: Two things are important before taking this information into the classroom and school. Remember that concepts and abstract thinking engage the executive functions, which are different for different age groups. Young children can understand symbols like Santa Claus and the meaning of telling the truth. These may have to be dealt with more concretely and need to be discussed. It has been our experience that elementary school teachers generally underestimate their students' ability to deal with abstract concepts like compassion and love. Children often don't have the vocabulary to express what they think and feel, and they are often not asked or given time to figure out what they actually understand (see Bransford, Brown, & Cocking, 2000, chap. 4).

We have already discussed how the survival response prevents access to higher-order thinking. It has been our experience (Caine, 2000) that students coming from high stress environments have real problems with abstract concepts. For certain populations, it is important to teach concrete facts first, then expand concrete facts and knowledge into rich and comprehensive categories. Teachers first need to give these students a sense of competence and confidence. Recall that self-efficacy counteracts the survival response, and that once students feel competent and safe, they can go farther.

TAKING IT INTO THE CLASSROOM

One of the crucial differences among the three teaching approaches is in the extent and depth of the patterning that students experience and master.

Instructional Approach 1 tends to operate at the sensory or concrete level. For such teaching, even important ideas that *should be* understood in depth become just facts to be remembered. Instructional Approach 2 expands to help students also grasp underlying concepts and connections, which usually moves thinking into the realm of the abstract. Instructional Approach 3 adds extra depth because, in addition to knowing essential facts and grasping concepts, students learn to think metaphorically, which uses the executive functions. That means, in part, that they can take concepts from one subject area and understand how to use them to make sense of other subject areas.

An Example of a Curriculum Standard for Writing

"The proficient writer uses organization that enhances the reader's understanding. The students will . . .

1. write a cohesive paragraph with at least three sentences.

2. organize a written piece with a beginning, middle, and end."

Kansas State Curriculum Standards, Third Grade, Standard 2, Writing, page 9, Benchmark 3.
(Notice how the above standard invites Instructional Approach 1 teacher directed and easily limited to memorization and practice).

Instructional Approach 1

The concepts in question are *sentence* and *paragraph.* The Instructional Approach 1 teacher knows the content and would probably begin with the steps outlined in the teacher's guide to give the students practice in writing a paragraph or story. The teacher would show them an example of a key sentence and demonstrate how two other sentences are used to expand upon the key sentence. The teacher would probably use worksheets with sample paragraphs for the students to analyze. Their own paragraphs would then be written.

This would be highly structured and deal explicitly with the precise requirements of the standard. However, the students would rarely grasp the fact that real paragraphs can express something important to them or that they tend to be formed over time, particularly with rewriting. They would be unlikely to get a feel for how supporting sentences and key sentences work together in the writing process, and while they may be able to recognize the difference between beginning, middle, and end, they would not grasp how these three parts of a composition actually work. This would emerge if actor-centered questions drove their search for understanding.

Instructional Approach 2

The Instructional Approach 2 teacher would use other techniques to help students make sense of the different components of a paragraph and stages of a story. The goal would be to get the concept of a sentence and a paragraph. For instance, the students might look at fairy tales to see how they are all put together in a way that helps the reader move from one event to another. The students could take story strips of events and put them in order, laying the foundation for organizing written material. There would be structure, but it would be supplemented by interesting material and additional approaches to help students grasp the core concepts. Some material used by traditional teachers would be included, but the entire process would generate much more student understanding.

Instructional Approach 3

Instructional Approach 3 would begin differently. A friend of ours, for example, once made use of a real-life playground conflict that the students had recently encountered. She "seized the moment" and used the playground conflict as a spontaneous global experience that led to an understanding of aspects of sentences and paragraphs.

The initial conflict raised issues and questions. Students discussed the events and put those events in a sequence (with a little guidance). Students discussed where things could have taken a different turn so as not to become a problem (see chain of escalating conflict in Chapter 6). The teacher recorded the discussion on the board.

Note that the central *concept* here was "sequence" but the teacher was expanding the context. She was using an apparently unrelated situation (resolving a conflict) and abstracted some qualities from that situation (the idea of sequence and clusters of incidents) to help students make sense of sentences and paragraphs. The class was getting a feel for how events develop over time and the order in which things do and could happen, and then applied that to understanding part of the process of writing.

Later, the teacher used that discussion as the basis for some writing. The notion of "paragraph" was achieved by working with the class to find ways to make the conflict understandable to an audience of peers. Each paragraph dealt with a particular aspect of the conflict. Then, students looked for key sentences within those paragraphs. The activity was extended when they were encouraged to add two sentences to make the key sentence clearer. The teacher actually used the experience on the playground as a metaphor to help students gain a deeper insight into how sentences and paragraphs work.

Under the guidance of the teacher, the students compared paragraphs with each other and gave each other suggestions about why some paragraphs were clearer than others. In this way, all the elements of the standard were introduced, but in a vital and meaningful way that kept the students engaged through a real-world example.

This teacher capitalized on a "teachable moment." By using real experience in a safe and effective way, she engaged the students' interest and had them involved in real analysis and decision making. The executive functions, in particular flexibility, of each student were being called upon in a very natural and meaningful way.

Opportunities for Instructional Approach 1 Teaching

The most important challenge for traditional teaching is to help students grasp the difference between concrete fact and abstract concept.

Renate's Story

A teacher was teaching biology using owl pellets. As many teachers know, owls eat various creatures like rodents and birds. They somehow digest the essentials and regurgitate the feathers and bones in what is known as "owl pellets." I was walking around a classroom where students had each been given one pellet to dissect. They were systematically pulling out the bones from the hair or feathers. With an answer sheet beside them, they checked off items that identified whatever creature had been swallowed.

The class was quiet as each student did the assigned task. I had so many questions! I turned to one student and asked, "How does the owl's stomach do that?" "Humans can't swallow a whole chicken and spit out the bones and feathers? Could you?" "How are our stomachs different?" The student I addressed and others who had overheard me looked at me as though I were crazy. What did that have to do with their assignment?

The students were engaged in their basic task, but almost none thought about the underlying concepts that were really important. Even the notion of digestion did not mean much to them. A powerful way to get them thinking is to ask basic questions such as, "Can you explain the difference between this and that?" or "In what way is this connected to that?"

Opportunities for Instructional Approach 2 Teaching

Expand the use of comparisons and multiple examples to help students get the idea that they need a broader idea or concept. Look for novel ways to introduce concepts and ideas into teaching, for instance, by using the arts.

Opportunities for Instructional Approach 3 Teaching

Practice noticing and using powerful moments as global experiences to lead into a concept. Practice thinking metaphorically and using different frames of reference to expand the meaning of concepts.

THE THIRD FOUNDATIONAL SKILL FOR ORCHESTRATED IMMERSION: SEEING AND TEACHING PATTERNS

As we mentioned early in this chapter, one key to improved teaching and raising standards is making the shift from dealing with facts to helping students understand concepts.

Teachers need to guide the ongoing activity of the students by constantly calling attention to those core concepts. At the same time, the teacher will be guiding students in finding and working with essential resources and in gathering information.

> Once students have embarked on a research project or are setting out to complete a project or solve a problem, they have to be able to "get" and work with core concepts.

Using Themes

Themes are powerful ways to link concepts (Kovalik & Olsen, 1997). Themes can be used for specific topics, for an entire course, and even as a way of integrating courses. Use themes that deal with the major questions raised by a topic and involve the core concepts. For example, the theme for the units dealing with the Civil War could be the following:

- War and peace
- Families divided
- Duty and freedom
- When beliefs clash
- Government and individual rights

Before launching into the global experience, post the theme in a conspicuous place on a board or wall. It can then be pointed to or referred to at will.

As students call out their questions, and ask you to help them find questions in common that they can work on together, refer to core concepts and themes. For example, one question from students that was very helpful was, "Why did people fight each other?" We liked this question because the standards inevitably call for students' mastering the causes of the war and we could tie this actor-centered question to addressing that standard.

Focusing Questions

As the students begin to think about how to begin researching their own questions, you (the teacher) use questioning to help students further clarify their focus. The range of questions that you ask depends to some extent on the sophistication and knowledge base of the students, as well as on the standards with which you are dealing. For example, if a student is interested in the question of why and how women fought in the Civil War, you could ask questions like these:

- Who knew about these women?
- How would it have been possible for a woman to serve as a soldier during the Civil War?
- How many women served?
- How do you relate this to the role of women in society generally?
- Were the women's motives for fighting in the Civil War different from the motives of the men?
- How did we come to know about them?

After you ask a question, allow students some time to talk and do additional research.

Guiding Research

You will need to guide students in their research. One way to begin is to have students share information about the resources with which they are familiar. It may be appropriate to see if some students can demonstrate how to use the resources. It will also become apparent that the ways in which students use resources depends on their grasp of the concepts involved. The reason is that the deeper their understanding of the concept, the more alternative resources can be seen to be useful.

Supervising the Work and the Learning

Research, projects, and problem solving are all ongoing processes. Information needs to be pulled together and sifted through, and an understanding of concepts usually takes place over time.

It is important to work with individual students and groups privately, sometimes guiding their thinking and sometimes guiding both their research and thinking with suggestions and questions. This is what we call active processing, and we provide some guidance for the additional use of questions in Part III of this book.

It may be necessary to bring the class together occasionally so that students can report on what they are doing, ask questions, and solidify facts and basic information. On these occasions, you can invite students to respond to each other's questions, and you can ask further questions of your own. Remember that repetition is still essential, even though facts, skills, and knowledge are inevitably embedded as students wrestle with concepts and ideas.

At times you will have occasion to bring them all together, if there is a common problem, need, or concept that should be addressed. Sometimes a brief explanation will be required from you. Sometimes there will be a mini topic within the topic, as you help all the students grasp a core concept. For example, the topic of the Civil War may be used to raise the issue of freedom. This is an issue that can be dealt with several times in several ways while student research is ongoing. One possibility would be to spend part of a class on aspects of the civil rights movement and then ask questions about the extent to which the same question was relevant to the causes and playing out of the Civil War. You can also have students role-play a Union and/or Confederate view of the conflict.

Student Self-Management

Managing time, staying on task, clarifying needs, and making decisions are all essential skills and capacities that students must have and will be developing. Most are related to the maturing executive functions. At this point, you may wish to review Part I on relaxed alertness. We will continue to address ways to deal with this need in the next chapter and in Part III of this book, primarily in the chapter on self-regulation (Chapter 15).

THE TRANSFORMATIONAL ADMINISTRATOR AND THE PROCESS FOR MAKING IT REAL

> Reinforce your teachers' needs to be very familiar with the standards they are responsible for at their grade levels. It makes sense that the more they internalize their standards, the better chance they have of seeing the patterns within their respective curriculum.

One rarely used and very powerful process is to invite teachers to work together to rethink the core concepts of their courses and then to relate their selection of core concepts to the standards. These can be brief discussions, and they can also be ongoing and very invigorating discussions. Sometimes learning circles work as very effective venues, but sometimes material may not be of equal value to every member of a learning circle. In the latter case, meetings of subject area specialists or teachers at the same grade level will work, still using aspects of ordered sharing.

We also suggest that you pursue the goal of making the school climate intellectually powerful and exciting. This is actually a natural outcome when teachers meet in learning circles. Schools that use learning circles consistently remark on their shift to more challenging and professional discussions, even in informal settings. Begin inviting staff to analyze and examine the basic concepts and ideas they use as the basis for their opinions. This could be the beginning of an insistence on evidence to support opinions about, say, how to connect with the community and why.

In tandem with the National Teaching Standards

Accomplished teachers draw on their knowledge of subject matter to establish goals and to facilitate student learning within and across the disciplines of the curriculum.

Teachers understand that meaningful learning arises from concepts drawn from a range of disciplines. To deepen students' conceptual understanding, teachers build on prescribed curriculum, but are not constrained by it. As students' needs dictate, they incorporate related topics, issues, and technology that stretch students' perceptions, extend their knowledge and understanding of the world, and thereby enrich their education.

—Standard II: Knowledge of Subject Matter

Continue your exploration with your process partner or learning circle by discussing the issue of the standards themselves. What, for instance, *is* a standard? Is it a criterion, a goal, a baseline, a statement about content? Even the organization of the curriculum into standards and the ways in which educators are held accountable reflect patterns of thinking that need to be better understood by all of us.

If we want to create enriched environments that help students learn, then we need to include all of the following:

- Engage their individual style and uniqueness
- Engage the physiology in learning
- Engage social interactions
- Engage their innate search for meaning
- Engage their capacity to recognize and master essential patterns
- Engage emotional connections
- Engage their ability to perceive both details and the larger view
- Engage both their ability to focus attention and learn from the peripheral context
- Engage both conscious and unconscious processing
- Engage their capacity to learn from memorizing isolated facts and biographical events
- Acknowledge and engage developmental steps and shifts
- Reduce threat and enhance self-efficacy

11

Engaging and Assessing Developmental Steps and Shifts in Learning

Brain/Mind Learning Principle 10: *Learning is developmental.*

 ## At the Core

Although all human beings have in common a somewhat predictable process of development, rarely do human beings develop in precisely the same way or at exactly the same rate. This applies to the development of the executive functions as well. All learning builds on previous learning, and we now know that this process is accompanied by changes in the physiology as it interacts with experience. While most educational systems tend to categorize and organize learners on the basis of their age or in some other logical or sequential fashion, this does not address the vagaries of human development. Performance, not age or grade level, provides the best evidence for future learning.

Capacity: All students can learn more effectively if individual differences in maturation and development are taken into consideration.

HOW DO WE KNOW THIS?

Psychologists have been investigating cognitive, emotional, and physical development for many years. Most educators have been introduced, for instance, to Piaget's theory of cognitive development or Eric Erikson's (1994) psychosocial developmental theory.

Neuroscience has recently added to the general understanding of stages of development. For instance, it is now known that there are two periods of extraordinary bursts of brain growth: one during the first 18 months of life and one in adolescence.

> We recommend two exceptional books that summarize the more general developmental path from a neuroscience perspective in a readable manner: *Magic Trees of the Mind* by Diamond and Hobson (1998) and *The Secret Life of the Brain* by Restak (2001).

As we have already discussed, it is known that development is a consequence of the interaction of nature and nurture, of genes and experience. Children's ongoing experiences have an enormous impact on how their brains develop. In particular, we want to note that although there are many commonalities, development in even "normal" children can vary by a matter of months or years, which is why binding grade levels to ages is potentially so self-defeating and limiting.

The Executive Functions

> In this book we focus on the executive functions because, as we have seen, it is through the development of executive functions that much cognitive and emotional maturity can be documented and achieved over time.

Infancy

Very basic foundations for executive functions develop in infancy. By six months of age infants can already attend and participate. By the end of their first year they are able to link the past, present, and future, and by 18 to 30 months of age they have mastered some self-control (Sternberg & Grigorenko, 2001). At this point their development of language (including sign language) becomes critical. If language is not acquired, further cognitive development is more difficult.

Detailing the Research

Researchers (Sternberg & Grigorenko, 2001) have found almost no differences in intelligence among children prior to six months of age. That includes children from low socioeconomic (SES) environments or racial or ethnic minorities. Differences appear after that and are most pronounced around age two, when language develops.

Mastery of language is beginning to be identified as a major factor in determining student differences in intelligence and achievement in school. The advantage is being determined before students even reach school. Diamond and Hobson (1998) summarize these early years in their chapter, "All You Need Is Love—and Language."

Early Years

Although parents and adults continue to be the proxies for incomplete development of executive functions in children, the early school years mark an incredible time for the brain. The child's brain is still extremely malleable (responsive and shaping itself on the basis of its experiences). Children are still naturally excited by the world around them, and they have an almost limitless capacity to learn. Besides figuring out how to do things in a concrete and hands-on way, children also need to be partially in charge of their own learning. Guided, self-directed learning is therefore equally important and is critical for engagement of the executive functions throughout the school years.

Adolescence

The adolescent years bring growth of a different kind. These are the most critical years for developing executive functions. In many ways, the adolescent brain is now going through a major shift, somewhat like adding the most sophisticated elements to a house. Metaphorically speaking, it is as if the house now participates in creating its own wiring for itself.

Something very special is happening in the adolescent brain as it undergoes its greatest changes since infancy. Neuronal proliferation occurs. This means that the brain suddenly "sprouts" an immense number of new connections—far more than are needed. This "exuberance of new connections" is followed by a kind of streamlining as, once again, neurons take on the "shape" of significant experiences while sloughing off connections that are not used (Restak, 1995).

This is actually a positive process in the sense that the brain becomes "lean and mean" or prepares itself for what will be needed as a mature adult. In a very real sense, adolescents must now take over from their parents who, it is hoped, have been supplementing their children's executive functions. Up to this point it has been parents or caretakers who (again, hopefully) made certain that adolescents think ahead in order to anticipate dangers or opportunities. Parents have had to tell their kids to "study hard to get into college," "organize your time," and generally help them make the best decisions.

The problem is that the adolescent is now becoming capable of taking over these functions but it doesn't happen automatically. Prior experience with decision making and reasoning now becomes critical.

There are a lot of surprises for parents as one day their adolescent appears to be mature and the next day appears to have lost any newly found ability to make sensible decisions. For one thing, the limbic area, which houses the hippocampus and emotions, is already well developed. Adolescents are often full of feelings that are difficult to control. In addition, they are continually exposed to too much information (also influenced by TV or peers), little of which is yet grounded in good judgment, analysis, or linked to potential consequences.

A Word About Drugs and Adolescence

Although the focus of this book is not on dysfunction, it is important to mention that when adolescents use drugs and alcohol, they are playing with a time bomb. Most drugs play havoc with prefrontal lobe development and executive functions (NIDA, 1974 to date). In addition, drugs can hijack the pleasure areas of the brain before students learn to love life and enjoy activities such as playing in a band, mastering a sport, singing in a chorus, and being with friends they respect (as many as possible of these positive emotional experiences need to be included in their early development). Almost 80% of adolescents addicted to drugs at this critical age never recover (Restak, 1995). At the very same time that adolescents must gain control over their sexual urges and aggressive or passive impulses, drugs rob them of the opportunity and capacity for self-control. Without positive social/emotional skills, including the ability to foresee the consequences of their behavior, they have little with which to harness and override their more basic urges.

Here are the characteristics of students who appear to be more resistant to drug use and the effect of drugs. They

- enjoy environments that include positive affect,
- have developed a sense of optimism,
- have strong social connections,
- experience self-confidence and empowerment,
- experience multiple interest and development of their own talents (enjoyment),
- have parents who do not abuse drugs or alcohol (see Restak, 1995).

Zone of Teacher Influence

Remember that development does not happen in isolation from a broader context. This is where a teacher or a mentor (or a parent or a guide) plays a very special role. Psychologist Lev Vygotsky (1978) suggested that in all student-teacher interactions there is a zone of proximal development. That means that there is a space for the next phase of learning—where the capacity of the teacher matches the student's expanding capacities. This means that the amount and quality of learning that is possible for a student in any situation depends to a large extent on his or her relationship with an adult or teacher. The question is not just, "How much development is possible?" but, for any teacher, "How much can I help that student develop given this particular situation?"

A further problem is that learning and human development are nonlinear and messy. There are forward, backward, and sideways steps even as there is general growth. It usually takes a fairly complex and lifelike environment to accurately assess what sort of progress a person is making. That is why the "in the moment" or fluid kind of teaching used in Instructional Approach 3 is so powerful.

PROCESSING THIS PRINCIPLE

Personal Connections

Take some time to look back over your life and reflect on your own growth and development.

- Have you ever learned something that had been puzzling you for a long time until someone showed you a way of relating it to something else that you knew quite well?
- Where, in your own life, are you becoming more competent and knowledgeable by building on what you already know?
- Can you recall a time when you (perhaps suddenly) acquired a new capacity or ability? What happened? How did you feel?
- Has your own development in any field been messy and nonlinear? How did you handle it? If others were teaching or guiding you, how did they handle it? Were you satisfied with what happened?

Going Deeper

> Development always presents a dilemma, because all children are unique and yet there are similar patterns of development.

All people learn best in an optimal environment where they feel both safe and challenged, where they have the opportunities to become competent and confident and to deal with their own interests. They need to be protected to the extent possible from being emotionally overwhelmed, yet have ample opportunities to make their own decisions.

One key to working with infants and children in the early years is to realize that complex reasoning, which has not yet been developed, must often be put on a back burner in favor of teaching some skills and procedures directly. At the same time, the teacher must empower children to take charge and make some basic decisions on their own. This can happen when teachers surround children with multiple opportunities to hear enriched vocabulary and grammatical expressions and provide them with many opportunities to speak, such as the following:

- Allow them to describe, explain, and share their plans.
- See each sharing as an opportunity to expand and reinforce their vocabulary and thinking by rephrasing or summarizing what they have said or want to say.

- Be patient and kind. Even if they don't get it right away, remember it is the exposure, not the immediate mastery, that counts at this age.
- Don't underestimate them! But do not overload them! Allow students to make decisions, but keep these manageable.

> Adolescents are similar but different. Their capacities to reason are biologically more advanced, so they need multiple opportunities to execute judgment and reasoning.

Adolescents need to apply intellectual information and to debate or engage in discussions of issues that are important to them. Because their emotions can be turbulent, they must have multiple opportunities to learn to monitor and regulate themselves and to develop more self-control and sounder judgment. They also need opportunities to interact with a broader context that includes real-world problems and dilemmas. All of this needs to be done in an emotionally safe environment where they are neither overwhelmed nor overstimulated.

Bridging to the Practical

Running in tandem with the development of body, brain, and mind is the fact that ideas and skills are also mastered developmentally. People do have to walk before they can run, and some basic mathematical operations are indispensable for higher levels of math. That means that all subject areas need scaffolding so that students can continually build upon what has been learned or experienced before.

At the same time, body, brain, and mind form an integrated system in which everything influences everything else. One of the great drawbacks of a fragmented curriculum and of schools based on age, grade, and separate subject matter is that developmental problems are often made worse because they are ignored. Part of the solution is to leverage the connections among skills, subjects, and experiences. Let's look at some examples:

Children can come to love music or a tune before they are taught to play the piano one note at a time. When their friends play an instrument, when parents participate in actual playing or singing, and when the teacher uses music in school, the context begins to support and encourage learning about music naturally, and playing an instrument becomes part of what is simply done.

Singing in a choir or learning to play a keyboard has been shown to develop spatial intelligence. Spatial intelligence is critical for understanding higher mathematics and determining how objects behave in space (Rauscher, Shaw, & Ky, 1995; Rauscher et al., 1997).

When teachers allow students to draw an object of their choosing, and encourage them to observe the object closely, they are helping students develop observational skills, which are critical to scientific observation (Root-Bernstein & Root-Bernstein, 2000).

> It is not possible to quantify all learning or control the developmental path. The brain/mind is complex; much of what it does is spontaneous and unpredictable.

In order to discover the world with its myriad patterns, teachers should consider the following:

- Do students have opportunities to observe, test, decide, and communicate their discoveries?
- Are they being helped to discover unique preferences and skills that emerge out of a love or fascination with music, art, science, or stories and writing?
- Are they being prepared to search continuously for knowledge and revel in possibility?
- Do we expose them to arts that support academic learning?
- Are they permitted to explore and learn in natural settings?

> "The search for the lessons of the new science is still in progress, really in its infancy. . . . In this realm, there is a new kind of freedom, where it is more rewarding to explore than to reach conclusions, more satisfying to wonder than to know, and more exciting to search than to stay put. Curiosity, not certainty, becomes the saving grace" (Wheatley, 1999).

TAKING IT INTO THE CLASSROOM

It should not be surprising to discover that the three instructional approaches deal with development differently. Here is an example from a curriculum science standard.

> ## An Example of a Curriculum Standard
>
> "Make wise choices in the use and conservation of resources and the disposal or recycling of materials."
> *Texas Elementary Curriculum Standards, Grade 4, Science 112.6 (b) Knowledge and Skills*

Instructional Approach 1

Students would follow the textbook, read a story, or watch a video, with the final goal being the ability to answer questions on a multiple-choice test. There would be little attention paid to developmental issues, and the executive functions would be largely ignored because there is rarely any student choice or decision making beyond doing what is required.

Opportunities for Instructional Approach 1 Teaching

A very good first step for Instructional Approach 1 teachers is to spend some time with colleagues to think about the basic assumptions that drive this approach. Is it really conceivable that all children should be on the same page at the same time or that they all learn in the same way and at the same speed? What are the basic assumptions underlying prescriptive teaching? Teachers need to answer these questions and questions such as "How do I learn? What do I do to learn about developmental differences in a way that will help me become a better teacher?" These questions and the discussion are very suitable for learning circles.

Instructional Approach 2

Let's say that the teacher, Bill, designed a global experience that gives students a sense of the critical importance of natural resources and energy consumption. He might ask the students to identify some places where energy is being consumed and energy is being wasted. Using this as an introduction, the teacher might then ask the students to work together in small groups to see if they can come up with ways to reduce the amount of wasted energy based on the research they generated as a class. Then he would give the students some freedom to develop a way to make their presentation to their peers and perhaps others (the principal, another class, parents, or other professionals).

Using a guided experience-based approach and small groups gives the teacher an opportunity to move around and gain a sense of what students know, how they interact, and what they need to know or develop. It also provides an opportunity to work with students individually and in their small groups in order to provide them with guidance that is appropriate for them. At the same time, the teacher would know that some students work better in groups than others, and that learners proceed at different rates.

As he assesses these factors, he becomes better equipped to help students adopt a problem of appropriate difficulty. He might help some students with their presentations while allowing others to work by themselves. He can also place students in groups that would tend to suit them. He would have an opportunity to address students at their developmental level because his classroom is more complex than an Instructional Approach 1 classroom. Nevertheless, the teacher would still be very much in charge and, therefore, miss many opportunities to see authentic student decision making and behavior.

Opportunities for Instructional Approach 2 Teaching

1. *Make the content and experiences relevant.* For many students, the more relevant and familiar the topic, the more they can and want to participate. For example, students tend to have a keen interest in and awareness of lifestyles. In the example above, when a discussion about recycling or disposing of goods is required, a direct connection can be made by asking,

"Are we a wasteful or conserving society?" This can lead to a discussion that engages higher-order thinking about recycling programs and can provide opportunities to brainstorm ways to rid the home of glass, aluminum, and wastepaper.

2. *Empower students to have a voice in how the class is working and to take action to solve any problems.* Remember that the fact that students may be at different developmental levels does not indicate a permanent condition. One of the best ways to deal with differences is for students to learn how to cope with them, act on them, and resolve them. For example, if they need more time they should be able, in most situations, to take a vote and then ask the teacher for time. If there is conflict, they should be able to use their own initiative to deal with it, including asking the teacher for assistance. That is why the foundational skills we introduce in Part I are so important. If concepts are difficult, the climate should make it easy for students to seek help from their peers as well as from the teacher.

Instructional Approach 3

The teacher would have a sense of what students already know from prior courses and classes. With that in mind the teacher, Carmen, would use global experiences to create situations requiring students to think, make decisions, and act. Sometimes an experience can be ongoing. An example might be a simulation. For example, in an elementary classroom where students are coming to terms with what it means to conserve and recycle, only a limited amount of paper might be available for everyone in the classroom and at home for approximately two weeks. A limit could also be placed on the number of pencils available over the same time period. Within this simulation, the teacher and students would gather ways to deal with the rationing taking place in the classroom. They would have to work as a community of decision makers in order to come up with a reasonable solution to these problems. She might take other simulation ideas and run full speed with them, opening up opportunities for the students to try to determine where conserving resources could be put to good use around the school or in their community.

Clearly this teacher already has higher expectations of *all* of her students and anticipates that they can function in complex ways. She will watch and intervene and support students as needed. But she will also have supported the creation of an excellent community. That means that students will be more likely to help slower students, rather than feel bothered by them. Because the situation is also more complex, students will have opportunities to show strengths (and win respect from peers) in ways that just aren't available in a more controlled classroom. For example, some people who read slowly may be better artists, and their art can begin to show. Students then have an opportunity to work with their unique strengths in order to explore different perspectives.

> As the situation becomes more complex, students begin to have more choices and make more autonomous decisions.

Opportunities for Instructional Approach 3 Teaching

1. *Look for additional ways to integrate other subjects into the curriculum.* This will open up opportunities for students to excel by calling on the different capacities and strengths that they might have.

2. *Expand your own knowledge base and become a learner along with your students.*

THE FOURTH FOUNDATIONAL SKILL FOR ORCHESTRATED IMMERSION: EFFECTIVE ASSESSMENT

Assessment is primarily for the purpose of determining a student's development. Its purpose is to help a student progress further.

Karl's Story

As we mentioned earlier, in doing some additional work with the Convergence Education Foundation (www.cef-trek.org), Karl uses the Segway, the new two-wheeled human transporter recently made available to the public.

During a session with some elementary students, Karl was responding to a number of questions being asked by the very curious students. How fast does it go? How do you stay balanced? How much does it cost? The questions kept coming at a furious pace. When a young man asked how far you can ride on the Segway, the response was ten to fifteen miles, which Karl then followed with, "And amazingly, when you recharge the batteries, it will only cost about ten-cents worth of electricity to do that!" A few minutes later, a delightful third-grade girl raised her hand. With a puzzled look on her face she asked, "Where do you put the ten cents?"

As Karl looked around at the others, he realized that the question was clearly on their minds as well. Many of these kids thought that the dime needed to be deposited into the machine somewhere! Of course!

Karl's activity provoked a question that revealed what some of those children actually knew and understood with beautiful clarity and in a way that gave him an opportunity to introduce new material and concepts at precisely the right teachable moment. That is how brain/mind assessment works. It shows the teacher what students really know. Assessment is an ongoing diagnosis of student learning and development (Cooper, 1998).

> Teachers have to know what to look for, how to look, how to interpret what they observe, and what to do with it. Most of this information becomes available in the moment and should guide the ways in which teachers act and respond.

Of course there are other reasons for assessing students. Parents and the larger community want to compare and contrast student development with that of others from neighboring communities and around the world. Employers want to know what capacities and skills students have. Many people want to know that their children are developing a genuine understanding of, and capacity to function effectively in, the world that constitutes their future. For this reason, some form of standardized assessment will most likely be with us, and students will be held to performance on such exams.

From the perspective of brain/mind educators, however, the primary objective of assessment is to give feedback that helps students learn.

Some Assessment Guidelines

Put standardized tests in perspective (Kohn, 2000; Popham, 2001; Sacks, 1998). The community insists on the use of standardized tests, and there is a place for them. With that in mind, it may be necessary to help students acquire some test-taking skills, but as they become proficient, competent, and confident, most will tend to do well on standardized tests naturally. This has been our experience (Caine, 2000; Caine & Anderson, 2003; Caine & Caine, 1997). We will focus on approaches to testing that are educationally useful and informative.

1. *Have clear expectations, but be willing to change your expectations.* Work with your colleagues regularly to clarify and articulate your expectations for your students. How well do you expect them to be able to read, to work together, to think critically, to manage their emotions? Although having expectations is essential, the danger is that they can become an upper limit. For example, one of the best early childhood programs in the world can be found in the province of Regio Emilia in northern Italy. Many American researchers who go there return saying that young children seem to be able to perform much better than is generally expected in other countries (Edwards, Gandini, & Forman, 1996).

2. *Know the standards and know your subject matter.* There is no way to adequately assess, nor is there a way to adequately teach at a high level, unless teachers are masters of their material.

3. *Use multiple modes of assessment.* This offers teacher and students more opportunity to see what the student does know and can help pinpoint developmental strengths and weaknesses not revealed by just one type of testing.

4. *In particular, focus on performance assessment.* Most of the time the best way to discover what people know or can do is to observe them in a real-world or semi–real-world context. Performance assessment should, therefore, be the norm; also make it a point to vary types of performance. Instructional Approach 3 is important in this regard because it creates so many natural opportunities for multiple modes of assessment.

5. *Design assessment to support instruction.* This does *not* mean a teacher just teaching to the test, although assessment should always be aligned with what is being taught. The key is to use assessment to provide information and feedback to both teachers and students in a way and at the times that allow both to benefit. It is vital, for instance, not to interrupt the flow of teaching too much and to avoid more-than-occasional formal testing.

6. *Students should know what you expect.* To the extent that students will be consciously acting on the basis of the feedback you give them, they should know what the criteria and expectations are. This is where teacher-student designed rubrics come in, and where students can learn from seeing the work of others. Many students may not clearly understand what is needed, despite your explanations. Seeing evidence of achievement by others can be a real eye-opener.

7. *As much as possible, engage students in self-assessment.* Students have to be able to know what they don't know and to take charge of their own learning. Participation in their own assessment (in systematic ways that have consequences) is an enormously powerful way to help students both gain a realistic sense of what they know and can do AND see how to go farther. In fact, good self-assessment by students is one of the best tools teachers have. Again, one way to begin is for teachers and students to work jointly on appropriate rubrics. This does not mean that their opinions automatically prevail. They need to show evidence of expertise and high standards and they need to learn how to compare what they know and do with those standards—something that a teacher helps them to learn.

8. *Design testing to fit naturally into instruction.* First, this does less to interfere with learning and student attitudes. Second, it makes it possible to use the testing to provide good feedback at the right times.

9. *Test your testing.* As Grant Wiggins (1993) notes, when you use a variety of tests and use them well, you become better able to successfully predict how students will do on other tests. Your ability to teach well depends on how well you REALLY know your students.

10. *Work with your colleagues.* Despite the best will in the world, every one of us filters information through our own expectations and mental models. Be willing to seek other evidence so that you do not bias your own findings.

11. *Regularly raise your expectations a notch* and act on that. The only way to keep raising students' standards is to keep raising your own.

Using Assessment to Teach

Instructional Approach 3 does not separate assessment from teaching and learning. The model we present invites you to have students engage in several different kinds of culminating activities that can also be used as a basis for assessment. These include exhibitions, portfolios, presentations, enactments, reports, multimedia, and more.

The key is to avoid a single, all-or-nothing presentation. Part of teaching lies in working with the students as they make decisions, plan, and develop their final product. Portfolios, for instance, are built over time. Exhibitions and reports should also be discussed with peers and adults. This helps the teacher include the standards and guide students in areas where they need more work. At the same time, it automatically engages students in self-assessment. The questions and procedures introduced in Part III, "Active Processing," will help guide you.

THE TRANSFORMATIONAL ADMINISTRATOR AND THE PROCESS FOR MAKING IT REAL

All learning is developmental, and that includes the learning of the staff. As a building or district administrator, empowering teachers to take the risks necessary to accomplish the type of teaching noted above has to come from you. Providing opportunities for teachers to work together and staying cognizant of their professional developmental needs is where some of your greatest challenges will lie. Teachers, like learners in the classroom, are expected to be in the process of becoming better.

The assessment philosophy spelled out here applies just as much to adults and the staff as it does to students, and having the staff use it will make its implementation for students much more authentic. There need to be standards for teaching. We use the National Standards and have identified a professional development path based on the three instructional approaches. We invite staff in their learning circles and in other forums to clarify the expectations for and of teachers, to work on appropriate modes of assessment, and to engage in self-assessment in order to test the testing.

> If the learning circles are solid and authentic, the issue of teacher standards and the developmental path identified in this book becomes a powerful topic for reflection and exploration.

In tandem with the National Teaching Standards

Accomplished teachers do not rely on a single method of assessing students, because behavior is influenced by the setting in which it occurs. They know that students have skills that will not emerge in certain settings or during the course of a single assignment. Their knowledge extends to creating various means for evaluation, such as portfolios, videotapes, demonstrations, and exhibits.

Accomplished teachers do not limit their assessments to verifying that students can repeat facts; they probe for evidence of higher-order understanding, the ability to connect and process various forms of knowledge, and an awareness of the complexity of the world.

They know that testing strictly for grading and ranking purposes may rob students of instructional and learning time. They also recognize the limited utility of standardized testing programs that are not well integrated with their curriculum or that assess a narrow range of skills. They focus their energies on enhancing student learning rather than on raising test scores as an end in itself.

—Standard IX: Assessment

We suggest that Instructional Approach 3 is the most useful vehicle for meeting the developmental needs of students. The National Standards on assessment support this approach. We invite you to discuss this in your learning circle. We also invite you to discuss whether it is possible to have an authentic assessment policy and practice for students unless the same philosophy also applies to the adults who are responsible for that development.

PART III

Active Processing

12

Introduction to Active Processing

The Art of Digesting Experience and Consolidating Learning

Experience is not what happens to a man; it is what a man does with what happens to him.

—Aldous Huxley (1894–1963)

 At the Core

Active processing is the art of digesting, thinking about, reflecting on, and making sense of experience and of consolidating learning. It ranges from systematic practice and creative rehearsal (for memorization) to the deeply probing and ongoing questions that test the limits of a learner's abilities to call on executive functions and respond within a real-life context. It can be done by both the learner alone and collectively with others, but ultimately it must be done.

One reason some project-based and experiential teaching does not work is because people do not automatically learn everything they need to know, nor do they adequately exercise their executive functions just by having an experience, no matter how well crafted. Even if a superb classroom and school climate have been established, and even if teachers are wonderfully innovative in their design of projects and activities, that is not enough. Although students can pick up values, attitudes, beliefs, and information just by being present in a particular cultural context, powerful learning and adaptive decision making require more action and effort by students. *Experience needs to be processed.*

The reason is simple: It has to do with depth of learning and the engagement of students. One issue is memory. We will show in the next chapter that there are several types of memory. Some of what students learn needs simply to be memorized by rote, because some aspects of consolidation involve practice and rehearsal. This engages the more complex capacities of the brain only minimally, however. In addition, memory is also "natural" and dynamic, as people use what they learn in reacting and responding in real ways in the real world. In so doing, they need to observe accurately, think, make good decisions in the moment, anticipate the future and plan for it, and monitor themselves, all of which require the executive functions. The way to develop that second sort of dynamic memory is to embed necessary skills and ideas in well-designed experiences and then to mine the experiences for the lessons and essential skills they offer.

> Active processing is probably the most overlooked and unappreciated aspect of powerful teaching.

Active processing is the key that enables a teacher to move away from providing information to ensuring that students have many, many opportunities to make personal sense of material and to learn in real depth. Because Part III relies heavily on application to practice, we have simplified the organization used so far. Sections will continue to include "How Do We Know This," "Processing This Principle," and "Taking It Into the Classroom," but "Personal Connections" and "Bridging to the Practical" will be subsumed under the above sections.

HOW DO WE KNOW THIS?

Every Brain/Mind Learning Principle is relevant; in this part of the book we focus on four principles not yet covered.

- There are at least two approaches to memory. One is to store or archive isolated facts, skills, and procedures; the other is to simultaneously engage multiple memory systems in order to make sense of experience.
- Learning involves both focused attention and peripheral perception.
- Learning is both conscious and unconscious.
- Each brain is uniquely organized.

Layers of Active Processing

There are several different ways to approach active processing. We introduce them here and explore them in detail, with strategies and suggestions, in the chapters that follow.

Practice and Rehearsal

Sometimes facts need to be memorized and skills practiced over and over again. Even in medical school, future doctors spend time simply memorizing parts of the body, symptoms of diseases, and other facts. There are many occasions in life when rote recall is needed. For such needs, active processing is basically a matter of finding the best, most effective, and creative ways to memorize. Rote learning, however, does almost nothing to enhance the executive functions. It is more like filling the shelves of our mental grocery store with products and ingredients that may one day be needed.

Observations and Questions

When people learn for the purpose of becoming really proficient in a skill or profession, or in order to gain a deep understanding of concepts and ideas, processing needs to be more sophisticated. The primary approach here is to increase a learner's powers of observation and to use questions that deepen thinking and understanding.

Every professional knows the steps to take to discover facts and get results. In the real world, good professionals process regularly to solve problems and to improve their own skills and knowledge.

Questions professionals use:

- Lawyers *ask critical questions* of clients, witnesses, experts, and others.
- Doctors are trained to *observe patients and make diagnoses* by asking questions about symptoms and patterns of aches and pains.
- Architects spend much of their time *relating the form of a building to the functions* that it must perform, assessing what is possible in a given location, and clarifying what clients want.
- Therapists continually *ask probing questions and listen* for what clients really mean.
- Coaches work with athletes to *constantly review* the athletes' *performance* and monitor their skill and attitude.
- Administrators work with staff and ask questions in multiple ways to *check on facts, test procedures, maintain systems,* and ensure that personnel concerns are dealt with.

Looking at this more closely, it can be seen that each of these professionals is making ongoing observations and continually asking questions to gain more information and make sense of things. In fact, some of the time they are guiding their clients and patients to make the observations and ask their own questions, because it is the clients who need to understand and use their executive functions.

For instance, two of us have recently been working with an architect to design a learning center. It has been a collaborative process as the architect asks what we want, we ask him to explain what he has proposed. He shows us his ideas, we point out what we need (say, to make sure that everyone can see a screen), and so on. For the purposes of teaching, this is what process looks like. It requires the use of observations and questions to help make sense of experience.

The aforementioned questions that professionals use can provide teachers with directions for processing. Teachers then use processing to consolidate technical/scholastic knowledge. They can:

- teach students to ask critical questions,
- help students observe and diagnose their own work and the work of experts,
- assist students in relating the form of what they are generating (creative writing or scientific research) to the functions their work is meant to address,
- encourage students to assess what is possible by asking probing questions and listening,
- encourage students to check on facts and details and to test their beliefs and conclusions,
- help students review their performance and monitor and assess their skills and attitude.

Self-Regulation

There is more. We have shown that, in addition to developing general skills and understanding, the key to optimizing the use of the brain is the development of the executive functions. This involves an increase in students' abilities to monitor their own actions and impulses and to regulate themselves (see, for example, Perry, 1998). In addition to learning all kinds of things, students are constantly learning how to learn. Much of the time, this is known as metacognition or thinking about the way one thinks. Active processing is an indispensable key to metacognition and improved self-regulation. In essence, students are presented with repeated opportunities to observe themselves in action, to gain insight into their own strengths and weaknesses, and to develop ways to improve. This is critical to their own maturation and to the enhancement of their own sense of competence and confidence.

Reflection may reveal a need to slow down and be less impulsive; it may lead to a realization that they need to develop more strategies for solving problems or dealing with difficult material; it may reveal a need to master new ways to interact with other people. The list of strategies and procedures for this sort of self-development are all part of another aspect of active processing, one that helps students realize that they are continually growing and becoming more mature and competent.

ACTIVE PROCESSING AND THE INSTRUCTIONAL APPROACHES

As we have said, there are three basic elements in brain/mind learning: creating the optimal climate and state of mind in the learner that we call relaxed alertness; immersing the learner in complex experience in which the curriculum and standards are embedded; and the active processing of that experience so that the learner does actually learn. Each of the instructional approaches deals with the elements slightly differently.

The essential difference lies in how instruction (or immersion) and processing are blended.

> The more control and emphasis on linear and sequential instruction, the less opportunity there is for adequate active processing.

Instructional Approach 1

In Instructional Approach 1 the teacher develops and presents information, and then the student works at memorizing it. Instructional Approach 1 relies heavily on practice and rehearsal. Limited opportunities are sometimes supplied for thinking and analysis, but not at the level that is needed for in-depth understanding or actor-centered decision making. Without student processing, the teacher has very little idea what a student has heard or understands. Unless they exchange information or engage in open-ended questioning, students can walk away believing that they understand, when in fact they don't.

Instructional Approach 2

Because Instructional Approach 2 is a more complex approach to teaching and involves experiences, group participation, and some student independence and creativity, the opportunities for active processing are much more extensive. Teachers find many occasions to use well-formulated and directed questions throughout the teaching cycle, and there are multiple occasions to engage the students in some genuine interactions leading to analysis and reflection. However, as the approach is still controlled by the teacher and tends to be moderately structured, much of the time it will seem as though instruction and processing are separate but connected activities.

Instructional Approach 3

For Instructional Approach 3, the three elements—relaxed alertness, immersion, and active processing—do not occur one after the other. It is much better to think of them as a triple helix, or as a braid that is created by intertwining three separate strands of hair. For example, very early in a course a teacher could use questions to find out what interests a student. Active processing helps the teacher help a student relax and reveal his or her own actor-centered questions.

> Because a student's interests and motivation play such a large role, and because the teacher still needs to ensure that the standards are covered, there will be many spur-of-the-moment issues to address and questions of different types to ask. Active processing becomes an aspect of immersion.

In addition, of course, there can be reflections and discussions during a project and once it has been completed. Active processing is also involved at the end of a course to help a student consolidate ideas and information.

Setting the Stage

It is essential to see processing in action. For that reason, we use at least one common topic throughout this section of the book that we have introduced in a variety of guises previously: the U.S. Constitution. This subject matter is covered in different but overlapping ways at several different grade levels and, for some people, in college. We will take much of the basic factual information for granted, though some facts will be added as needed.

THE TRANSFORMATIONAL ADMINISTRATOR AND THE PROCESS FOR MAKING IT REAL

One of the most useful ways for staff to engage in professional development is to process their day-to-day experiences. We are not talking about the sort of discussion that involves complaints and stories. Rather, the key to becoming more professional is to learn to observe and listen to what is actually happening in a classroom and in one's own mind. The work is the experience. Process the experience, and the work becomes easier and more enjoyable.

The learning circles are designed so some time can be spent in every meeting for the purpose of genuine processing. Just as in a classroom, the place to begin is with respectful listening and a safe environment. The reason is that when people process they reveal what they really think and reflect on how to deal positively with what appear to be problems and mistakes.

We suggest using the practices and strategies introduced in the next four chapters, modifying them as needed. Sometimes it will be a matter of asking ourselves and each other probing questions; sometimes it will be a matter of working alone or with colleagues to observe what actually transpires in a classroom; sometimes other processes will suit.

You, along with your staff, need to take your time and not rush any of this.

- Allow your teachers (and yourself) time to process all that is going on.
- Work through these complex issues as a living system, intent on supporting each other through the wonderfully coordinated materials we have provided for you.
- Rushing ahead into territory unknown, without time to process, will not allow for understanding to develop.
- Model active processing and make it part of the regular rhythms active in your school/district.

In tandem with the National Teaching Standards

Accomplished teachers realize that the most powerful learning comes from questions generated by students themselves. They structure their classrooms so that students actively pose questions and seek to answer these questions. Teachers work to help students to acquire the mental operations, habits of mind, and attitudes that characterize the process of inquiry.

—Standard II: Knowledge of Subject Matter

A central theme of the National Teaching Standards is the use and pursuit of questions that start students thinking and reflecting. Active processing is specifically designed to make that happen.

Engage their individual style and uniqueness

Engage the physiology in learning

Reduce threat and enhance self-efficacy

Engage social interactions

Acknowledge and engage developmental steps and shifts

Engage their innate search for meaning

Engage their capacity to learn from memorizing isolated facts <u>and</u> biographical events

Engage their capacity to recognize and master essential patterns

If we want to create enriched environments that help students learn, then we need to include all of the following:

Engage emotional connections

Engage both conscious and unconscious processing

Engage both their ability to focus attention and learn from the peripheral context

Engage their ability to perceive both details and the larger view

13

How to Capitalize on Different Aspects of Memory

Brain/Mind Learning Principle 9: *There are at least two approaches to memory. One is to store or archive isolated facts, skills, and procedures. The other is to simultaneously engage multiple systems in order to make sense of experience.*

 At the Core

Memory is what makes any type of performance possible, so memory is indispensable for survival and success. However, there is a great deal of confusion about how memory works, and this confusion is one of the reasons why the goals of education are often conflicted. The key distinction that educators need to make and understand is between rote memorization, which is the hallmark of traditional approaches to teaching, and the dynamic memory that is engaged in everyday experience. Sometimes facts and procedures do need to be memorized, but rote learning engages the executive functions in only minimal ways. In dynamic memory, the executive functions are more likely to be engaged naturally as people sift through what they have stored in order to make decisions in new contexts.

Capacity: All students can learn more effectively when taught through experiences that engage multiple ways to remember.

HOW DO WE KNOW THIS?

Memory has fascinated thinkers for thousands of years. In recent times, cognitive psychologists and neuroscientists have attempted to identify and list different types of memory and different memory systems (e.g., Squire & Kandel, 1999). For example, they have distinguished between the following:

Declarative memory—memory for facts

Procedural memory—memory for skill and procedures

Episodic memory—memory of events in one's life

Semantic memory—memory for the meanings of words

Emotional memory—memory involving emotions

There are many other ways of talking about memory as well, including the distinctions that tend to be made between short-term memory, working memory, and long-term memory. We have focused on working memory, for instance, as being a central aspect of the executive functions.

The problem is that this list of memory systems just does not help educators very well, primarily because all the memory systems interconnect when educators are teaching for meaning. In fact, researchers are continually adding to the types of memory systems. For example, one current distinction researchers are exploring is between explicit and implicit memory. Explicit memory is what people can consciously recall and store intentionally. Implicit memory is what people just pick up indirectly as a consequence of being in a situation or environment. Implicit memories are rarely consciously recalled.

We believe that the notion of implicit memory is valuable for educators. Our way of dealing with it is spelled out in Chapter 14.

MEMORY AND DECISION MAKING

Essentially, educators need to distinguish between memory as an archive (memory that is consciously stored and recalled) and memory that is generated in context in the moment of acting and making decisions. Active processing can then be used to enhance both types of memory.

Memory as an Archive: Memory Stored and Recalled as Veridical Knowledge

When people think of memory, they think of memorizing vocabulary words, facts, skills, and specific procedures. We know all of these to be critically important to any practice or profession. The essential point is that every subject and every discipline has a body of information and procedures that need to be stored—or archived—so that they can be retrieved when necessary.

It is difficult to imagine a doctor without specialized vocabulary that allows for describing specific diseases or for prescribing medicine. It is equally difficult to imagine a neuroscientist who has not committed to memory a very large amount of information about specific regions and functions of the brain. Lawyers, engineers, teachers, writers, and mechanics all need to memorize specific vocabulary and procedures that allow them to practice.

Education acknowledges the critical role that memorization plays in learning, and most Instructional Approach 1 teaching focuses on mastering the essentials for multiple disciplines using teacher-directed practice and rehearsal. Yet this is far from the whole picture, because so much of what is memorized in this way is static—it tends to be fixed and relatively unchanging.

> Almost all standardized tests are concerned with the retrieval of "stuff" that has been archived in this way. In effect, memorization alone supports veridical decision making because people remember just specific skills and "what the facts are."

Memory in the Moment of Acting: Memory for Active Decision Making

In the real world, memorized facts and procedures are integrated from moment to moment as people solve actual problems and make decisions about how to act. Almost invisible, but absolutely critical, are the essential patterns we have discussed so far that require executive functions.

> Recall neuroscientist Elkohnon Goldberg's (2001) distinction between veridical knowledge and adaptive decision making. Just as a heart specialist would not get very far without knowing what a pulmonary valve is, that same doctor would not go very far without knowing how to make a decision about a particular patient—a decision that includes analyzing all kinds of information and data unique to this particular individual. A professional unable to synthesize or analyze complex information in order to make critical decisions is a professional who is lacking critical abilities that are often more essential than mastering vocabulary and basic procedures. So the essential point is that critical information and procedures must be easily accessed and used "in the moment."

Teacher training provides an example close to the heart of every teacher. A great deal of instruction focuses on memorizing facts and theory prior to entering the classroom (veridical). Often such preparation becomes irrelevant when teachers can't translate what they memorized for tests into genuine responses to spontaneous and unplanned dilemmas that arise in the classroom (adaptive). The real problem with taking classes and passing tests that are independent of actual lived experience is that things memorized become veridical knowledge.

Veridical knowledge, including memorized information or procedures, is sometimes referred to as static knowledge. It is not easily translated to dynamic situations where many unpredictable factors come together and call for appropriate action. This ability to integrate veridical or static knowledge in order to adapt to a new context is sometimes referred to as transfer of learning (Haskel, 2000). Transfer of learning is essential to adaptive decision making.

> In effect, memory called upon in the moment of acting is at the core of adaptive decision making because the facts are continuously being assessed and used in context.

PROCESSING THIS PRINCIPLE

Let's take a moment to explore memory personally. Think back to some facts and procedures that you have had to memorize or learn by rote.

- What was it?
- How did you learn?
- How much time did it take?
- How long have the memories lasted?
- To what extent can they be retrieved (if you want) irrespective of the context in which you find yourself?

Now look at a skill that you use in everyday life, one that does improve with experience. Notice the extent to which what you do is automatic and takes place without the effort of conscious thought. A good place to look is at language—ranging from everyday conversations to writing letters and reports.

- Have you improved with experience?
- Do you make use of information, ideas, and procedures without consciously thinking about them?
- What sort of moment-to-moment decisions do you make in the exercise of this skill (e.g., whether or not to talk to someone, what sort of language to use, and what issues to discuss)?

You will find that, even in the mastery of complex skills, some information and procedures will be called on that were once acquired by rote learning and memorization. But most of what you do with what you learned, and even the way in which you use what was once memorized, is a result of action and practice in real-world situations.

TAKING IT INTO THE CLASSROOM

Storing veridical knowledge is important, and is more directly emphasized in Instructional Approach 1 than Instructional Approaches 2 and 3. Almost all direct instruction is based on the fact that students will need to memorize what has been presented. Where memorization, practice, and rehearsal are important, we suggest that you make some of them creative by using games, puzzles, and other enjoyable activities. This follows in the path of a 2,000-year-old tradition of working with mnemonics to assist memory. These strategies will be even more helpful for Instructional Approach 2 and 3 teaching.

Example

One of the authors once needed to memorize the kings and queens of England. The first king of England after the conquest by the Normans (from France) in 1066 was William the First. He was followed by William the Second, Henry the First (also known as Harry), Stephen, Henry the Second, Richard, John, Henry the Third, Edward the First (also known as Ned), Edward the Second, and so on. He came across the following doggerel, which he remembers to this day.

Willy, Willy, Harry, Steve,
Harry, Dick, John, Harry Three.
One, Two Three Neds, Richard Two,
Henry Four, Five, Six, then who?

Here, then, are some ideas. Keep every one of them simple to begin with, and keep the classroom mood and atmosphere positive. Learning this way is geared primarily to memorization but allows for students to be creative. These ideas also invite novelty and humor—all of which enhance memory. It is very easy to gradually increase the degree of difficulty as the teacher and students acquire more experience. As an example, when teaching about the U.S. Constitution using Instructional Approach 1, an enormous amount of basic information, ranging from names and dates to aspects of the various documents themselves, can be memorized in the following ways.

1. Games Based on Quiz Shows. *Jeopardy, Wheel of Fortune,* and other games provide excellent formats for memorization. In the initial stages the teacher can create the games, using course material as the basis for questions. We have found that, with a little practice, students love to set the questions for each other.

2. Songs and Stories. Have the students make up songs or poems like the one we used as an illustration. They can also create make-believe stories in which the facts and people and events are included. Especially in the beginning, it is easier for students to do this in groups of about three.

3. Repetition in Rounds. Have students create songs made up of information to be memorized. Some songs lend themselves to being sung in rounds or with several different parts. This is fun for the students; when the parts are changed, it adds variety.

4. Puzzles. Puzzles are good because they can be a first step in encouraging students to think about relationships. One example is to use course material to create a mystery with clues. Another, where you have some visual information or pictures, is to create a jigsaw puzzle. An advance on this is to have teams of students create puzzles for each other.

5. Exaggeration, Imitation, Modeling. Students often like to act things out if the pressure is not too great. An easy introduction is for students to start imagining what some figure from science or history might have looked and sounded like, and then to pretend to be that person— exaggerating gestures and movements and language. Another way to begin is to have students pretend that they are at a conference. Invite them to talk about a subject, but to begin with all they have to do is use the words and not really make any sense! They can pretend to be experts, and can crack as many jokes with the vocabulary as they like. The reason for doing this is because one of the biggest hurdles to helping students get a feel for a subject is getting them to use the vocabulary, and this is a surprisingly effective first step.

6. Visualization. Great athletes and actors often visualize a performance ahead of time. You can see this just before skiers begin a slalom run, and almost all professional golfers tell us that they visualize what a shot will look like before they hit the ball. Students can do the same thing. A teacher can, for instance, read about an event in history or a chemical process and invite students to do their best to vividly imagine what is going on. Rehearsals have been used for imaging a best performance. Students can imagine what their best performances would look like and actually edit their performances in their visualizations.

THE FIRST FOUNDATIONAL SKILL FOR ACTIVE PROCESSING: THE EFFECTIVE USE OF QUESTIONS

Much of our emphasis in Instructional Approaches 2 and 3 has been on the need to immerse students in orchestrated experiences that are deeply engaging. Walking hand in glove with this philosophy is the need to mine those experiences in such a way that students learn enough from them. One process, discussed in the next chapter, is to help students improve their powers and skills of observation. Another is to ask useful and effective questions.

We know of a wonderful high school biology teacher near Pittsburgh, Pennsylvania, who had an inherent understanding of the need to process with students before, during, and after their immersion experiences.

A nearby stream was available as a major focal point for his curriculum. The textbook became a resource, not a recipe. The stream was the provider of opportunities, guided by the interests of the students. As his students researched the aquatic environments and their connectedness to the grander environment and society, he engaged in "free-flow" processing. When they had questions, he would help them be more precise. When they made an observation, he would sometimes ask for more detail, or for what a student thought the implications might be. When students compiled their reports, he would ask questions about their evidence and the logical inferences that led to their conclusions. He would challenge them to double-check spelling. He knew that the best time to get the students to think deeply about what was happening in and around those "objectives" is when they were there, in the field. They were engaged. *And* they were thinking. *And* his students won repeated victories at state-level competitions in science.

> Well-used questioning is a superb way to help students observe and come to understand the ideas and skills that they are learning, while simultaneously absorbing and retaining a great deal of information.

There are many ways to frame questions, and the skill develops with experience. Here are some approaches that we have found to be very effective.

An Introductory Step

For those fairly new to the use of questions, the following four questions provide a very useful foundation. They work when students are engaged in a project that had some student choice involved. While the students are working on the project (alone or in teams), the teacher asks:

What do you want (or need) me to see?

Don't ask the question in a hostile way to keep discipline but in an authentically inquiring way to help students accurately describe their project in their own words. This is a very good way to help them begin to look more clearly at details.

Why did you select to do this, particularly? What is your goal?

Be cautious of the answer, "Because the teacher says I have to do it." Sometimes it is quite true, but sometimes it is an excuse for not thinking. This question can help a student begin to see the reason for the project or activity, and that is a major step in making sense of it.

Can you explain it?

This question is often a big transition. Now students are being called upon in real time to speak about and recall and elucidate on central ideas and concepts.

What would happen if . . . ? Or what would have happened if . . . ?

This question is the leaping-off point for introducing new possibilities and ideas. It forces students to spell out their thinking and conclusions and go beyond obvious answers. This prepares the path to deeper thinking.

Imagine, for instance, that you are teaching about the Constitution and the Bill of Rights, and a student expresses an interest in slavery and in Jefferson's ownership of slaves. The teacher's questions could vary from the very large: "Can you explain why the Bill of Rights applies here?" to the more specific, "Can you explain how the Constitution dealt with slavery?" You could use hypothetical what-ifs to get the students thinking. For example, you might ask, "What do you think would have happened if Jefferson had given up owning slaves?"

Notice that students are no longer simply recalling essential facts and skills in isolation. If the immersion was successful, students will be embedding essential vocabulary and concepts in their answers to you. Also note that all these questions are marvelous ways to assess students' knowledge and understanding at the same time you are helping them to recall and express or demonstrate their own learning. The format should not be standardized (except, perhaps, for the first few times while you are trying it out).

If you allow yourself to be flexible and to ask the questions in any order, you will find that as the student talks, the next appropriate question begins to occur to you. In this way, you can engage in a fairly natural conversation with the student, which will help everyone to relax, allowing you to teach.

Questions to Make First Connections

These questions can be asked at different times. They can be used shortly after the global experience, and they can be used while students are carrying out their research. They can also be used with the class as a whole, with individuals, or with individual groups. Suggested questions include the following:

- How does this relate to what we did last week?
- Can you remember where we encountered this before?
- Is that an example of what we called an inclusive concept?
- What other works of literature do you recall that dealt with a similar theme?
- Can you help us say this in a different way?

Questions That Expand Understanding by Using Analogies and Metaphors

Every subject and skill is full of metaphors.

Many concepts from basic physics are used to make sense of other subjects. You might like to take a day to observe how often, and in how many different contexts, people use the terms "force," "momentum," "inertia," "lever" (as in "leverage"), "orbit," "field effect," and "particle."

Here is something to do alone or with a colleague: Take some time to spot metaphors and analogies in any subject that you teach. Make a list of them, and then select at least three that you regard as most important. When you ask students questions to help them understand what you are teaching, use these analogies and metaphors. The core question to ask is:

In what way is this (idea . . .) like (the analogy or metaphor . . .)?
For example:

- In what way is a civil war like a family feud?
- In what way are opinions like weeds or flowers?
- In what way is the brain like or not like a computer?
- In what way is the political process like a game or a game show?

Note: Many people have developed the use of metaphors to a fine art. Those who are interested in taking the process farther might like to explore the ideas and techniques called *synectics* (Gordon, 1968).

From a Teacher's Journal

We had written poetry about trees, gathered our knowledge into books about trees, moved as trees do, identified leaves and their parts with a microscope, observed branches and bark, made a question board on trees from recorded details, and created art projects, all to explain the whats and wherefores of trees. I was beginning to be "treed out" when one of my fourth-grade students, who rarely spoke, came up and said, "I've been thinking about how our classroom is like a tree. The roots are all the things that make up the space we are in, it is where our learning is nourished. The trunk is the form we take as a group as we learn and grow. As we change, our cambium layer puts out another ring. Our branches and leaves are all the ways we do things together (projects, class meetings, etc.) and the seeds are our new ideas. Yeah, I think we are like a tree." I loved his insights, and the fact that he had gone way beyond the textbook and topic into metaphorical thinking.

Ask Questions That Help Students See the Story

The objective is to dive deeper into the facts in a way that helps tie them together naturally. In Chapter 9 we described stories as being natural wholes. Here is a way to use questions to help bring information together in a story format.

- What is the real story here?
- What happened?
- Who/what was involved?
- Describe the physical setting.
- When did it all happen?
- Identify critical moments and events.
- What else do you think might happen?
- Who/what else might be involved?
- What is the message or moral?

Imagine using these questions in discussing the discovery of radio-activity or the double helix, the signing of the Declaration of Independence, the invention (by two people simultaneously: Newton and Leibniz) of calculus, the birth and demise of rock and roll, and so on. Most of these questions tend to be useful for acquiring concrete knowledge and are simple and straightforward for some Instructional Approach 1 teachers as well as for teachers using Instructional Approaches 2 and 3.

The Socratic Method

When high standards are important, it is sometimes essential to ask hard questions that force students into really deep thinking about their opinions and concepts. The Socratic method is used by most great law schools and business schools. The teacher has the student read law cases or business scenarios and then begins to ask questions that call for more and more insight. Is there an end? No. There is always more, which is why the use of such questioning is an art.

If one were teaching about the Constitution, the process, which includes questions and actions, might look something like this:

- What is meant by the separation of powers (referring to the legislative, executive, and judicial branches of government)?
- How are the branches of government really separate? The probing then could deal with what is meant by "separate."
- What does it mean to legislate and how do courts make law?
- Discuss cases such as *Marbury v. Madison* (1803) in which the U.S. Supreme Court gave itself final power to interpret the Constitution. Was this a legislative act? If not, what sort of act was it?

> The key to this art lies in noting a core concept used by a student and then "unpacking" it by examining each of the defining characteristics, looking for generalizations and unstated assumptions.

Be aware of the fact that this approach to teaching can be intimidating. It is important to have an excellent classroom climate (relaxed alertness) and for a teacher to know and accept that sometimes he or she can be wrong.

Student Questions

The ideal is for students to begin using questions naturally and to take over much of the questioning. They should learn how to question each other—AND their teacher. One way to get student questioning started is in the context of the final reports and exhibitions that tend to bring a topic to an end.

From a Teacher's Journal

For the assessment portion on the Constitution, students wanted to share their understanding in their own unique way. The room was full of activities as, day after day, research, productions, and general teenage enthusiasm filled the air. I kept conferencing with each group, asking questions, reviewing standards, and providing resources as we were in process. Many students were working on their own time at home, some were coming in during their lunch time or before and after school. The big day arrived with groups volunteering to present. One group had the class divided into thirds, each representing a perspective on why we should adopt the Constitution. One third for, one third against, and one third to decide which position to accept (a real-life debate). The room was draped with student-made banners from American flag collages to the Seal of the United States. Desks were moved as needed so that the class could be fully engaged. A musical selection was played to back up the group members as they presented an essay, poetry, lists, and so on. These represented what was important about the Constitution from each member's own perspective. Another group had an overhead projector presentation with music while others made a personal video, including interviews of local citizens on their perspective of what made the Constitution important. The whole class applauded and critiqued each group. The air was full of STUDENT questions such as, "Why did you do that? Who said that? What happened when . . . ? How could you say that if . . . ?" You could feel the individual pride in what each one had contributed. Their depth of understanding of the concept of a government built on the Constitution was palpable. I had not forced their learning, but the overall support and guided questioning had energized them marvelously. The students had taken charge of the learning and their depth of understanding was remarkable.

Reflection: Something to Think About

In what situations (in any field of life) has the questioning of a mentor or colleague helped improve your understanding of and memory for some idea or process? When has your questioning helped someone else?

THE TRANSFORMATIONAL ADMINISTRATOR AND THE PROCESS FOR MAKING IT REAL

We invite you and the staff to begin to explore the nature of memory in some depth along the lines developed in this chapter.

One of the most powerful levers to help people make a shift in teaching is their grasp of the fact that memory is actually strengthened by insight, and that when concepts are understood in depth, it is much easier for students to remember relevant facts.

One way to work at this level is for participants in the learning circles to start reflecting on what they remember easily and what presents them with problems. They would need to get beyond the obvious (faces, names, food) and start really examining how their memories of and for their specialties developed.

A second step is to begin practicing the art of asking questions. To some extent this has already begun with effective listening. However, being able to formulate questions really well and being able to go in depth from answer to answer is a skill that requires practice. In addition, the staff might find it useful to work with each other on the feeling tone they use and the manner in which they ask questions. The objective is to develop a high-powered skill without threatening the person being questioned. In our experience, the use of questions also becomes invaluable in helping members of staff to clarify issues, work with the community, and generally improve communication in a school or district.

In tandem with the National Teaching Standards

As teachers listen to, interpret, and assess student responses, they give students opportunities to frame the work of the class or shape independent studies in which they explore their own questions and interests and focus attention on defining their purpose and audience.

—Standard V: Meaningful Learning

Teachers' knowledge of their students, subject matter, and resources helps them choose compelling topics and materials that make the best use of their own time and that of their students.

The ability to vary their approach to major topics, themes, and skills allows teachers to slow or accelerate the pace of instruction or to change the focus of discussion in response to student performance.

—Standard VII: Multiple Paths to Knowledge

One task of teachers is to "change the focus of discussion" in response to student performance. The development of questioning skills such as we introduce in this chapter is invaluable for this purpose.

Engage their individual style and uniqueness

Engage the physiology in learning

Reduce threat and enhance self-efficacy

Engage social interactions

Acknowledge and engage developmental steps and shifts

Engage their innate search for meaning

If we want to create enriched environments that help students learn, then we need to include all of the following:

Engage their capacity to learn from memorizing isolated facts and biographical events

Engage their capacity to recognize and master essential patterns

Engage both conscious and unconscious processing

Engage emotional connections

Engage both their ability to focus attention and learn from the peripheral context

Engage their ability to perceive both details and the larger view

14

Powerful Learning Requires the Integration of Attention and Context

Brain/Mind Learning Principle 7: *Learning involves both focused attention and peripheral perception.*

 At the Core

It is well known that before human beings can learn or make effective decisions, they must pay attention. Attention is a natural phenomenon guided by interest, novelty, emotion, and meaning. Attention is critical to memory. What is less understood is the fact that human beings also learn from a context they rarely consciously attend to. This is how the nuances of our cultures are taught and how children "pick up"

(Continued)

behaviors, beliefs, and preferences or dislikes without ever having paid direct attention to how they were learning these (Schacter, 1996). Educators need to engage students in situations that call for the exercise of the executive functions, thus invoking and engaging students' natural and inborn need to attend and make decisions. Educators also need to understand how the context teaches and how to use that context to support the more explicit learning required of all students.

Capacity: All students can learn more effectively when their attention is deepened and multiple layers of the context are used to support learning.

HOW DO WE KNOW THIS?

The place to begin is to note that attention is critical to survival. This is true for those who are finding their way through a jungle, for those who are wandering through a new city, and for those who find themselves in a classroom.

The core idea is that the brain/mind is immersed all the time in a field of sensations, images, and input and continuously selects what to attend to and what to ignore. Attention itself is natural and tends to be driven by what is of most interest or relevant to the satisfaction of wants and needs. Here are some of the basics:

Novelty

The brain/mind is designed to immediately respond to novelty, a job in part for the reticular activating system (RAS) of the brain, which monitors incoming data. There is inevitably tension, therefore, between what a person is already attending to and other things that are calling for attention. The more novel, new, or different in some way incoming information is, the more likely students will attend. Attention is influenced, for instance, by a new person entering the classroom (student, teacher, aide, guest). Boredom, the other side of novelty, tends to get students to create novelty for themselves or among themselves, something most traditional teachers would identify as discipline problems.

Emotion

Attention is both hooked and sustained by emotion (Sylwester, 2002). As people walk through a mall, for instance, what they tend to focus on depends on how much they like shopping, who else is there, how important this shopping expedition is, and so on. The same set of factors applies in any classroom and in any project in any subject. Whether a subject is liked or disliked, the imminence of a test one is prepared for, excitement over a project, listening to background music while having time to muse or reflect, or preparing for an award or meeting a celebrity, all include emotional reactions that heighten attention.

People tend to pay more attention to things about which they feel strongly. This is true of scientists and artists and professionals who are consumed by a problem to solve or an issue to understand. This is evident in the passions that are ignited by political and religious discussions. Remember, however, that merely paying attention does not automatically lead to learning something new.

As individuals navigate through their world, several additional factors coalesce in the focusing of attention, many of which have already been introduced through the Brain/Mind Learning Principles.

Meaning

Because the search for meaning is innate, individuals are more likely to attend to what is personally meaningful, and the more meaningful, the greater their engagement. People who are relationship oriented might put more effort into being on good terms with those with whom they are working than on the task itself. Purpose and meaning guide what people pay attention to. That is why many educators want the curriculum to be relevant to the student and why actor-centered adaptive decision making is so important to motivation and learning.

Patterning

Walking though a strange city is more disorienting for some people than walking in one's own neighborhood because they prefer familiar patterns around them. But for others, the need for excitement and novel or new experiences is critical. These people learn best by traveling to distant cultures where they can have access to totally new information, acquire a new language, and master the nuances of an entirely different world. The same phenomenon plays out as students move to a new school, meet a new teacher, and come face to face with a new and strange subject.

> Because individuals perceive the world differently, the patterns they search for or events that will excite them cannot always be predicted.

Helplessness

We have shown that complex learning is inhibited by threat associated with helplessness and/or fatigue. Thus, when people feel helpless they pay more attention to the thing that threatens them, which means they lose the ability to see other cues in their environment that might be very important. Psychologists call this the narrowing of the perceptual field (Combs, 1999; Sapolsky, 1998). People literally cannot see what is in front of them or hear what is being said.

Note that controlling attention is a key feature of the executive functions. As students mature, and as learning becomes more actor-centered, students become responsible for deciding what to notice, choosing how much effort to put into a problem or issue and how long to persist, evaluating what is important and not important, and generally using attention as the foundation for making effective decisions.

Peripheral Perception

The peripheral environment, that part of the context to which people are not paying direct attention, nevertheless has an influence.

Some evidence of the impact of what is not quite seen comes in the form of implicit memory (Schacter, 1996). Let us say that you are in a room full of items. After you leave the room, someone asks you to recall as many items from the room as possible. You might recall only one or two, yet research shows that if experimenters give you the option to identify different items from a list, you are likely to choose those that were actually in the room, even if you don't remember seeing them!

Commercials work in this way. Even if you see something only once or out of the corner of your eye, and argue vehemently that you did not see the name of the product, given a number of choices in a store you are likely to select or prefer the product you claim not to have seen. That is why advertisers position their advertisements in the context of programs that stimulate identifiable desires and fears in selected audiences.

Diane Halpern (1989) tells of a conversation she once had with a cab driver. She and the driver had been discussing the way in which laundry products are advertised on television. The cab driver insisted that he never paid any attention to such advertising and that he always just got the blue bottle that got out the "ring around the collar." Halpern goes on to say,

"Although he believed that he was not allowing the advertising claims to influence him, in fact, they were directly determining his buying habits" (p. 132).

All of this has immense importance for education because it means that children in school are actually being profoundly influenced by the total environment. "What are the colors saying to them?" "What messages are being conveyed by buildings designed like factories and prisons?" "How do they respond to bells?" and "What about the presence of police with guns and metal detectors?" The important message here is that the context teaches. Students learn a great deal from each other, from how the adults interact, and from what those adults value.

What is the impact of the content and emotional color of the actual conversations to which students are exposed? It is clear, for example, that body language and facial displays that signal respect or contempt, patience or impatience, confidence or insecurity all have an impact on the learner. That is why the design of the peripheral environment, and the state of mind and behavior of teachers and staff in a school, all impact how and what students ultimately learn to value and adopt.

Integrating Attention and Context

One issue we are addressing here is the need to use and orchestrate the context in which learning takes place so it guides the learner's attention and supports the learning and teaching. At the same time, the teacher is always seeking to engage and sustain the attention of learners and to help learners use attention effectively.

PROCESSING THIS PRINCIPLE

We invite you to take a moment to examine some aspects of the way your attention works and to explore some ways in which your peripheral environment influences you.

Perceiving Sensory Input

Find a scene or bring to mind a scene, such as sitting in a favorite restaurant or sailing on a lake. It is worth your time to actually observe or recall some event or scenario.

- Notice the direct sensory input—the colors, the lighting, the motion, the rustle of wind and/or the roar of traffic, and so on. Notice how your other senses are responding.
- Now notice how the things you are observing are the context that tells you where you are. Notice how unique this context is as well as how it adds to your pleasure and experience.

The first goal of this activity is for you to become more aware of the sensory foundation of all the input you experience. The second goal is to confirm that everyone automatically organizes this sensory input into familiar patterns that have been acquired over time.

One of the primary reasons why what people teach may not make sense, and why students may not pay attention, is that educators often provide words and symbols—dry language—without engaging the sensory modalities that accompany whatever is to be learned.

Selecting and Sustaining Attention

In order to explore the ways in which people select what to attend to and how much attention they give to it, we invite you to keep a notebook with you for, say, a few hours of a working day. As often as you can remember to, note the events and incidents that attract your notice. Do your best to grasp what actually gained your attention—and what actually led you to continue to attend or to shift focus to something else. Ask yourself questions such as these:

- *What did I really care about?*
- *How much energy did I invest in attending?*
- *What else was going on in my mind at the time?*
- *What did it take for my attention to be diverted?*
- *How important was novelty?*
- *To what extent was my capacity to pay attention influenced by stress, excitement, health, or fatigue?*

You might also reflect on the ways in which you constantly scanned the environment for what was going on:

- *Was there anything that you were on the lookout for?*
- *Was there much going on that you simply ignored?*
- *How might this relate to your teaching? To your students?*

Reflect upon this last question. Perhaps discuss it with others. You will see that the dance between context and attention is a dynamic one. The two are intimately related, and students are definitely caught in that dance with you.

TAKING IT INTO THE CLASSROOM

As with every other facet of the Brain/Mind Learning Principles, how attention is engaged and harnessed and its interaction with and support from the peripheral environment depend on the instructional approach at work. Let us look at how the instructional approaches both engage attention and utilize the learning environment. It is only through Instructional Approach 3 that the two are fully integrated.

Engaging Attention

Instructional Approach 1 tends to rely on control in order to make students pay attention.

Classroom management techniques are used to ensure that students face the teacher or the blackboard at the front of the room. When attention is needed the teacher simply urges students to "Pay attention!"

Instructional Approach 2 involves the use of activities that trigger a student's sense of novelty or fun.

Humor and brief multimedia presentations are often used. In addition, the teacher may introduce novelty by asking questions such as, "Look carefully and you will see something strange. What is it?" Such teaching can also tie content to students' personal backgrounds and invite comments or discussion.

Some teachers also harness attention through the use of novelty or excitement. They sometimes do this by creating a sudden, unexpected event in a classroom (perhaps by coming into the room dressed up as George Washington or an alien, or by creating a unique experiment to demonstrate some principle of physics).

From a Teacher's Journal

We were just starting classes (seventh grade) at our new site. One morning I was beginning a lesson on medieval history. Out from behind the sliding white board a four-foot gopher snake appeared. After placing the students out of danger, I opened the back door to the room and requested the snake leave, which it promptly did. Instead of returning directly to the history lesson, we discussed what happened. The students jointly asked questions: "Why was the snake there?" "What had happened to its environment?" "What might it have been looking for?" and "How had our building the new school affected the area the snake called home?" We then used art from the medieval period to get a sense of how the people of that time felt about their environment. The snake became a segue into our original topic. Later we used the experience in our writing projects. We wove the snake into our class and thus the incident that would have been much on the minds and attention of the students was not a lost opportunity, but an opportunity to harness the excitement the students felt and to focus attention on the topic.

Instructional Approach 3 uses questions and processes that stir up genuine student interest "in the moment." In other words, the more that teachers recognize and use global experiences, the easier it is to introduce questions—a key aspect of active processing—very early. That is why the global experiences introduced in Chapter 8 are intended to be partially open ended so that a teacher can say something like the following:

- "What interested you?"
- "What questions do you have?"
- "What did this remind you of?"

Designing the Context

The central point is that the context can be very useful. First, because attention wanders, teachers and administrators can design the context so that the wandering eye falls on something that actually supports what is being taught. Second, because people pick up some things naturally, the environment can be designed to help them just "pick up" some of what needs to be taught.

Instructional Approach 1

Most of Instructional Approach 1 involves the use of a bulletin board of some kind and the occasional use of charts.

The primary challenge for Instructional Approach 1 teachers is to increase the use of visual supports by making them colorful and interesting (provided there is not so much that it is overwhelming and distracting).

Instructional Approach 2

Instructional Approach 2 usually involves the substantial use of charts and guides around a room, many of which are powerful and useful.

Instructional Approach 2 teachers also tend to organize their classroom peripherals to emphasize different areas that have different functions.

There are many ways to increase the power and value of these "peripherals":

- Use charts and posters that convey essential information that is visually accessible to students from different locations in the classroom. This can be enhanced by moving the posters and changing the content regularly.

- Use intriguing artifacts and post pictures and questions on the wall. In other words, bring in, and position around the room, material that can be used to generate interest and questions without necessarily providing immediate answers or information. Examples range from bones, to photographs, to new types of technology, to puzzles or sayings that have impact but no specific answer, such as, "Everything is separate and connected."

- Use great works of art to convey or suggest a general theme that is being explored. For instance, Van Gogh's *Starry Night* can be used in a course on astronomy, and any of Escher's drawings can be used to illustrate and support exploration about human perception.

The challenge is to develop a sense of design. First, it is important that students not be overwhelmed and distracted by the sheer quantity of stuff on display. Second, the material on display should interconnect. It really helps to bring to classroom displays the same aesthetic eye used to design one's own living space. It is also important to change the environment in order to create novelty and ongoing interest.

Instructional Approach 3

Instructional Approach 3 is actor centered. Students can be called on to contribute to their own learning environment and to design their own context. In addition to taking charge, part of the art of this approach lies in making occasional contexts lifelike. For example, in one upper-level Spanish class that we know, students and teacher generate a special event every Friday. The class is divided into residents and tourists (who will use vocabulary and material covered during the week and the year to date). The residents have free reign to design the classroom in any way they like so that it suggests a Spanish-speaking town with a focus on the material being covered in the course.

Some teachers, particularly in the lower grades, like to turn their classrooms into the settings that students are exploring, from regional habitats to nearby cities. A "theater set" approach can be very effective for secondary classrooms as well. When teachers and students become accustomed to designing these "environments," the design itself can become part of the teaching and assessment process. The method is simply to ask, "Why use this item?" "What does it tell us?" "Why not something else?"

and "Why put it next to Einstein's picture and not Newton's?" In fact, much of the thinking that goes into designing a set for a great movie or TV series can be applied to designing peripherals for a classroom.

THE SECOND FOUNDATIONAL SKILL FOR ACTIVE PROCESSING: CAPITALIZING ON ATTENTION THROUGH THE EFFECTIVE USE OF OBSERVATION

One of the great problems with attention is that learners may look but not see very much. Yet really seeing clearly is indispensable for really effective learning. It is all very well to get students excited and have them rush off to do research or work on a project. What matters, however, is how effective their research is and what they learn as they work on the project.

One of the most important skills of great artists and great scientists is their capacity to observe phenomena in detail and perceive the patterns that are there. In fact, more scientists who win Nobel Prizes have an arts-based hobby than those who don't (Cole, 1998).

> All too often students find the "right" words or draw interesting pictures without ever exploring the subject or idea or skill in depth.

The Art of Seeing

Here is a way to begin to teach the skill of observation. It will help improve all instructional approaches.

1. *Ask students to describe objects they see.* A first step is to help students enhance their sensory awareness so that they increase the quality and quantity of information gathering. Students can work in pairs or triads. Sometimes they can pool their observations, while at other times they may individually need to describe things.

You can begin with something very simple like a rock or a leaf. Be sure to give specific instructions or ask specific questions, such as, "What color is it?" "How big is it?" "What does it feel like?" "How heavy is it?" "What does it remind you of?" "What is unfamiliar?" and "Describe some of the smallest details."

Note: Students work at very different speeds and may end up seeing very different things. As teachers become more comfortable with the process, it is easier to deal with this sort of student diversity.

---

2. *Expand to include context.* Some items can be examined as independent entities. However, many critical features depend on the context in which an item is found or a process occurs. A good way to help students learn to see something in context is to use videos. You can select videos on

any topic ranging from enactment of an historical novel (such as *Pride and Prejudice*) to outdoors activities (such as the Animal Planet series, *The Crocodile Hunter*) to the vast number of fascinating studies of scientific matters (such as the many new series on the brain).

Again, student observations need to be guided by questions and directions. Questions include the following:

- Who is involved?
- What do they look/sound like?
- What are they wearing?
- Describe the physical environment.
- What period of history is suggested?
- What features of the environment support your view?

This process can be used in any course or subject where something concrete is involved. For instance, we have seen this process used to teach computing, theater, biology, chemistry, and social studies.

Here are some important hints to help students make observations: First, do not let them give up too soon. They may complain, and they may need help, but allow the process to continue for several minutes. Second, they may stare very hard, but the key is to help them look in a more relaxed way. Staring often interferes with seeing.

3. *Seeing concepts and hidden agendas.*

> Although you do want students to pay attention to specific details, you are also inviting them to see in new ways and to discern patterns that may not be immediately obvious. This is the point at which innovative insights and creative thinking begin to flourish.

One technique is to use some of the practices of media literacy. You might select a video or a computer clip of a documentary or one or two popular commercials. A cigarette or soft drink commercial is often used.

a. Introduce the process by sharing with the class the fact that advertisers often try to influence people without being noticed. Tell them that you will play a commercial and then everyone will work together to see what the advertisers tried to do (Healy, 1998).

b. Play the commercial for the entire class.

c. Use active processing and have students work together, either in the large group or in small groups, to describe what was happening. Use questions and instructions such as these:
   - Describe the setting.
   - Who were the main characters? (age, gender, race, other features)
   - What was the main activity?
   - What product was being sold?

d. Play the commercial again and have the students assess the accuracy of their descriptions.

e. Next, analyze the features of the commercial or video that are intended to indirectly influence the viewer. This is done with questions such as these:

- Why do you think that type of music is being used? How does it affect you?
- Why are the people the age they are and dressed in those clothes—why not something else? What impact would different outfits have on the viewer?
- What concepts and themes are being promoted? (This is the point at which you really begin to dig into the standards you are addressing, ranging from media literacy to economics to communication to any other topic that you are setting out to teach.)
- Is there any additional or hidden message in the commercial that is not immediately obvious? What might it be? What is your evidence?

Note: Many other items can be used, including news shows, documentaries, and excerpts from soap operas and movies. Adjust your questions to the material you use. With a news show you can ask questions like these:

- What types of topics were selected?
- What key concepts and ideas are being expressed?
- What points of view were being promoted? How?
- Describe the style and mannerisms of key people (e.g., expressing opinions as fact without examining evidence).
- How was the show staged (e.g., politicians who always have flags behind them when they make statements)?

4. *Gaining deeper insight into concepts and ideas.* We mentioned in Chapter 8 that some of us have used the superb documentary *Gettysburg* (Turner Pictures & Maxwell, 1993) to create a global experience for the purpose of launching the class exploration of the Civil War. The strategies introduced above make it possible to use that same documentary to take student learning to additional depths and to investigate complex aspects of the history of the constitution. Some of the questions used above are unfolded and taken to additional depths.

For instance, you might select two or three powerful themes that are played out in the documentary. One might be the issue of slavery. Another might be how the preservation of the Union was supported by the Constitution. A third might be the notion of freedom.

Again, have students work together, either in the large group or in small groups, to describe what was happening and to make sense of it. Use questions and instructions such as these:

- Describe the setting.
- Who were the main characters? (age, gender, race, rank, profession, and other features)
- What were the main activities?
- Where was the issue of (slavery, the union, freedom) addressed?
- Who was involved? What did they say? Describe the context. What impact did it have on you?

As you begin to identify the key ideas and the key players, you can ask more complex questions, all the time going back to the documentary itself.

- Were there competing points of view?
- What were they?
- Describe the settings in which those differences were expressed.
- In what ways were you affected?

At the same time as students begin to see more, they begin to get more involved, their motivation is heightened, and their self-confidence increases. This means that the power of attention is being used to enhance the state of mind of learners—to increase relaxed alertness—and that the executive functions are engaged and higher standards of learning occur naturally.

Reflection: Something to Think About

This chapter has discussed Brain/Mind Principle 7: "Learning involves both focused attention and peripheral perception." Let us look at our own teaching for a moment. Take a particular unit of study and look at it through the initial questions posed on improving attention:

- How might you engage student attention?
- How do you help students see the basic patterns more clearly?
- How do you help students see beyond the obvious?

Now look at your classroom.
- How can you use the space to immerse the students in the unit through peripherals?
- Can they help you do this?
- Can colleagues lend you materials?

THE TRANSFORMATIONAL ADMINISTRATOR AND THE PROCESS FOR MAKING IT REAL

All of the processes for developing attention in students can be of value to adults. Rather than simply exploring how to help students, participants could take some time to examine what they do and do not pay attention to and how their own attention works. This will not only assist students, it can also be invaluable in other facets of life.

Administrators can help teachers, and each other, design good classroom environments. For instance, a very excited principal was raving to one of us (Karl) about one of the classrooms in his school. "This teacher is awesome, wait until you see his room!" We walked up to the third floor, turned the corner, and crossed the threshold. "Isn't this amazing?" he asked. My brain was screaming! There was so much "stuff" on the walls, hanging from the lights, stuck to the bulletin boards, taped to the desks and windows that I couldn't even see the back of the room! It would be very difficult for the brains in that room to remain attentive to the topic of the moment.

If this exciting teacher were in your building, proudly working hard for his students, you might want to help him "settle down" his classroom. See if he might rotate the students' work so that not everything every student has done is always on display. Maybe you could revisit Brain/Mind Learning Principle 4: "The search for meaning occurs through patterning." He could "theme" the room so that related information across disciplines was displayed at the same time. Perhaps you could help him with organizing the displays so they represent quality work and aren't up just for the sake of display.

In addition, it can be very useful to pay attention to the quality and design of the general environment of the school, because the *entire* context teaches. Here are some questions to guide analysis and reflection in the learning circles:

- What is the ratio of living plants to concrete, both inside and outside the building?
- Is there any good art on display?
- Do you hear singing anywhere (other than the music room or "choir")?
- How is time organized, and how are time periods communicated?
- Is the environment joyful?
- To what extent is the language of adults in the school filled with the subject matter that is taught in classes?
- To what extent does the language and behavior of adults indicate that reflection, critical thinking, high standards, and an open mind are natural aspects of everyday life?

In tandem with the National Teaching Standards

Teachers constantly seek opportunities to expand their base of instructional resources by drawing on theory, research, technology, accomplished practice, and nontraditional sources. These resources challenge students and reveal to them the complexity and texture of the social, cultural, ethical, and physical worlds in which they live. Such efforts bring to the students' attention a broad array of resources that will make them more capable and independent learners.

—Standard III: Instructional Resources

An important point here is the way in which teachers bring to the students' attention a broad array of sources. It is easy, but relatively ineffective, to "tell" students what is available. Much more powerful is the art of using the context and the dynamics of attention so that students genuinely become aware of, attend to, and work with the world of resources that are available.

If we want to create enriched environments that help students learn, then we need to include all of the following:

- Engage their individual style and uniqueness
- Engage the physiology in learning
- Engage social interactions
- Engage their innate search for meaning
- Engage their capacity to recognize and master essential patterns
- Engage emotional connections
- Engage their ability to perceive both details and the larger view
- Engage both their ability to focus attention and learn from the peripheral context
- Engage both conscious and unconscious processing
- Engage their capacity to learn from memorizing isolated facts and biographical events
- Acknowledge and engage developmental steps and shifts
- Reduce threat and enhance self-efficacy

15

Including the Conscious and Unconscious in Learning

Brain/Mind Learning Principle 8: *Learning is both conscious and unconscious.*

 At the Core

Learning involves layers of consciousness. Some learning requires a person to consciously attend to a problem that needs to be solved or analyzed. Some learning at a deeper level requires unconscious incubation in the same way that the creative insights of artists and scientists sometimes occur after the mind has done some unconscious processing. Beyond that, really successful learners are also capable of monitoring themselves—a central feature of the executive functions—so that they know their own strengths and weaknesses and can take charge of how they learn. In order to help their students attain high standards, educators must be able to work at all three levels with students.

Capacity: All students can learn more effectively when given time to reflect and acknowledge their own learning.

HOW DO WE KNOW THIS?

Ever since the 19th century and the time of Freud it has been known that everybody is working in both conscious and unconscious ways, and that the unconscious aspects of the mind can have a very powerful impact on how one thinks, feels, reacts, and behaves (Neville, 1989).

In recent years it has become even clearer that much thinking is unconscious in the sense that it operates "beneath the level of cognitive awareness" (Lakoff & Johnson, 1999, p. 10). This means that much of the "thinking" or processing that an individual does in order to come to understanding happens without conscious awareness.

The neurosciences have taken a more physiological approach to the unconscious but have not, by any means, disputed that awareness is multilayered (LeDoux, 1996; Sapolsky, 1998; Siegel, 1999).

Others who have known this are those who research and write about creativity (see, for example, Perkins, 2001).

Creative Insight

People searching for a solution to a problem or a creative insight are advised to engage in a mixed process. On the one hand, they need to focus very clearly on the question they want answered and then work to find as much information as they possibly can. On the other hand, they are advised to relax and let go so their minds can "incubate." Very often, the solution occurs when they are *not* thinking about the problem. Incubation is just another term for unconscious processing.

One example is the story of how the sewing machine needle was discovered. Elias Howe had been thinking and thinking about how the needle could be attached to the machine, go through the fabric, turn around, and go back up through the fabric. This seemed impossible to do. One night he dreamed that he was in the jungle and pigmies were throwing spears at him. All the spears had holes in the front at the sharp edge. He woke up realizing that he had to put the hole for the thread in the tip, not the top of the needle. The sewing machine was ready!

Another example is the way Kekule discovered benzene's structure. He worked on it for ages. One night he fell asleep and dreamed about snakes intertwining. When he woke up he knew he had dreamed about something important but couldn't remember what it was. The next night he dreamed about it again and woke up remembering and understanding that the pattern he had seen was the answer to his question. (For an interesting look at the power of dreams, read *Our Dreaming Mind* by Robert Van de Castle, 1995.)

The practical implication is quite startling. If educators want their students to use more of their minds, they have to help them with both their conscious and unconscious processing. On the one hand, educators need to help students focus clearly on issues; penetrate the meaning of ideas; and gather, organize, sort, and compare facts, figures, and processes. Many of these are grounded in the effective development and use of the executive functions. On the other hand, students need help in priming their own minds so that more unconscious thinking and organizing takes place. Active processing is extremely useful because it works at both levels.

Making the Unconscious Conscious: Metacognition

An essential key to improving performance in any field, and to improving learning, is to become aware of how one functions and then to intentionally develop additional capacities. This is possible because at the heart of all learning is a very basic feedback loop.

An individual does something, gets feedback about what happened or how it worked, and that feedback provides him or her with an opportunity to make adaptations or appropriate changes. Beyond this is our capacity to observe our own performance while it is taking place, to assess what is happening, and to make changes midstream, as it were. Donald Schon (1983) calls this *reflection in action.*

The critical word here is *reflection.* Psychologist David Perkins (1995) offers another way of approaching the issue. He shows that most people can develop what he calls reflective intelligence.

Reflective intelligence is "coming to know your way around decision making, problem solving, learning with understanding, and other important kinds of thinking. . . . The stuff you get is very diverse—strategies, habits, beliefs, values and more—but it's all part of knowing your way around" (Perkins, 1995, p. 236).

People tend to know that they procrastinate or are impulsive, for instance, when they take the time to observe themselves. The key is the capacity to be conscious of one's own behavior.

In education, the notion of thinking about one's own thinking is called metacognition, and it has been studied extensively (see, for example, Perfect & Schwartz, 2002). In fact, working with metacognition is essential for enhancing the executive functions, all of which are strengthened as people become aware of their own behaviors, capacities, and predispositions.

By way of example, in a wonderful video produced by Dorothy Fadiman (1988), *Why Do These Kids Love School,* a youngster in seventh grade at a middle school is talking:

When 10:15 comes around, sometimes, and math time comes, I just get this kind of . . . a reaction of, "Oh no, it's math. I don't want to do math." But then . . . I say, "Ease up . . . There's nothing wrong with it. So, go ahead and do your math."

He has grasped the art of examining his own attitude and changing it. In so doing, he changes his performance, the quality of his experience, and the quality of his own learning.

Working Both Consciously and Unconsciously

Educators can best help their students by working with various layers of consciousness. We dealt with direct attention to the task at hand in Chapter 14. Here we will look at additional ways in which educators can help students access creativity and take charge of their own thinking, feeling, and functioning.

PROCESSING THIS PRINCIPLE

We invite you to briefly examine both sides of consciousness in your own life and learning by using the basic strategy for creative problem solving. This is a metacognitive activity: You need to take charge of and observe some of your own functioning. It requires you to let go and let your unconscious mind do much of the work. The assumption in this activity is that you already know a moderate amount about the problem in question.

Step 1: Identify a manageable problem that needs an insightful solution. Talk it through, discuss it, write it down, express it in different ways. One example might be an article that you want to write; another might be a need to design part of a building or your garden within some tight parameters.

Step 2: Gather all the information you can. Ask questions. Talk to people. Read books or articles on the subject. Watch videos. Observe related activities, places, and events.

Step 3: Elaborate playfully. Find a variety of ways to think about and experience the problem and the information. Go to the top of a tall building and think about perspective. Play with a map of the world and think about interconnectedness. Pretend to be different people and think about different points of view.

Step 4: Incubate. Leave the problem alone in your mind for a while, even though doing so can be very difficult. In fact, you are likely to experience some confusion and frustration. That is why you may need to get so involved in something else that you actually do not have the time or energy to bother about your problem. Sometimes it is a matter of simply taking a break—exercise, relax, go to a movie, do some gardening. Sometimes it is a matter of consciously giving yourself permission to think about other things—for an hour, a week, or longer.

Step 5: "Aha!" solutions emerge. Be awake to them. You may have a dream in which an insight is embedded. You may overhear a remark in a conversation that points the way. You may get a sudden urge to act—to begin writing or drawing or (in the case of your garden) just moving something. When the insight arrives, make a note of it or begin action as appropriate.

Step 6: Test the insight. This test can be difficult because your idea may be contrary to conventional wisdom or your own prior beliefs. Find ways to try it out in practice. Perhaps discuss it with people who you know to have open and questioning minds.

Step 7: Reflect on the experience. Ideally, all members of the learning circle will also experiment so that you can dialogue and reflect together.

- How long did it take?
- What was easy and what was difficult?
- What aspect of formulating the problem and of preparation seems, in hindsight, to have been most useful?
- If you were to improve your technique, what would you do and what would you change?

Commentary

Although the process we describe has been used for many years, most people do not relate it to learning in school. Yet to a very large extent, meaningful learning guided by actor-centered questions involves the same process as insightful problem solving, if not always to the same degree. Even confusion is a friend if dealt with appropriately. It takes experience with, and awareness of, the process to appreciate what is really happening in student minds and how best to support student thinking.

TAKING IT INTO THE CLASSROOM

The extent to which students can benefit from strategies that prime the unconscious depends on the instructional approach being employed. That is partly because the strategies require a combination of system and freedom, and partly because the results will lead to innovative answers to questions that teachers must be willing to deal with on their merits.

Instructional Approach 1

In tightly structured classrooms, where the primary indicator of effective learning and teaching is observable in terms of "time on task," it is very difficult to introduce the strategies we deal with here. Our suggestion is to go back to Chapter 13 and begin to use some of the memory strategies that require creative practice and rehearsal.

Instructional Approaches 2 and 3: Invoke the Arts

The arts are valuable in their own right. They are also extremely useful as a vehicle for helping students understand the curriculum and for priming unconscious processing.

Adding More Depth to Immersion

The obvious way to expand upon the use of the arts is to be more artistic in the entire orchestration of instruction. There are many ways to do this. An excellent way to begin in many subjects is to partner with an arts colleague. For example, we have seen a history teacher and a teacher in the visual arts work together to cover the same period in history in order for students to gain a better grasp of both the history and the art. We have also seen a physics teacher work with a computer artist to help students explore complex ideas through the development of visual models.

Use Different Art Forms to Process Experiences and Insights

One strategy is to give students an opportunity to express their emerging understandings and insights in some art form. This will take some practice if students are unfamiliar with the arts or, in the case of computer art, with the necessary software.

One reason why the early childhood program in Reggio Emilia (introduced in Chapter 14) is so good is that the adults there know that children can use a multitude of art forms to learn and express quite complex concepts and ideas at a very early age. Students have permission to draw, mold, sculpt, and move to convey their understandings in different, expressive ways.

We have used the following processes in classes ranging from the early grades to college:

- Draw a picture or diagram to illustrate key concepts or processes.
- Write a poem or short play that reveals your understanding of . . .
- Create a multimedia presentation as your way of exhibiting core ideas and processes.

Educators at all levels can use exactly the same process. Whether a topic is in social studies, humanities, or the earth sciences, students can be offered the opportunity to use the arts to convey their understanding. Many of today's students love to use multimedia for this purpose. Some are willing to spend days creating a slideshow, a Web site, or a video but would be reluctant to spend a few minutes simply writing an essay.

Use the Arts Combined With Powerful Questioning

The primary task for educators is to process the art form and to insist on, and help, students truly understand the content they are studying. This is done by using questions and observations in the right way. For instance:

- What are you setting out to describe and explain?
- Which images (for instance) make this clear? How?
- What alternatives did you consider?
- What criteria did you use to choose your approach and form?

- This part seems to suggest two possibilities to me (explain). How would I know which one you were emphasizing?
- There are several different elements to this concept (mention one or two). Are they all here? Which are left out? What was your reasoning? If you were to do it again, how might you incorporate those other elements?

Depending on the relationship between students and the atmosphere built up in a class, a teacher could then further expand student understanding and learning by helping students compare and contrast their work and exhibitions with those of other students. The key is to continually use opportunities to introduce, examine, and explore underlying ideas and concepts that need to be mastered. For instance, here is how two groups might be guided in working together and learning in more depth.

- Who else was working on this particular concept and material?
- Let's see what Group A and Group B had in common and how they differed.
- What art forms did you use?
- In what ways are they similar? In what ways are they different?
- How did each form evoke the core ideas?
- Did each form seem to leave something out? How did that happen? Which form seems to go into more depth? In what way?
- Here is an idea that doesn't seem to be expressed in either approach—how would you introduce it into what you did?

THE THIRD FOUNDATIONAL SKILL FOR ACTIVE PROCESSING: SELF-REGULATION

> At the heart of self-regulation is students' ability to recognize what is happening to them. The key is for students to become aware of what they are experiencing, what the dilemmas are, and that alternatives are available.

Recognizing Situations and Making Choices

A good introductory example can be found in Dorothy Fadiman's video, *Why Do These Kids Love School?* introduced earlier. A group of three- and four-year-olds is painting outdoors, waving their brushes around and generally having a good time. A teacher sees that one youngster is unhappy. He comes to her saying, "Jim splashed paint in my ear." The teacher asks him if he wanted to be splashed. When he says no, she asks if he told Jim not to do that. You can literally see the lights go on in this young man as he pivots around and goes back to Jim and tells him, "Jim, don't splash paint in my ear." The teacher continues by turning to all the children saying, "Jim is spattering. Do you want to spatter?" Some nod their heads and a few say "no." She then says, "Well, you may want to step away." The commentary goes on to say that one of the first goals is to help children become aware of what they feel. Once they know what they feel and they can see options, they can begin to exercise choice. This is the first step in self-monitoring and self-regulation.

A teacher can help students of every age become more aware of their situations, feelings, dilemmas, and possibilities. As this happens, a teacher can also help students to consciously develop new strategies for coping and for success. This approach to teaching marks the beginning of actor-centered decision making.

Here is a caution: *Always* remember that skills and interactions with others are shaped by the instructional approach being used. A really useful and powerful suggestion for Instructional Approach 3 may, in the hands of an Instructional Approach 1 teacher, be harmful to the student. For example, when students misbehave, they need to be called on it. But there is a world of difference between confronting students using threat and power, and allowing the students to participate fully in a process that enhances their own understanding and responsibility.

Mastering the process takes time and requires teachers to develop a set of personal qualities. These include patience, tact, empathy, and a capacity to be direct without being hostile.

Journaling as a Tool to Help Students See Themselves

We suggest that educators practice in their learning circles and that they use some quality peer coaching as they expand the range of their communication with their students.

A popular general procedure for learning to examine oneself and to assess personal strengths and weaknesses is through journaling or sketching.

A very simple activity is to invite each student to have a notebook and divide the page in half (sometimes called a dual-entry journal). On the left side, there is room for specific questions; on the right there is room for open-ended comments and sketches. At the top of the page the student selects some event or project and describes it briefly in two or three sentences. Then on the left the student could respond to the following questions as appropriate:

- What did I want to do?
- What did I do?
- How did it work out?
- What could I have done differently?
- What do my feelings and impressions tell me about this?
- What is it about me that makes me see it this way? What's my filter?

The right-hand page is also for any general thoughts or feelings or ideas or personal observations that come to mind.

Notes

1. Be careful with this process. On the one hand, because students can be vague and wishy-washy, the teacher needs to help them be specific and develop clarity. On the other hand, many of a student's thoughts should be private. While teachers may want to help students learn together, they must also be very careful not to embarrass a student. In particular, do not try to "do therapy" and solve a student's life problems! Stay focused on curriculum issues and the standards.

2. As students develop their capacity both to observe more clearly and to understand themselves, the groundwork is being laid for effective authentic assessment. The goal is for students to assess their own work accurately, to note their own strengths and weaknesses, and to begin to take charge of what they need to learn. Teachers can work with students to begin to use their journals for this purpose by providing some seed questions. Some examples follow:

- What aspect of (this skill or concept) am I using effectively? Give a reason and an example.
- What aspect of (this skill or concept) do I need to work on?
- Who seems to have mastered (this skill or concept) quite well? Why?
- What do they do that is different from what I do?

3. A state of relaxed alertness is necessary for the success of this process. The more fearful and helpless students feel, the less able they are to see themselves, and the more reluctant most of them are to share with others.

From a Teacher's Journal

Ashley was confident but quiet. She was happy to work both alone and in groups, but always chose to work with people she liked and tended to take a backseat. On one occasion we used a process meeting to deal with the concept that everyone has strengths and weaknesses and that all of us have something to contribute and something to learn. After a discussion, the class decided we should address our next project from the perspective of what we wanted to study (the topic) instead of who would be in our group. The class then addressed topics they were interested in learning about in earth science and formed groups based on those interests. Ashley wanted to study glaciers and found herself with people she had never worked with before. As she walked out of the class the day her project was finished, she made a comment to me in passing, "That was the first time I ran a group—and I loved it! I want to try doing that again." Ashley learned something about herself.

Living the Learning

Students are just like the rest of us. It is possible to learn about something, even a personal quality, and yet not implement the learning in new situations and new contexts.

Teachers also need to be aware of the skills and qualities that students are working to develop. This requires teachers to be genuinely interested in the students as people and to develop some capacities to interact and relate authentically. That is why we devoted the first section of this book to relaxed alertness and the classroom climate.

As students begin to have insights about themselves, teachers need to offer them multiple opportunities to practice in new situations and then to reflect again and again.

The interactions we describe are nearly impossible at Instructional Approach 1 and are still difficult and time-consuming for Instructional Approach 2. Our experience is that all this becomes easier as teachers approach Instructional Approach 3. One reason is that the more students work alone, effectively, and without supervision, the more time a teacher has for one-on-one conversations. As students begin to grasp the idea of process, they can begin to help each other. Ashley's processing could also have occurred as part of a group reflection or as an entry in her journal.

To be successful, teachers need to have a wealth of options at their fingertips, so that if students do not choose situations in which to practice their new skills, opportunities can be provided and suggested. For example, in the note from the teacher's journal above, Ashley indicated that she wanted more opportunities to run a group. She had just experienced a taste of leadership. A good teacher would be on the lookout for more leadership opportunities for Ashley to try. They would need to be appropriate, but they could range from running discussions and assessing class opinions to taking charge of some aspects of a field trip.

The key: The teacher would need to spend a little time with Ashley to process the experience. This could take the form of questions such as the following:

- What did you do?
- What was easy and what was difficult?
- What worked well?
- What would you do differently?
- What did you learn about leadership?

Students Taking Charge

As students begin to feel empowered, and as they develop greater understanding and competence, many will want to take greater charge of how the classroom works. A wonderful little example is recounted by an associate of ours who used to teach a combined second- and third-grade class of low SES students in California. One of the matters she addressed regularly was the daily and monthly calendar. One day a student suggested to her (to a chorus of agreement) that the students should be allowed to take over the calendar because they would do a better job! Our associate was delighted with the suggestion, agreed to let it happen, and was equally delighted with the results.

For students to begin to "take charge" *and* work at very high standards, a different type of listening and questioning is needed. Teachers need to know their material very well and have a great deal of self-efficacy. A good climate that fosters relaxed alertness needs to be established. Teachers need to be able to listen for what is really happening in the classroom and ask questions or make suggestions based on what is heard. At this point, teachers are primarily asking questions such as the following:

- What is happening here?
- What do the students seem to find interesting?
- Is there a way to connect this with that?
- What can I bring in or introduce that would further inspire them?
- Does x or y seem to need an opportunity?
- When does x or y flourish?

And, after trying something out, teachers need to go on asking themselves questions like these:

- What seemed to work? For whom? Why?
- How was this different from that?
- Who can I talk this over with?
- What did I find really exciting?
- What else can I do?
- Is there anything I need to learn so I can do this better?

> The secret to improving student metacognition is for educators to improve *their* metacognition and to live what they teach.

Reflection: Something to Think About

When looking at learning as both conscious and unconscious and considering all the suggestions in this chapter, remember to take things a step at a time. What will be your first step to help students "prime" their own minds? How will you engage active processing to assist the students' unconscious learning? What will you do to help students begin to take charge of their own functioning and learning?

THE TRANSFORMATIONAL ADMINISTRATOR AND THE PROCESS FOR MAKING IT REAL

In many communities there is an energy that appears to provide a sense of safety and balance. A positive and welcoming feeling exists that is difficult if not impossible to measure, but is palpable. There are also schools into which people can walk and almost stop in their tracks because the feeling of the building is cold or unwelcoming.

This seems to be getting back to the notion of climate and relaxed alertness—and it is. One of the best ways to create that climate is for adults to have opportunities to be creative and to be in charge of themselves and the situation. We are not talking about gaining more power in the district. Rather, the key is for adults to practice the skills and master the qualities described in this chapter.

Reflective intelligence is the hallmark of effectiveness and is a critical factor in professional development and peace of mind.

We invite administrators to use learning circles and to work with staff on adult versions of the strategies and processes introduced in this chapter. They are very powerful.

In tandem with the National Teaching Standards

Accomplished teachers require students to confront, explore, and understand important and challenging concepts, topics, and issues and to improve skills in purposeful ways.

Teachers help students acquire the metacognitive skills to begin to guide their own learning and assume the role of lifelong learners. Such teachers craft tasks and problems that extend students' abilities and habits to think deeply, creatively, and incisively about the world and their place within it.

—Standard V: Meaningful Learning

Accomplished teachers consider reflection on their practice central to their responsibilities as professionals to extend their knowledge, improve their teaching, and refine their evolving philosophy of teaching. They examine their strengths and weaknesses and employ that knowledge in their analysis and planning. Ultimately, self-reflection contributes to teachers' depth of knowledge and skill and adds dignity to their practice.

—Standard X: Reflective Practice

Metacognition is the bridge to much higher-order functioning. The processes and principles in this chapter are a gateway to meeting the National Teaching Standards and, therefore, to helping teachers and students help themselves raise their own standards.

If we want to create enriched environments that help students learn, then we need to include all of the following:

- Engage their individual style and uniqueness
- Engage the physiology in learning
- Engage social interactions
- Engage their innate search for meaning
- Engage their capacity to recognize and master essential patterns
- Engage emotional connections
- Engage their ability to perceive both details and the larger view
- Engage both their ability to focus attention and learn from the peripheral context
- Engage both conscious and unconscious processing
- Engage their capacity to learn from memorizing isolated facts and biographical events
- Acknowledge and engage developmental steps and shifts
- Reduce threat and enhance self-efficacy

16

Teaching to Unique Students

Brain/Mind Learning Principle 12: *Each brain is uniquely organized.*

 At the Core

The paradox that faces education is that human beings are both similar and different. For example, every human being is an expression of DNA, and that process is universal. Yet every individual has a unique genetic blueprint. To genuinely raise standards, educators have to grasp and deal with the commonalities of their learners and, at the same time, address each student as a unique individual with unique characteristics, capacities, and needs. Ultimately, it is only by adequately developing their executive functions that students and teachers will be able to cope successfully with the issues of sameness and diversity in their lives.

Capacity: All students can learn more effectively when their unique, individual talents, abilities, and capacities are engaged.

HOW DO WE KNOW THIS?

This book is grounded in the Brain/Mind Learning Principles, which spell out similarities between people. In particular, each one of the learning principles spells out how every person learns, irrespective of age, culture, and other factors. Everyone has the capacity to develop executive functions and, for instance, engage in adaptive decision making.

At the same time, this book also acknowledges that given the commonalities, each learner is different. The brain is shaped and influenced by experience. The combination of a unique genetic heritage and unique experiences ensures that everyone's brain and physiology is organized differently. Thus, people make their own decisions based on their own perception of what is happening in life.

The neurosciences, using technology such as PET scans and FMRI, have permitted researchers to see the brain at work on specific tasks and in a wide variety of situations. This, along with continually advancing technology, is helping researchers map the ways in which different parts of the brain perform different functions, ranging from language to observing sensory processing to maintaining one's balance. On the basis of these observations, there will hopefully emerge a more refined picture of individual differences and unique "intelligences" that combines the best thinking of educators, psychologists, and neuroscientists. Educators would benefit from such clarification.

Learning Styles and Multiple Intelligences

Beginning in the 1970s, educators became interested in research that indicated that different students learn differently. Methods of teaching emerged that made it possible to deal with various styles differently. Simultaneously, teachers were encouraged to allow students to express what they were learning using their preferred style (see, for example, Dunn & Griggs, 1988).

Another issue has been the attempt to reconceive intelligence and go beyond a limited set of abstract cognitive abilities. Among the pioneers doing this work are Howard Gardner (1993), Robert Sternberg (1988), and David Perkins (1995).

Sternberg suggested that there are three primary "types" of intelligence: *Creative Intelligence, Analytical Intelligence,* and *Practical Intelligence.*

Creative intelligence refers to the ability to see how to do things or think about something in multiple ways. Creative people question assumptions and search for new ways to approach a problem or a situation.

Analytical intelligence refers to the ability to consciously formulate and solve structured problems, such as mathematical puzzles, as well as to apply strategies and evaluate results accurately.

Practical intelligence refers to the capacity to learn readily in action-oriented situations where knowledge is used to solve a problem or is applied to everyday life (Sternberg, 1997).

Each of these types of intelligence engages some—but not all—aspects of the executive functions.

Better known to educators are Howard Gardner's eight different types of intelligences. They include the following (Armstrong, 2000):

1. *Linguistic intelligence* (ability to understand and work with language)

2. *Logical-mathematical intelligence* (ability to work with numbers, categorization, and reasoning)

3. *Spatial intelligence* (ability to visualize things accurately and transform images accurately)

4. *Bodily-kinesthetic intelligence* (ability to master one's bodily movement, the handling of objects)

5. *Musical intelligence* (ability to master music, including pitch, rhythm, and timbre)

6. *Interpersonal intelligence* (ability to understand and identify others' feelings, emotions, and motivations)

7. *Intrapersonal intelligence* (ability to understand oneself through insight)

8. *Naturalist intelligence* (ability to classify objects in the environment)

Personality Styles

Personality styles are more generic individual perspectives or "lenses" that also shed light on how individuals process experience. Perhaps the best known instrument is the Myers-Briggs Type Indicator (Briggs-Myers & McCaulley, 1985), which is available for adults. It is based on a psychological theory developed by Carl Jung. Other learning styles instruments are based on which senses predominate in an individual.

The Caines (1999) have developed a very simple four-style profile based on dominant sensory modalities. They distinguish the styles as follows:

- **Adventurers** (multisensory)
- **Directors** (sense of sound dominates)
- **Evaluators** (sense of vision dominates)
- **Nurturers** (emotions dominate)

Naturally, the Caines' styles overlap; it is important to be careful not to make them too rigid or absolute. However, they do help students (and adults) see some of the patterns they have in common with others and to highlight differences.

A larger issue, of course, is that there are also cultural and other social differences. Fields of research ranging from anthropology to sociology deal with such questions.

Given this wealth of material and the multiplicity of solutions, educators are in a quandary. Which approaches and instruments are most useful for education? How do educators work with groups of students covering similar subject matter and at the same time ensure that each student is being treated as an individual and is making personal sense of the curriculum?

PROCESSING THIS PRINCIPLE

As a way to begin, we suggest that you explore an individual styles instrument of your own choosing and discuss the differences on which it is based. By way of introduction, we briefly describe the four perceptual styles mentioned above (Caine, Caine, & Crowell, 1999). Read the following descriptions and identify where you might (mostly) fit. Also keep in mind students you are currently teaching and see if these descriptions help you recognize their sensory style.

Adventurer (Multisensory)

Change and variety are very important to you, including a variety of sensory experiences. For example, you might love shopping or visiting new places but can literally get lost (lose direction, lose your sense of time, or forget your goal) in an environment that provides too much sensory stimulation. You tend to anticipate what is going to happen in the future. You often feel comfortable guessing or rationalizing rather than bothering about the accuracy of details. Embellishing on a story is almost natural for you. This is probably because you prefer excitement and a bit of drama in your conversation with others. You are spontaneous and creative. The risk is that you lose a sense of orderliness and respect for other people's perspectives and needs. You love sensation, variety, and fun and often find yourself involved in several projects and ideas at the same time.

Director (Sense of Sound Dominates)

Words and sounds are very important to you. You value challenge and you like to direct others. You tend to make decisions quickly and stick to them. You want the facts before making decisions, but you tend to be impatient with detail and look for the big picture. You can easily put pressure on others, even if you hate being under pressure yourself. You can also be very direct and blunt, something that will offend sensitive individuals. You tend to be a leader, but you may alienate people by seeming not to care about them personally or being too sharp or abrupt.

Evaluator (Sense of Vision Dominates)

Order and system are very important to you. How things look, either in the real world or in your mind, is also important. Your first impression of a person or place is based on what you see. You also care what other people think of you and how you look to them. You are systematic and a good planner, and you like things to take place according to your plans. That means you can also be inflexible and may find it difficult to adjust when something unexpected happens.

Nurturer (Emotions Dominate)

Relationship and feelings, both your own and how you imagine others feel, are extremely important to you. So is working with your hands. You need people around you and can become depressed and morose when alone. Because you care so much, you like to help others. You work hard for causes that you believe in. Your desire to work hard means that you can also be used by others, because you are anxious to please them. You may end up giving too much and then feeling hurt and resentful.

Questions

Aspects of all of these styles are found in everyone, but usually one style dominates. For example, imagine that four people, each of a different style, decide to go out to dinner followed by a movie. Who would be more likely to organize the whole thing? Who would be most concerned that everyone was equally included and was enjoying himself or herself? Who would be more likely to visualize the entire event beforehand, including what they would eat and wear? And who would be more likely to decide to change the restaurant or agreed-upon movie at the last minute?

How might persons with each of the above styles assess a situation? What would they examine first and deem to be most significant? Would there be differences in the ways in which they adapt to situations and use their executive functions?

Here are additional questions you may wish to consider:

1. How might these different styles act when in the survival response? (In the case of threat, who tends to retreat and who tends to attack?)

2. How might these different styles relate to new people? Do some come close and others stay away? Do some act while others react?

3. What decision and leadership tendencies would you expect? Would some individuals leap in while others sit on the fence? Are there natural leaders and followers? Do some like detail while others begin with a big picture?

5. What are the implications for your work as an educator?

6. To what extent might *you* have to adapt in order to communicate effectively with different types of people and students? How might you go about that sort of adaptation?

Cautions

There is a great danger in overreliance on types of differences. It is possible to inappropriately label and pigeonhole people, and by so doing limit their and our capacity to grow. For example, a person could ignore the fact that some differences are context dependent, which means predictions about others might not be reliable given a different context. Are there contexts where you have seen this happen?

TAKING IT INTO THE CLASSROOM

From a Teacher's Journal

A teaching friend of ours works in a large, urban school system as a fifth-grade teacher. An exciting conference was being held at the nearby convention center, and her class was invited to this remarkable, international technology event. Sadly, she had to decline the offer because all of the teachers had been told that "field trips" were not being permitted at that time. It seems the administration determined that all outside-of-school trips were frozen until their new, highly prescriptive reading curriculum was put in place. Therefore, no students were to leave the building for any learning excursions, even if the event was right down the street and would not involve any expense to the school or students.

Here was a chance for students to enter an event that had music, art, engineering, science, math, reading, and excitement! Enough to engage all the students in some way.

That school functioned at Instructional Approach 1 and simply did not grasp how individual differences could be addressed and learning enhanced by means of a rich dose of experience.

The developmental path we have employed throughout this book is a powerful tool and essential framework for successfully dealing with similarities and differences in students.

Instructional Approach 1

Instructional Approach 1 treats students as almost identical and are organized by age and grade. The curriculum for each age/grade level is mandated. Instruction is relatively linear and sequential. Teachers manage the classroom by keeping control, and so most individual student issues, styles, characteristics, and attributes are usually seen as irrelevant.

Instructional Approach 2

Instructional Approach 2 permits much more variety. Students can work alone and together. Variety is used in presentation and assessment. Some choice is available. Several assessment tools tend to be used. The teacher makes more use of the classroom climate and student support in order to get things done. One thing yet to be mastered is how to provide substantial and authentic student choice and actor-centered decision making. Another relates to the range of experiences to which students are exposed.

Instructional Approach 3

Instructional Approach 3 optimizes the possibilities for the teacher and the range of choices for students. They can function in a multiplicity of ways and roles that help them learn and that increase the range of possible assessment.

Caveats and Cautions

There are always caveats.

First, the fact that students may not like something does not exempt them from dealing with it. We do not want to give the impression that if students do not like to write, alternatives are always acceptable. High standards of the information age require high standards in literacy. The key is to work with individual differences, providing students with varying situations that allow for learning to be layered in ways that lead to more success.

One solution is to broaden the ways in which students can be called upon to write while at the same time embedding very sophisticated analysis. Teachers can capitalize on some aspects of individual differences by finding different points of view and perspectives that students like to adopt. For instance, a project can be written up and described from the perspective of

- A financial journalist
- A reporter for a tabloid
- A consultant for a property developer
- A civil rights activist
- A budding politician
- An environmentalist
- A teacher
- A local parent
- And more . . .

Second, some students have become used to Instructional Approach 1. Our own experience is that almost all students end up preferring Instructional Approach 3 in the long run, but teachers can expect some initial resistance before students make the shift if they have been exposed only to Instructional Approach 1 for most of their school years.

Third, some students need more structure and direct instruction than others. It may be a matter of coming from an inconsistent and unreliable environment outside of school. If they have been in a survival state the majority of the time or if they have missed out on acquiring some foundational habits and skills, these students do need to catch up.

The developmental path we use in this book allows for individual needs because the instructional approaches are *not* exclusive. Instructional Approach 2 includes aspects of Instructional Approach 1 as appropriate and needed. And Instructional Approach 3 includes aspects of approaches 1 and 2 as appropriate and needed.

Self-Monitoring and Working Together

It seems to be a fact of life that people are often impatient with, and critical of, those who are different. This can make it very difficult to work together on projects and in teams. The creation of a good classroom climate based on relaxed alertness is an essential foundation.

In addition, children love to find out something about their learning styles. Adolescents in particular are struggling with developing their own identity, and they really seem to enjoy finding out more about why they are the way they are and how they differ from others. This also helps students work better in teams, and it helps teachers organize and form groups and teams.

Using a version of the Caines' learning styles in the form of an adolescent identity profile, we can work with students to develop a much better sense of community and teamwork through students' processing their own views and differences. When they do this they collectively can better understand more about each other and themselves. For example, we work with groups by asking the following kinds of questions:

- Are you having trouble beginning this project?
- Who wants to plan it all out first?
- Who wants to just get going?
- Why do you think these approaches are different?
- How could we compromise and work together?

In effect, the teacher helps the students see that there are differences, that the different ways of doing things all have something to offer, that sometimes one is preferred over others, and that learning about themselves is critical to effective functioning. This means that adaptive decision making and the executive functions are built into the ways in which students work together.

There is a further benefit to working with individual styles in this way: *The goal must always be to maintain the state of relaxed alertness.* One interesting feature of learning and personality styles is that people of different styles move into survival in different ways. As Perry's distinction between a hypervigilant and a dissociative response indicates, some students who feel threatened will tend to withdraw into themselves, become quiet, and just not participate. Other students who feel helpless or threatened tend to become angry and obstreperous. In addition, some students slow down; others speed up. In our experience, as students and adults become aware of their different styles, they also become aware of their own ways of surviving. They can see it in each other and, over time, see that a person is not "bad" or "wrong," just experiencing fear with helplessness. This awareness builds patience and acceptance and is a powerful tool for sustaining relaxed alertness.

THE FOURTH FOUNDATIONAL SKILL FOR ACTIVE PROCESSING: ADVANCED QUESTIONING

> Active processing is essentially the art of listening and questioning.

We introduced a range of strategies and examples in the preceding chapters. Here, we want to illustrate the fact that there is no limit to the depth that is possible, and that much of the key to reaching and engaging students is a matter of increasing their options, then listening with more depth and questioning with more skill.

This is a way to expand the range of questioning. It is primarily for Instructional Approach 3.

Use Big Ideas and Broad Themes

Every concept can always be understood as being part of a larger concept. That is why some curriculum frameworks now use umbrella concepts like "patterns" as the bedrock for an entire subject. Big ideas and themes transcend individual subjects. They become a natural way of linking material and integrating the curriculum. The notions of "order" and "chaos" can be applied to a novel or play, crucial moments in the history of any nation, the way that forces interact in the world of physics, changes in art forms, and in every other subject.

> One approach we have found to be very powerful is to have a set of complex, universal themes that can be introduced anywhere. We call them *Principles of Connectedness*.

The Caines have used these principles of connectedness as the basis for ordered sharing in their workbook *Mindshifts* (1999, coauthored with Sam Crowell):

- The whole is greater than the sum of the parts.
- Reality is both linear and nonlinear.
- Inner and outer reflect each other.
- Order emerges out of chaos.

- Reality consists of matter, energy, and meaning.
- Everything is both part and whole simultaneously.
- What is, is always in process.
- Everything is in layers.
- Stable systems resist change—dynamic systems exist by changing.
- Rhythms and cycles are present everywhere.
- Everything is both separate and connected.

You might like to have these listed somewhere. Create a chart with them and post it on a wall. Select any one of them and use it to frame questions. They are also superb topics for an ordered sharing.

Use the Principles of Connectedness by Asking Questions

Perhaps the easiest way to begin is to use one of the principles of connectedness to ask some questions in a class in order to provoke discussions about the link between the material being studied and big ideas. For example:

- What rhythms and cycles can be seen in (this novel or event in history or process in science)?
- Can you see how order emerges out of chaos in (this scientific discovery or this political event)?

The very use of the big idea naturally introduces topics and concepts from across the curriculum, giving you a powerful tool for integrating the curriculum.

> In addition, themes are marvelous vehicles for connecting with the interests and hobbies of students and for linking those interests to the standards.

THE TRANSFORMATIONAL ADMINISTRATOR AND THE PROCESS FOR MAKING IT REAL

No matter what the topic is, and no matter what people say, there is always more going on in their minds and hearts.

The business world and the world of therapy have both developed processes for going deeper and helping others to see more deeply. One approach that we strongly recommend for your learning circles is to start working with dialogue. This is not a matter of just talking to each other more politely, but of learning to hear the deeper flow of meanings (e.g., Isaacs, 1999).

One suggestion is to *listen to the listener*. Sometimes people get so opinionated or take things so for granted that they cannot even hear themselves and are not aware of their own assumptions and mental models. We suggest that, in your learning circles, you explore the notion of listening to the listener, and keep on revisiting it. This will equip you to hear your students better and to hear yourself better while you are teaching.

Another suggestion is to *observe the observer*. This refers, in part, to the fact that people can only walk the walk if they notice how they are walking. Again, the key to success is not just to master a tool or process in practice, but to live it so that it becomes a part of the way an individual functions. We invite you to use the learning circles to develop ways to observe the observer.

The journey never ends. Active processing can now be seen to do more than simply help instruction. Much of the joy of life, and much of the growth that should ideally occur in every job, emerges out of the ways in which people process their experience on the job and in all of education.

Therefore, the one thing we strongly recommend is that processing itself, and the consistent use of learning circles, be deeply entrenched in a school's culture. That is the way to develop the spirit of continuous deep learning, which, in the end, is the essential spirit that should infuse a school.

Our suggestion is to make learning circles an ongoing part of the educator's life and work. They become an oasis of professional growth and a way for educators to be continually supported and challenged.

In our experience, after some time the circles become very tightly knit and may need to re-form. This is a matter of art and feel, but the process of the learning circle should be a constant.

In tandem with the National Teaching Standards

Accomplished teachers model and promote behavior appropriate in a diverse society by showing respect for and valuing all members of their learning communities and by expecting students to treat one another fairly and with dignity.

The choice of whole-class, group, or individual activities and of texts for study and discussion attests to a commitment to engage all students in learning. In grouping students for cooperative assignments, for example, teachers may bring together individuals from varying backgrounds, or teachers might establish leadership roles to prevent gender or other stereotypes from restricting participation.

Teachers create environments that help students learn about one another and understand that all individuals have unique capacities and limitations.

—Standard VI: Respect for Diversity

People are both different and alike. This applies to students and to staff. The key is to find a way to work so that the differences and similarities become useful instead of a distraction. That is when diversity can be truly appreciated.

Resource A

The Brain/Mind Learning Principles Wheel

12 — Each brain is uniquely organized.
11 — Complex learning is enhanced by challenge and inhibited by threat associated with helplessness.
10 — Learning is developmental.
9 — There are at least two approaches to memory: archiving isolated facts and skills or making sense of experience.
8 — Learning always involves conscious and unconscious processes.
7 — Learning involves both focused attention and peripheral perception.
6 — The brain/mind processes parts and wholes simultaneously.
5 — Emotions are critical to patterning.
4 — The search for meaning occurs through patterning.
3 — The search for meaning is innate.
2 — The brain/mind is social.
1 — All learning is physiological.

Human Beings Are Living Systems

© Caine and Caine, 2000

Three interactive elements emerging out of the principles

Relaxed Alertness	Orchestrated Immersion in Complex Experience	Active Processing

Brain/Mind Learning Capacities
Creating an Enriched Environment for Learning

According to Brain/Mind Learning Principles, all learning engages the following.
Our job is to orchestrate learning so that as many aspects of learning are engaged as possible.

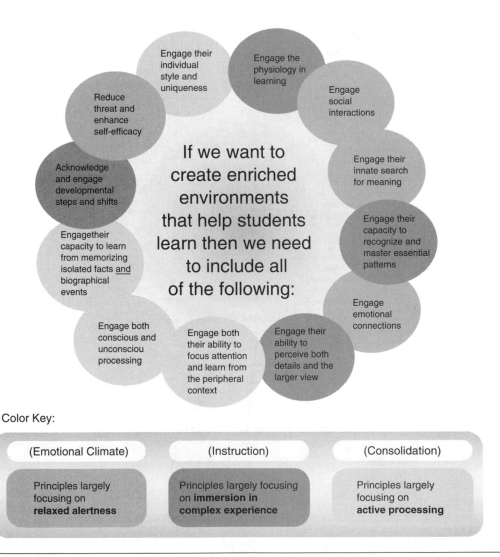

If we want to create enriched environments that help students learn then we need to include all of the following:

- Engage their individual style and uniqueness
- Engage the physiology in learning
- Engage social interactions
- Engage their innate search for meaning
- Engage their capacity to recognize and master essential patterns
- Engage emotional connections
- Engage their ability to perceive both details and the larger view
- Engage both their ability to focus attention and learn from the peripheral context
- Engage both conscious and unconsciou processing
- Engage their capacity to learn from memorizing isolated facts and biographical events
- Acknowledge and engage developmental steps and shifts
- Reduce threat and enhance self-efficacy

Color Key:

(Emotional Climate)	(Instruction)	(Consolidation)
Principles largely focusing on **relaxed alertness**	Principles largely focusing on **immersion in complex experience**	Principles largely focusing on **active processing**

Resource C

How to Develop Learning Circles

FIRST STEPS

1. Successful Professional Development

Professional development programs work when they

- make sense to participants,
- are useful and practical,
- are interesting,
- are sustained,
- are supported,
- are real.

• Educators need to know that the most powerful learning for students occurs when students become aware of how a concept or skill works in the real world.

• Educators need to know that constructivist learning and teaching produce students who know their subjects really well *and* who can score well on tests.

• We need to use a process that is personally interesting and enjoyable and that provides adequate support.

2. Learning Circles

One way to support professional development that is compatible with the Brain/Mind Principles is the use of small groups.

The groups are suitable for any adult working in or with a school or larger educational unit. Participants are usually teachers and administrators, but you can invite special resource personnel, librarians, psychologists, secretaries, custodians, and teacher aids.

The reason for including all adults is that every adult contributes to the community that is created for students, and students learn from every adult. Ideally, all adults should have a common mental model of how people learn, and their roles and functions should be mutually reinforcing. For instance, a positive and pleasant atmosphere in the school office and on the playground indirectly helps all teachers maintain orderliness and build a good learning environment in their classrooms.

3. Learning Circle Format

The learning circles should adapt to suit themselves. In the initial stage, we suggest that—ideally—each meeting of the group will contain all four of the following elements and phases. However, each element can also be very useful as a process that stands alone and that can be employed in a variety of situations.

Phase 1: Ordered Sharing
The purpose is to make it easier for people to listen and speak their own truth.

Phase 2: Reflective Study
The best way to make sense of new material is to both analyze it and personalize it through reflection on personal experience.

Phase 3: Implications for Practice
Nothing works until it is tried. New skills are built by experiment, feedback, practice, and reflection.

Phase 4: Regrouping
The way to fully benefit from a group session (and any other experience) is to regroup it by reflecting on what is happening and what was learned.

PHASE 1: ORDERED SHARING

1. Sit in a closed circle.

2. Examine the core material. This should be some issue or pithy saying or topic with a very large number of legitimate points of view.

3. Each person says something about the chosen subject, with a time limit of, perhaps, one or two minutes. People can share personal experiences or wax philosophical. The person on the left goes next. The direction of sharing continues around the circle.

4. No one makes any comment whatsoever about what another says. There is no opposition nor is there verbal support. However, every silent member pays full attention to what is being said.

5. The group leader monitors timing and participation. No one needs to speak for their full allotted time, and no one should exceed their allotted time. Ideally, everyone should say something and not just "pass."

6. If people pass, go back to them (continuing to the left) after everyone else has shared.

Key: Deep Listening

This is the art of listening to oneself and others at the level of mental models and hidden assumptions. One essential key here is to recognize that when a person has a strong emotional response to an idea or a behavior, that may disclose a deep belief or an unarticulated belief that the person has.

Skills

Nonjudgmental listening to oneself and others

Patience

Beginner's mind (being open)

PHASE 2: REFLECTIVE STUDY

Select the material to study ahead of time. Those who are becoming brain/mind constructivists would begin with the Brain/Mind Learning Principles and examine one principle each group meeting. Ideally, group participants would read a little before the group meeting. Because there may not be much time for reading this, the facilitator should have some essential material available for participants to read during this phase of the group process.

Once the material has been read, participants should spend time discussing and personalizing it.

In part the discussions are used to analyze and think about what the material means. In addition, every participant should think and talk about some personal experience related to the material.

For example, if you are exploring the fact that the brain/mind is social, you would discuss times when you worked well in groups and when you worked better alone, what the differences were, and so on. The goal is to see how the principle operates in your own life and in your own learning.

A very powerful further step is to use activities such as role-playing to experiment with the idea or skill being studied. After the activity, participants should reflect on and share their personal experiences and reactions.

Key: Active Listening

This is the art of paying full attention and of asking questions that enable the speaker to clarify his or her own thoughts.

Skills

Asking clarifying questions

Reflecting on one's own experience

Tolerating confusion and ambiguity

PHASE 3: IMPLICATIONS FOR PRACTICE

Participants should take some time to think about some aspect of the material that has direct application to their work. That is the basis for deciding what to try the following week.

This aspect of the process can be carried out in different ways. Participants might like to work alone or in pairs and small groups. They can decide to try different processes or to experiment individually with the same process.

The facilitator should prepare some questions that set the stage for what participants will work on during the following week. Here are some examples:

- Does the material studied seem to apply most to some aspect of teaching, discipline, or assessment?
- What should I experiment with next week?
- How will I do it?
- What do I expect to happen?
- What responses or outcomes should I look for?

Key: Making Material Practical

This is the art of translating abstract ideas and suggestions into real-world applications.

Skills

Developing a systematic approach to practice

Action research

Peer coaching

PHASE 4: REGROUPING

Every group meeting works at two levels. One level is the content of subject matter that participants work on, such as a Brain/Mind Learning Principle. The other is the skills that the group process teaches, such as the art of listening without judgment or of asking good questions.

The process itself is designed to help participants master the content. The final phase—regrouping—helps participants with skill development.

In this phase, the facilitator should provide at least one or two questions that participants can think about privately or discuss with others. Questions can be general or specific, and can be on many topics. For example,

- What did you learn during this group session?
- What did you learn about listening during this group session?
- Did you become aware of any assumption that you have about learning or teaching that you want to reexamine?
- What aspect of asking questions is easiest and what aspect is most difficult for you?

And so on.

We suggest that participants use the ordered sharing process for their responses to these questions. In that way, everybody shares what they are learning, everybody hears what others are learning, and the practice of listening to everyone fully is reinforced.

Key: Learning to Learn

This is the art of developing insight and skills by capitalizing on experience.

Skills

Active processing of experience

Sharing with others

Learning together

GETTING STARTED

Volunteers

It is absolutely essential that group participants be volunteers, because that is the first element of safety.

Group Size

The ideal number of participants is between 7 and 12.

Forming Groups

Adapt to your own circumstances.

Location

Wherever possible, meet away from your normal place of work.

Time and Duration

Ideally, meet once a week for one and a half hours at a time.

Facilitators

The goal is for everyone to be both a leader and a follower.

PROCESS PRINCIPLES

1. Have a degree of routine and ceremony with beginnings and endings.
2. Be aware of the energy and focus of the group.

3. Stay or go, but don't come and go.

4. Maintain psychological safety by keeping all comments in the learning circle confidential.

5. Slow down to speed up.

6. There are no prescribed outcomes!

7. Honor individual differences while collectively committing to the process.

8. Do not give each other advice.

9. Maintain the process.

CAUTIONS

The Mindshifts process is a way to learn about ourselves and others. Thus, it may become quite personal.

1. Conflict Resolution

People sometimes find themselves in conflict. Our primary suggestion is that those who do not subscribe to the philosophy of the process do not participate. We also suggest that, should the need arise, you invest some time (including group time) in developing skills and procedures for conflict resolution (see Chapter 6).

2. Relevance for Children and Students

The process developed here is for adult volunteers. It can provide the foundation for working with students very effectively but needs to be modified based on your professional skill and judgment. In particular, students are not volunteers and they have limited abilities to protect themselves, so care should be taken to avoid personal disclosures that can be embarrassing or hurtful. A modified approach to the ordered sharing for use with students is described in Chapter 3.

A FINAL WORD

There is always more. Professional development and group building are complex processes, and many questions will arise. For example,

- How long does the group continue?
- When do groups change membership and focus?
- How do new groups form?
- What patterns tend to occur in group dynamics?
- Do cliques ever form?

- What is the best way to combine individual group processes with the larger community that is forming in the entire organization?

The answers to these and other questions are partly a matter of experience and partly a matter of learning together. Leaders may also need to develop additional facilitation and processing skills, such as the following:

- Helping participants identify their learning and perceptual styles
- Building rapport and adapting to the actual competencies and beliefs of participants
- Using questions and feedback to help people process their experience and guide them in their learning
- Creating a safe, orderly, and supportive environment for learning

For assistance in these areas, consult a good facilitator or colleague or contact us at http://www.cainelearning.com.

Resource D

Guided Experiences Presentation Cycle

What follows is a model that facilitates a more advanced brain/mind approach to teaching. This model focuses on the guided experience. These guided experiences will always be different in many ways, but the described phases will be present regardless of subject matter, focus, or discipline.

Before you begin:

• It is critical to remember that the following will work only if the teacher and students have established an authentic community with shared procedures and expectations.

• Be sure that, as the teacher, you have internalized as many of the standards as possible and have access to the rest.

• Collect and display examples that represent excellence in the instructional discipline on which you are focusing. Leave these available throughout all four phases. You may refer to them or simply have them openly available, encouraging student investigation and questions.

• Although official guidelines may suggest that you must limit yourself to a single topic, broaden your investigation into a concept that covers several related topics. Selection of topics should be left to the students.

• Maintain a clear sense of essential skills and knowledge that you want students to master. This will allow students to choose topics to explore while you will have a sense of control over the necessary outcomes. The standards, essential skills, and knowledge will guide your active processing and will help in the design of rubrics and authentic and paper/pencil assessments.

Phase I: Creating an initial sense of "Felt Meaning"

Purpose:

To facilitate an introduction to new and largely unsolicited subject matter

How Done:

A global experience that invokes an emotional reaction and intellectual understanding

Phase 2: Forming preliminary connections to new subject matter

Purpose:

To encourage student exploration and "buy-in." Students decide how they want to explore this concept or topic.

How Done:

Allow for open questions, comments, and reactions to a global experience.

Once students have expressed an interest in any aspect of the subject, have them agree on and write out what they want to explore and research.

Phase 3: Deep exploration through research and projects

Purpose:

To develop a project that demonstrates unique aspects of the subject being investigated. This phase allows students to access input from a wide variety of sources, including literature and books, the Internet and software, teacher guidance, information, and expert knowledge. The exploration phase helps students continuously improve, refine, and process what they are learning.

How Done:

Provide students with multiple sources of information. Have them define and describe their project. Collectively and individually process rubrics and clarify them for all concerned.

Active processing throughout all phases, but particularly Phase 3

Purpose:

The teacher's job during Phase 3 is to actively process student work in an ongoing fashion, keeping high standards, critical skills, and disciplinary knowledge and the rubrics in mind. It is the teacher's responsibility to see that all students master basic knowledge in the field despite divergent research and/or projects.

How Done:

Open-ended questions, guiding comments, direct instruction when needed in order to consolidate essential knowledge and skills (see Part 3, "Active Processing").

Phase 4: Consolidation

Purpose:

The teacher's job during Phase 4 is to document learning. Also, products, presentations, exhibits, or projects are finalized; knowledge gained is consolidated; and critical aspects of learning are articulated in multiple ways.

How Done:

Although assessment will have been ongoing through active processing, it is in this phase that various modes of assessment may be used as a culminating activity. For example, understanding is demonstrated through authentic assessment of all types. Students can design and take exams covering critical elements. The teacher engages students in oral and written exams in order to process essential learning and to ensure that students can use acquired knowledge in new and spontaneous situations.

It is also in this phase that the teacher determines what needs to happen next and how best to tie that to student interest and begins to design a new global experience.

Resource E

Guidelines for the Guided Experiences Model

TEACHER PREPARATION	LEARNING CYCLE	ACTIVE PROCESSING
Know the standards	Create authentic community	Process continuously for standards:
Identify critical concepts students need to master	Develop global experience	Critical concepts
	Engage research questions	Critical facts and skills
Know all critical facts and skills to be mastered	Organize preliminary research groups	
	Develop class rubrics for research	
	Allow for student research	
	Support in-depth research	
	Assist in planning documentation of research	
	Develop rubrics for documentation	

Global Experience Design Wheel

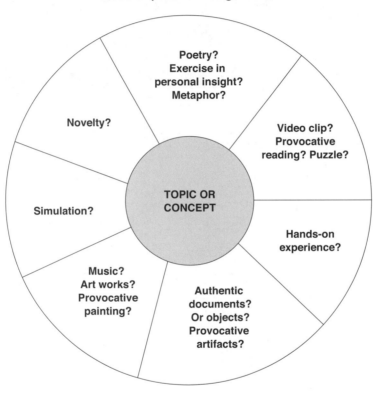

Questions to Guide You	Suggestions
Where is this topic in real life?	Most of these happen while brainstorming.
What is the concept behind it?	Start small.
How can *you* make students *experience* it?	Begin with your area of expertise.
	Make use of the artists among you.
	Look for poetry or music that expresses the metaphor.
	Don't overdo emotional connections.

References

Armstrong, T. (2000). *Multiple intelligences in the classroom* (2nd ed.). Alexandria, VA: ASCD.

Ashby, F., Isen, A., & Turken, U. (1999). A neuropsychological theory of positive affect and its influence on cognition. *Psychological Review, 106*(3), 529–550.

Austin, J. (1998). *Zen and the brain.* Cambridge: MIT Press.

Bandura, A. (1973). *Aggression: A social learning analysis.* Englewood Cliffs, NJ: Prentice Hall.

Bandura, A. (2000). Self-efficacy: The foundation of agency. In W. J. Perrig (Ed.), *Control of human behavior, mental processes, and consciousness* (pp. 17–33). Mahwah, NJ: Lawrence Erlbaum.

Barratier, C., Mallet, Y., & Perrin, J. (Producers) and Nuridsany, C., & Perennou, M. (Directors) (1996). *Microcosmos* [Motion picture]. Burbank, CA: Miramax Films.

Barzakov, I. (1986, July 14). [Unpublished workshop notes. Optimalearning™ Workshop.]

Baudrillard, J. Available from http://www.egs.edu/faculty/jeanbaudrillard.html

Baudrillard, J. (2001). *Impossible exchange* [C. Turner, Trans.]. New York: Verso.

Benesh, B. (1999). *The brain and learning: ASCD Professional Inquiry Kit—8 activity folders and a videotape.* Alexandria, VA: ASCD.

Bickmore, K., Goldthwait, P., & Looney, J. (1984). *Alternatives to violence: A manual for teaching peacemaking to youth and adults.* Akron, OH: Peace Grows.

Boekaerts, M. (1996). Self-regulated learning at the junction of cognition and motivation. *European Psychologist, 1*(2), 100–112.

Bowers, G. H., & Sivers, H. (1998). Cognitive impact of traumatic events. *Development and Psychopathology, 10,* 625–654.

Bransford, J. D., Brown, A. L., & Cocking, R. (2000). *How people learn: Brain, mind, experience, and school.* Washington, DC: National Academy Press.

Briggs-Myers, I., & McCaulley, M. (1985). *Manual: A guide to the development and use of the Myers Briggs Type Indicator.* Palo Alto, CA: Consulting Psychologists Press.

Brothers, L. (1997). *Friday's footprint: How society shapes the human mind.* New York: Oxford University Press.

Caine, G., & Caine, R. (2001). *The brain, education and the competitive edge.* Lanham, MD: Scarecrow.

Caine, G., Caine R., & McClintic, C. (2002, September). Guiding the innate constructivist. *Educational Leadership, 60*(1), 70–73.

Caine, R. (2000, November). Building the bridge from research to classroom. *Educational Leadership, 58*(3), 59–62.

Caine, R., & Anderson, J. (2003). *Raising test scores by aligning teaching with the California standards for the teaching profession.* Manuscript submitted for publication.

Caine, R., & Caine, G. (1997). *Education on the edge of possibility.* Alexandria, VA: ASCD.

Caine, R., & Caine, G. (in press). *Making connections: Teaching and the human brain* (Rev. ed.). Thousand Oaks, CA: Corwin Press.

Caine, R., Caine, G., & Crowell, S. (1999). *Mindshifts* (2nd ed.). Chicago: Zephyr.

California Teachers Association (CTA) Leadership Training. (1989). Fist of Five workshop, Yucaipa, CA.

Church, C. (1998). Pie Jesu. On *Voice of an angel* [CD]. New York: Sony Music.

Claxton, G. (1997). *Hare brain, tortoise mind: How intelligence increases when you think less.* Hopewell, NJ: ECCO.

Cole, K. (1998, August 13). Why the arts are important to science. *Los Angeles Times*, p. 8.

Combs, A. (1999). *Being and becoming.* New York: Springer.

Community Board Program. (1987a). *Conflict resolution: A secondary school curriculum* [Workshop materials]. San Francisco: Author.

Community Board Program. (1987b). *Conflict resolution: An elementary school curriculum* [Workshop materials]. San Francisco: Author.

The Convergence Education Foundation. Available from http://www.cef-trek.org

Cooper, C. (1998). *Learner-centered assessment.* Hastings Point, NSW, Australia: Global Learning Communities International.

Costa, A., & Kallick, B. (2000). *Habits of mind: A developmental series.* Alexandria, VA: ASCD.

Csikszentmihalyi, M. (1993). *Flow: Psychology of optimal experience.* New York: Perennial.

Damasio, A. (1994). *Descartes' error: Emotion, reason and the human brain.* New York: Avon Books.

Damasio, A. (1999). *The feeling of what happens: Body and emotion in the making of consciousness.* New York: Harcourt Brace.

Damasio, A. (2003). *Looking for Spinoza: Joy, sorrow, and the feeling brain.* New York: Harcourt.

Davies, L. (2002). Ten ways to foster resiliency in children. Available from http://www.kellybear.com/TeacherTip25.html

Detweiler, J., Rothman, A., Salovey, P., & Steward, W. (2000, January). Emotional states and physical health. *American Psychologist, 55*(1), 110–121.

Diamond, M. (1988). *Enriching heredity: The impact of the environment on the anatomy of the brain.* New York: Free Press.

Diamond, M., & Hobson, J. (1998). *Magic trees of the mind.* New York: Penguin Putnam.

Dunn, R., & Griggs, S. (1988). *Multiculturalism and learning style.* Westport, CT: Praeger.

Edwards, C., Gandini, L., & Forman, G. (1996). *The hundred languages of children: The Reggio Emilia approach to early childhood education.* Norwood, NJ: Ablex.

Egan, K. (1986). *Teaching as story telling: An alternative approach to teaching and curriculum in the elementary school.* Chicago: University of Chicago Press.

Ekman, P., & Davidson, R. J. (Eds.). (1994). *The nature of emotion.* New York: Oxford University Press.

Ericson, K., & Smith, J. (Eds.). (1991). *Toward a general theory of expertise: Prospects and limits.* Cambridge, UK: Cambridge University Press.

Erikson, E. (1994). *Identity and the life cycle.* New York: W. W. Norton.

Fadiman, D. (1988). *Why do these kids love school?* (Video). Menlo Park, CA: Concentric Media.

Festinger, L. (1957). *A theory of cognitive dissonance.* Stanford, CA: Stanford University Press.

Finn, J., Gerber, S., Achilles, C., & Boyd-Zaharias, J. (2001, April). The enduring effects of small classes. *Teacher College Record, 103*(2), 145–183.

Fredrickson, B. (2000, March). Cultivating positive emotions to optimize health and well-being. *Prevention and Treatment, 3* (Article 0001a). Available from http://journals.apa.org/prevention/volume3/pre0030001a.html

Fullan, M. (2001). *Leading in a culture of change: Being effective in complex times.* New York: Jossey-Bass.

Gardner, H. (1993). *Frames of mind: The theory of multiple intelligences.* New York: Basic Books.

Gendlin, E. (1982). *Focusing.* New York: Bantam.

Gillham, J. (Ed.). (2000). *The science of optimism and hope: Research essays in honor of Martin E. P. Seligman* (Vol. 2). Radnor, PA: Templeton Foundation Press.

Goldberg, E. (2001). *The executive brain: Frontal lobes and the civilized mind.* New York: Oxford University Press.

Goleman, D. (1997). *Emotional intelligence: Why it can matter more than I.Q.* New York: Bantam Books.

Gopnik, A., Meltzoff, A., & Kuhl, P. (1999). *The scientist in the crib: Minds, brains, and how children learn.* New York: William Morrow.

Gordon, T. (1977). *TET: Teacher effectiveness training.* Harlow, Essex, UK: Longman Group.

Gordon, W. (1968). *Synectics: The development of creative capacity.* New York: Macmillan.

Greenough, W., Black, J., & Wallace, C. (1987). Experience and brain development. *Child Development, 58,* 539–559.

Halpern, D. (1989). *Thought and knowledge: An introduction to critical thinking.* Hillsdale, NJ: Lawrence Erlbaum.

Hart, L. (1978). *Human brain and human learning.* New York/London: Longman.

Haskel, R. (2000). *Transfer of learning: Cognition, instruction, and reasoning.* Burlington, MA: Academic Press.

Hassard, J. (1999). *Science as inquiry: Activated learning, project-based, Web-assisted and active assessment strategies to enhance student learning.* Santa Monica, CA: Goodyear.

Healy, J. (1998). *Failure to connect: How computers affect our children's minds—for better and worse.* New York: Simon & Schuster.

Huttenlocher, P. (2002). *Neural plasticity: The effects of environment on the development of the cerebral cortex* (Perspectives in Cognitive Neuroscience). Cambridge, MA: Harvard University Press.

Isaacs, W. (1999). *Dialogue and the art of thinking together: A pioneering approach to communicating in business and in life.* Garden City, NY: Doubleday.

Kohn, A. (1999). *Punished by rewards.* Boston: Houghton Mifflin.

Kohn, A. (2000). *The case against standardized testing.* Portsmouth, NH: Heinemann.

Kokko, K., & Pulkkinen, L. (2000). Aggression in childhood and long-term unemployment in adulthood: A cycle of maladaption and some protective factors. *Developmental Psychology, 36*(4), 463–472.

Kovalik, S., & Olsen, K. (1997). *Integrated thematic instruction: The model* (3rd ed.). Covington, WA: Books for Education.

Lakoff, G., & Johnson, M. (1999). *Philosophy in the flesh: The embodied mind and its challenge to Western thought.* New York: Basic Books.

Larrivee, B. (2005). *Authentic classroom management: Creating a learning community and building reflective practice.* Boston: Allyn & Bacon.

Lazear, D. (1991). *Seven ways of knowing: Teaching to the multiple intelligences.* Palatine, IL: Skylight.

LeDoux, J. (1996). *The emotional brain.* New York: Simon & Schuster.

LeDoux, J. (2002). *The synaptic self.* New York: Penguin Group.

Llinas, R. (2002). *I of the vortex: From neuroscience to self.* Cambridge: MIT Press.

Loescher, E. (1986). *How to avoid World War III at home.* Denver, CO: Conflict Center.

Luckner, J., & Nadler, R. (1997). *Processing the experience: Strategies to enhance and generalize learning* (2nd ed.). Dubuque, IA: Kendall/Hunt.

Lyon, G., & Krasnegor, N. (Eds.). (1999). *Attention, memory, and executive function* (2nd ed.). Baltimore, MD: Brookes.

MacLean, P. (1978). A mind of three minds: Educating the triune brain. In J. Chall & A. Mirsky (Eds.), *Education and the brain* (pp. 308–342). Chicago: University of Chicago Press.

McEwen, B. (2001). *The end of stress as we know it.* Washington, DC: Joseph Henfry Press.

Miller, B., & Cummings, J. (1999). *The human frontal lobes.* New York: Guilford.

Molfese, D., & Molfese V. (2002). *Developmental variations in learning.* Mahwah, NJ: Lawrence Erlbaum.

National Board for Professional Teaching Standards. Available from http://www.nbpts.org

National Center for Education Statistics. (2000, December 5). Highlights from the Third International Mathematics and Science Study-Repeat (TIMSS-R). Available from http://nces.ed.gov/timss/highlights.asp

NCATE. (2003). Summary data on teacher effectiveness, teacher quality, and teacher qualifications. Available from http://www.ncate.org/resources/factsheettq.htm

Neville, B. (1989). *Education psyche: Emotion, imagination and the unconscious in learning.* North Blackburn, Victoria, Australia: Collins Dove.

NIDA/National Institute on Drug Abuse. Available from http://www.drugabuse.gov/NIDAHome.html

Nye, B., Hedges, L., & Konstantopoulos, S. (2003, Spring). The long-term effects of small classes in early grades: Lasting benefits in mathematics achievement at grade 9. *Journal of Experiential Education, 69*(3), 245–257.

Pajares, F. (1996). Self-efficacy beliefs in academic settings. *Review of Educational Research, 66*(4), 543–578.

Pajares, F., & Schunk, D. (2001). The development of academic self-efficacy. In A. Wigfield & J. Eccles (Eds.), *Development of achievement motivation.* San Diego, CA: Academic Press.

Panksepp, J. (1998). *Affective neuroscience.* New York: Oxford University Press.

Peale, N. V. Available online at http://www.quotationspage.com/quotes/Norman_Vincent_Peale

Perfect, T., & Schwartz, B. (2002). *Applied metacognition.* Cambridge, UK: Cambridge University Press.

Perkins, D. (1995). *Outsmarting IQ: The emerging science of learnable intelligence.* New York: Free Press.

Perkins, D. (2001). *The Eureka effect: The art and logic of breakthrough thinking.* New York: Norton.

Perry, B. D. (1996). *Maltreated children: Experience, brain development and the next generation.* New York: Norton.

Perry, B. D. (2003a). Keep the cool in school: Promoting non-violent behavior in children. Available from http://teacher.scholastic.com/professional/bruceperry/cool.htm

Perry, B. D. (2003b, October 8). Workshop: 2nd Annual Southwest Family Violence Conference, presented by the Alternatives to Domestic Violence and Prevent Child Abuse Council of Southwest Riverside County, CA.

Perry, B. D., Pollard, R., Blakely, T., Baker, W., & Vigilante, D. (1995). Childhood trauma, the neurobiology of adaptation and "use-dependent" development of the brain: How "states" become "traits." *Infant Mental Health Journal, 16*(4), 271–291. Available from http://www.trauma-pages.com

Perry, N. (1998). Young children's self-regulated learning and contexts that support it. *Journal of Educational Psychology, 90*(4), 715–729.

Pert, C. (1997). *Molecules of emotion.* New York: Scribner.

Peterson, C., Maier, S., & Seligman, M. (1996). *Learned helplessness.* New York: Oxford University Press.

Piaget, J. (1976). *To understand is to invent: The future of education.* New York: Penguin.

Popham, J. (2001). *The truth about testing: An educator's call to action.* Alexandria, VA: ASCD.

A Private Universe [Motion picture]. Pyramid Film and Video. Available from http://www.pyramidmedia.com

Rauscher, F., Shaw, G., & Ky, K. (1995). Listening to Mozart enhances spatial-temporal reasoning: Towards a neurophysiological basis. *Neuroscience Letters, 185,* 44–47.

Rauscher, F., Shaw, G., Levine, L., Wright, E., Dennis, W., & Newcomb, R. (1997, February). Music training causes long-term enhancement of preschool childrens' spatial-temporal reasoning. *Neurological Research, 19*(1), 2–8.

Reivich, K., & Shatte, A. (2002). *The resilience factor.* New York: Broadway Books.

Restak, R. (1995). *Brainscapes.* New York: Hyperion.

Restak, R. (2001). *The secret life of the brain.* Washington, DC: Joseph Henry Press.

Robbins, B. J. (2003, May-June). *Awe, gratitude and compassion: Common ground in a will-to-oneness.* Paper delivered at conference on Works of Love: Scientific & Religious Perspectives on Altruism, Philadelphia.

Root-Bernstein, R., & Root-Bernstein, M. (2000). *Sparks of genius: The thirteen thinking tools of the world's most creative people.* Boston: Houghton Mifflin.

Rumbaugh, D., & Washburn, D. (1999). Attention and memory in relation to learning: A comparative adaptation perspective. In G. Lyon & N. Krasnegor (Eds.), *Attention, memory, and executive function* (pp. 199–219). Baltimore, MD: Brookes.

Sacks, P. (1998). *Standardized minds: The high price of America's testing culture and what we can do to change it.* Cambridge, MA: Perseus Books.

Sapolsky, R. (1998). *Why zebras don't get ulcers: An updated guide to stress, stress-related diseases, and coping.* New York: Freeman.

Schacter, D. (1996). *Searching for memory: The brain, the mind, and the past.* New York: Basic Books.

Schmahmann, J. (Ed.). (1997). *The cerebellum and cognition.* San Diego, CA: Academic Press.

Schon, D. (1983). *The reflective practitioner: How professionals think in action.* New York: Basic Books.

Schunk, D. H., & Pajares, F. (2002). The development of academic self-efficacy. In A. Wigfield & J. Eccles (Eds.), *Development of achievement motivation* (pp. 15–31). San Diego: Academic Press.

Schwartz, J., & Begley, S. (2002). *The mind and the brain: Neuroplasticity and the power of mental force.* New York: HarperCollins.

Seligman, M. (1998, April). Positive social science. *APA Monitor, 29*(4), 11.

Siegel, D. (1999). *The developing mind: Toward a neurobiology of interpersonal experience.* New York: Guilford.

Sosniak, L. (1989). From tyro to virtuoso: A long term commitment to learning. In F. Wilson & F. Roehmann (Eds.), *Music and child development: Proceedings of the 1987 Biology of Music Making Conference* (pp. 274–290). St. Louis, MO: MMB Music.

Squire, L., & Kandel, E. (1999). *Memory: From mind to molecules.* New York: Freeman.

Sternberg, R. (1988). *The triarchic mind: A new theory of human intelligence.* New York: Viking.

Sternberg, R. (1997). *Successful intelligence: How practical and creative intelligence determines success in life.* New York: Plume.

Sternberg, R., & Grigorenko, E. (2001). *Environmental effects on cognitive abilities.* London: Lawrence Erlbaum.

Stipek, D., Feiler, R., Daniels, D., & Milburon, S. (1995). Effects of different instructional approaches as young children: Achievement and motivation. *Child Development, 66,* 209–223.

Sylwester, R. (2002). *A biological brain in a cultural classroom* (2nd ed.). Thousand Oaks, CA: Corwin Press.

Turner, J. C. (1995). The influence of classroom contests on young children and motivation for literacy. *Reading Research Quarterly, 30,* 420–441.

Turner Pictures (Producers), & Maxwell, R. F. (Writer/Director). (1993). *Gettysburg* [Motion picture]. Atlanta, GA: Turner Pictures.

Van de Castle, R. (1995). *Our dreaming mind.* New York: Ballentine.

Vygotsky, L. (1978). *Mind in society.* Cambridge, MA: Harvard University Press.

Wallenstein, G. (2003). *Mind, stress and emotions: The new science of mood.* Boston: Commonwealth Press.

Wheatley, M. (1999). *Leadership and the new science: Discovering order in a chaotic world* (2nd ed.). San Francisco: Berrett-Koehler.

Wiggins, G. (1993). *Assessing student performance: Exploring the purpose and limits of testing.* San Francisco: Jossey-Bass. *American's children: Key national indicators of well-being, 2003.* Population and family characteristics. Available from http://www.childstats.gov/americaschildren/

Zimmerman, B., & Martinez-Pons, M. (1990). Student differences in self-regulated learning relating grades, sex, and giftedness to self-efficacy and strategy. *Journal of Educational Psychology, 82*(1), 51–59.

Contacts

Caine Learning LLC: http://www.Cainelearning.com

2 Perspectives, Learning and Leadership Consulting: http://www.2perspectives.org

Index

CORWIN PRESS

The Corwin Press logo—a raven striding across an open book—represents the union of courage and learning. Corwin Press is committed to improving education for all learners by publishing books and other professional development resources for those serving the field of K–12 education. By providing practical, hands-on materials, Corwin Press continues to carry out the promise of its motto: **"Helping Educators Do Their Work Better."**